The Economics of Regulating Road Transport

The Economics
of Regulating
Road Transport

Erik Verhoef

Department of Spatial Economics,
Free University, Amsterdam

Edward Elgar

Cheltenham, UK ○ Brookfield, US

Published by
Edward Elgar Publishing Limited
8 Lansdown Place
Cheltenham
Glos GL50 2HU
UK

Edward Elgar Publishing Company
Old Post Road
Brookfield
Vermont 05036
US

A catalogue record for this book
is available from the British Library

Library of Congress Cataloguing in Publication Data
Verhoef, E. T.
    The economics of regulating road transport / Erik Verhoef.
    Includes bibliographical references.
    1. Roads—Government policy—Netherlands. 2. Roads—Government
policy. I. Title.
    HE363.N22V445 1997
    388.1'1—dc20   96–27073
                                                                  CIP

ISBN 1 85898 364 9

Printed and bound in Great Britain by Hartnolls Limited, Bodmin, Cornwall

TABLE OF CONTENTS

PART I INTRODUCTORY CHAPTERS

PART II EFFICIENCY OF REGULATION

PART III EQUITY ASPECTS AND SOCIAL FEASIBILITY OF REGULATION

PART IV CONCLUSION

FIGURES

TABLES

PREFACE

DEAR SIR OR MADAM WILL YOU READ MY BOOK?
IT TOOK ME YEARS TO WRITE, WILL YOU TAKE A LOOK?
(Lennon & McCartney)

"Transport policy is at the cross-roads", says the European Commission's latest Green Paper on transport. Various environmental and social problems arising from transport, and from road transport in particular, are becoming more serious almost by the day, and transport policy makers and scientists face great challenges finding ways to deal with them.

During my PhD research at the Free University of Amsterdam, I studied these problems from the economic perspective, trying to offer some insights into the economics of road transport regulation. This book is the main tangible result of this research project. The work presented here, of course, would not have been possible without the support and cooperation of many persons, and this seems the right place to thank them.

First of all, I would like to thank my promotors Peter Nijkamp and Piet Rietveld for the super-additive benefits I enjoyed from their supervision — or should I say superb-vision? They manage to create an extremely stimulating research environment at our department, and I really enjoyed working with them. I certainly learned a lot, and I absolutely look forward to the continuing cooperation in the next years.

I would like to thank Jeroen van den Bergh, Ken Button and Richard Emmerink for providing me with valuable comments on my work at various stages, and for the very inspiring cooperation we have had working on the joint papers. A number of anonymous referees also provided me with detailed comments, and I would like to take this opportunity to thank them for their time and efforts.

The 'Stichting VSB-fonds' provided financial support for the research project 'Transport and Environment', one of the results of which is this book. I would like to thank this foundation for their funding.

I would also like to thank the people at Edward Elgar Publishing Ltd. for the very pleasant cooperation. They were extremely helpful in the process of turning a thesis into a book.

Finally, I would like to thank my friends and relatives for their 'moral support', and for the interest, true or fake, they have shown in my work. One of them I would like to mention personally; and Inge, that is not only because you're so excited about the idea of having your name in print all over the world...

Amsterdam   Erik Verhoef
June 1996

ACKNOWLEDGEMENTS

The work contained in this book has been carried out within the VSB foundation project 'Transport and Environment'. Financial support from the Stichting VSB Fonds is gratefully acknowledged.

Although non of the chapters in this book exactly duplicates earlier publications, most chapters draw heavily on earlier or forthcoming articles. Without the kind permission of various journals and publishers to use this material, the present publication would not have been possible. I would like to thank these institutions for their kind cooperation.

For Chapters 2, 5 & 6:
With kind permission from Elsevier Science Ltd, The Boulevard, Langdon Lane, Kidlington OX5 1GB, UK; and Elsevier Science − NL, Sara Burgerhartstraat 25, 1055 KV Amsterdam, The Netherlands.

For Chapter 3 & 10:[1]
With kind permission from the Journal of Transport Economics and Policy.

For Chapter 4:
With kind permission from the Journal of Urban Economics.

For Chapter 9:
With kind permission from Transportation Planning and Technology.

For Chapters 7, 8 & 11:
With kind permission from Pion Limited, 207 Brondesbury Park, London NW2 5JN, UK.

---

[1]At the moment the present publication was finalized, the paper on which Chapter 10 is based was being refereed for the *Journal of Transport Economics and Policy*.

PART I

INTRODUCTORY CHAPTERS

1 INTRODUCTION

1.1 Background

Government intervention in transport dates back to times way before anything like the current science of economics was even in its infancy. Classic(al) examples are the 'time of day' chariot, where chariots were banned from the ancient city of Rome at certain times of day (Banister and Button, 1993a), and the publicly provided Roman road network. Ever since, and presumably also before, governments have intervened both in terms of the supply of infrastructures, and in terms of regulating the demand for their usage. Economic theory has subsequently not only justified and rationalized some particular forms of such government intervention, but also has provided useful insights and tools for its further specification and evaluation. Moreover, given the ongoing growth in mobility and its unwarranted side effects, the role of government intervention in transport increasingly has become an issue of great and urgent social importance in addition to its mere academic interest.

The present book deals with this field of government intervention in transport. The focus will be on the regulation of road transport externalities, which has come to the forefront as one of the most important issues in transport policy debates (Barde and Button, 1990; Banister and Button, 1993b; Button, 1993a, 1993b; Nijkamp, 1994). This is, in part, a direct consequence of the increasing general environmental awareness that has arisen since the report of the Club of Rome in the early 1970s (Meadows, Meadows, Randers and Behrens, 1972), and which has subsequently been boosted with landmarks in environmental policy such as the publication of the Brundtland Report (WCED, 1987), the Rio Declaration on Environment and Development (UNCED, 1992), and the United Nations Framework Convention on Climate Change (UN, 1994).

Transport affects the local and global environments in many ways, and for a number of pollutants, the transport sector, in particular road transport, is one of the most important contributors to environmental externalities (see Figure 1.1). Furthermore, transport is one of the main causes of noise annoyance; for instance, over 50% of the Dutch population is hindered by noise from road transport. In addition to environmental concerns, congestion has become one of the main problems facing urbanized areas

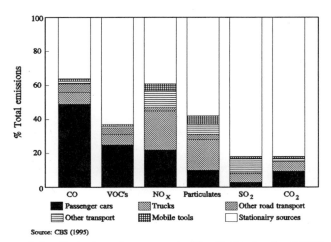

Source: CBS (1995)

Figure 1.1   Emissions by source in The Netherlands (1993)

nowadays. Last but not least, accidents and fatalities — about 1200 each year in The Netherlands — due to road transport can be mentioned as the fourth main negative side effect of road transport. Therefore, notwithstanding the central role that transport plays in modern societies, it is increasingly recognized that current and predicted road transport activities pose potentially excessive pressures on social and ecological environments, and more stringent regulation of road transport seems necessary. This is reflected in policy plans at various spatial levels, such as the European level (EC, 1992a, 1992b, 1995; see also Van Wee, 1995), the national level (for The Netherlands, the most recent national policy plan in this context is the so-called Second Structure Scheme on Traffic and Transport, abbreviated in Dutch as *SVV-II* (Tweede Kamer der Staten-Generaal, 1989−90)), and the local level.

This book studies such regulation of road transport externalities from the economic perspective. The growing concern for the environment has induced a large body of literature on the economics of the environment and the regulation of externalities (see Baumol and Oates, 1988; Pearce and Turner, 1990; Cropper and Oates, 1992; and Tietenberg, 1994). Although many of the principles developed hold equally for transport as for any other sector, some particular features of road transport deserve closer consideration. A range of complications specific to the road transport sector necessitates looking at the regulation of road transport externalities from a variety of angles, and will successively be addressed in this book. The research questions addressed may be summarized as follows:

This study seeks to offer welfare economic evaluations — in terms of efficiency and effectiveness as well as equity and social feasibility — of regulatory policies and policy mixes directly aiming at, or indirectly connected to the containment of externalities in road transport; varying from analyses at the level of individual actors and firms up to the behaviour of spatio-economic systems, and varying from theoretical studies and simulation models to applied empirical analyses.

Therefore, the book aims at providing insight into the economics of regulating road transport externalities, explicitly taking account of and focusing on complexities that are particularly relevant for the road transport sector. The next section, by presenting the structure and contents of the book, gives a first impression of such complexities.

1.2   Structure of the book

Figure 1.2 summarizes the structure and contents of this book. After the present introduction, in which also a general discussion of the economic fundamentals of regulation will be given, Chapter 2 gives an overview of the various externalities of road transport and the attempts that have been made to express these external effects into monetary values.

PART I INTRODUCTORY CHAPTERS

1 Introduction	2 External Effects and Social Costs of Road Transport

PART II EFFICIENCY OF REGULATION

3 Second-best Regulation of Road Transport Externalities	4 Second-best Congestion Pricing with an Untolled Alternative	5 Information and Pricing in Regulating Stochastic Congestion	6 Regulatory Parking Policies	7 Transport, Spatial Economy and the Global Environment

PART III EQUITY ASPECTS AND SOCIAL FEASIBILITY OF REGULATION

8 Efficiency and Equity in Externalities	9 The Trade-off between Efficiency, Effectiveness and Social Feasibility	10 The Social Feasibility of Road Pricing	11 The Social Feasibility and Effectiveness of Parking Policies at the Firm Level

PART IV CONCLUSION

12 Towards Efficient and Socially Feasible Regulation

Figure 1.2   Structure of the book

Part II is dedicated to efficiency aspects in the regulation of road transport externalities. A first important feature of road transport is the large number of generators of externalities. Consequently, externalities may be both intra-sectoral, such as congestion, or inter-sectoral, such as environmental externalities. In addition, road transport externalities range from instantaneous effects at the local level (for instance, congestion and noise annoyance) to long-term threats to the global environment (the emissions of greenhouse gases). However, each of these externalities will vary across individual road users according to specific characteristics such as the vehicle used, the time of driving, the area of driving or even the route chosen, and the length of the trip. In contrast then to the textbook model of externality regulation with one producer and one externality, one will usually face a heterogeneity problem in regulating road transport externalities. Moreover, since road users are by definition mobile, it is not guaranteed beforehand that each of the individual externality generators will indeed be reached with a certain regulatory policy. Such problems will become particularly relevant in more realistic second-best situations, for instance when regulatory policies are pursued which do not allow for perfect fee differentiation, or which do not affect all road users involved. These issues are analysed and discussed in Chapter 3.

A next specific feature is that road transport activities take place in a network environment. Therefore, regulation on a certain part of the network may lead to unwarranted spill-overs onto the rest of the network. The implications for the regulation of congestion are analysed in Chapter 4, both for the situation where a social planner regulates the network, and for the case where the network is partly or entirely controlled by a revenue maximizing private supplier.

In Chapter 5, uncertainty in congestion is considered. In particular now that real time drivers' information systems and congestion pricing schemes are likely to become reality in the foreseeable future, it is important to gain insight into the relative efficiency of, and possible interactions between these instruments in terms of their impact on congestion.

Next, the regulation of road transport externalities is often pursued by means of regulating complementary activities, such as parking policies. These are considered in Chapter 6. Moreover, this chapter is the first in the book explicitly to consider the spatial dimension of road transport by studying regulatory parking policies in the context of an urban equilibrium model.

The final chapter in Part II investigates complications that arise when it is recognized that transport demand is a derived demand. Probably more than any other sector, transport is interconnected with other economic sectors. Particularly when studying the relation between transport and global environmental sustainability, it is important to consider the interdependencies between transport and the spatio-economic system in one analytical framework, as a partial approach to transport regulation may actually suffer from second-best biases. In Chapter 7, these issues are analysed in the context of a spatial price equilibrium approach.

The regulation of transport may have a large impact on virtually every citizen, because practically everybody demands transport services on a daily basis, be it in terms of personal mobility, or through the consumption of goods that somehow have to be transported to him or her. The sort of transport regulation pursued, therefore, may strongly affect future developments in the structure of our societies. As a result, the social feasibility of regulation will also vary across alternative policies, and will probably turn out to be a key factor for the viability of policies. Part III is dedicated to issues of equity and social feasibility, and to the tension between these concepts and the more traditional narrow goal of economic efficiency as the central aim of regulation.

Chapter 8 explicitly includes the receptors of externalities as relevant actors in the regulation of externalities. The chapter analyses the question of to what extent the optimization and the compensation of an external cost are compatible under different schemes of regulation and internalization, and in different model settings.

In Chapter 9, we return to the regulation of road transport externalities. The chapter discusses the trade-off between efficiency, effectiveness and social feasibility in the regulation of road transport externalities, and identifies some possible ways of minimizing the problems associated with this trade-off.

Part III concludes with two empirical chapters. Chapter 10 contains the results of a large survey under peak hour road users in The Netherlands, aiming at the assessment of the social feasibility of road pricing. Chapter 11 concerns the social feasibility and effectiveness of regulatory parking policies at the firm level.

Finally, the concluding Chapter 12 in Part IV contains a summary and a general assessment of the policy lessons that can be drawn on basis of the preceding chapters.

With these contents and this structure, the book aims at doing sufficient justice to the breadth of the regulation of road transport externalities. Still, a number of issues will of course remain uncovered. Some of these omissions will be touched upon in the next section, which gives a brief discussion of the economic theory of regulation, in particular insofar as relevant for road transport.

1.3   Regulation in road transport: economic motivation
Traditionally, mainstream economists have been quite reserved in the advocation of government intervention in the economic process.[1] It is broadly accepted that economic science should aim at providing preferably 'value-free' descriptions and analyses of human choice, and the associated social processes, under conditions of scarcity. As it is not possible to construct a value-free social welfare function according to some ethically

---

[1]This especially holds for micro-economics; practices in macro-economics have been otherwise.

objective criterion, welfare economics has an inherent tendency to rely on quite humble welfare criteria for the evaluation of different possible outcomes of the economic process; for instance, under different forms of government intervention.

Among these, the strict and potential Pareto criteria are without doubt the ones most often employed (for a comparison of these Pareto criteria with other social welfare criteria such as the minimal state, the egalitarian criterion, the Benthamite criterion and the Rawlsian criterion, see Atkinson and Stiglitz (1980, pp. 336−343)). The *strict Pareto criterion* classifies some policy (change) to be socially desirable if, as a result, everyone is made better off (in its weak version), or at least if one person is better off, while no one else is made worse off (in its strong version). For most policy choices however, both losers and gainers will be involved, and the strict Pareto criterion becomes of limited use in the sense that it does not provide any basis for choice between the feasible alternatives. In such cases, one usually relies on well-known *potential Pareto criteria*, or compensation criteria, as suggested by Kaldor (1939) and Hicks (1939). Then, a change is classified desirable if the winners are able to compensate the losers such that everyone is better off after the change has occurred (Kaldor), or if the losers are in the initial situation unable to compensate the winners such that both groups would prefer to stay in the initial situation (Hicks). Actual compensation however, needs not occur according to these principles.

The related concept of *Pareto efficiency* is defined as a feasible situation, usually in terms of the allocation of goods and production factors, for which there exists no other feasible situation that is weakly preferred to it by all agents. Therefore, if an economy attains a Pareto efficient allocation, there remain no mutually beneficial exchanges to be exploited. Unlike the strict Pareto criterion, the potential Pareto criterion will always rank any Pareto efficient allocation above any Pareto inefficient allocation. However, neither the strict nor the potential Pareto criterion can say anything about the relative desirability of different Pareto efficient allocations (see Atkinson and Stiglitz, 1980; and Johansson, 1991).

The economists' reservation in advocating government intervention then, is closely related to a number of basic welfare economic theorems (see Varian, 1992, ch. 17). The first of these is known as the First Theorem of Welfare Economics, stating that under certain conditions (see below), a competitive equilibrium, if it exists, is Pareto efficient. In addition, the Second Theorem of Welfare Economics asserts that essentially all Pareto efficient allocations are competitive equilibria for appropriate distributions of endowments. Next, a welfare maximum for any social welfare function that satisfies welfarism (social welfare depends only on the utility of the households) and is Paretian (it satisfies the strict

Pareto criterion) is necessarily Pareto efficient. Finally, Pareto efficient allocations are welfare maxima under concavity assumptions for some choice of welfare weights in a welfaristic Paretian social welfare function. Varian (1992, ch. 17) presents the formal derivations of these theorems.

Consequently, as it is not possible to make a value-free comparison between different Pareto efficient market outcomes, the logical step for the economists is to advocate regulation merely if the 'certain conditions' necessary for the free market to attain Pareto efficiency, and hence a welfare maximum given the distribution of endowments, happen to be unfulfilled. The question of the desirability of the resulting distribution is then often left aside as an ethical one, beyond the domain of economists. Alternatively, the issue of equity is dealt with either in the light of the initial distribution of endowments, however artificial the bench-mark concept of lump-sum[2] distributions may be in practice, or in terms of the 'efficiency price' that has to be paid for attaining a desirable or satisfactory distribution through distortionary taxes and subsidies.

The non-fulfilment of the above mentioned 'certain conditions' for the First Theorem of Welfare Economics to apply is often referred to as 'market failure': markets fail to accomplish Pareto efficiency. The following forms of market failure are usually distinguished: (a) increasing returns to scale over the relevant range (falling marginal and average variable cost curves); (b) non price taking behaviour (market power); (c) external effects; (d) public goods; and (e) imperfect information.[3] Apart from these, two other important reasons for government intervention often mentioned are (f) distributional or equity considerations; and (g) (de-)merit good arguments.

It is from this perspective of market failures that the field of government intervention in road transport will be approached in this book. The blind spot involved with the tendency to ignore equity aspects in efficiency based policy evaluations, and the natural limit to the extent to which democratically elected governments can freely choose among

---

[2] A lump-sum tax or subsidy is defined as one which is independent of the behaviour of the affected agent. It therefore induces no substitution effect. As it usually will have an income effect, it is not correct to claim that it has *no* effect on behaviour (Atkinson and Stiglitz, 1980, p. 28).

[3] A somewhat different terminology may be encountered in the literature, where one speaks of 'externalities' to indicate what is called 'market failures' above. Bator (1958), for instance, uses 'technical externalities' to indicate 'scale economies'; 'public good externalities' to indicate 'public goods'; and 'ownership externalities' to indicate 'externalities' - which here only refer to 'technological externalities', as opposed to 'pecuniary externalities', in the terminology of Viner (1931) and Scitovsky (1954). Reversely, the term 'market failure' is sometimes reserved solely to indicate a market's 'failure to exist', which is the fundamental reason for technological externalities to occur.

various feasible efficient welfare distributions, are considered in Part III. In the various chapters, the risk of so-called *government failures* as opposed to market failures (see Barde and Button, 1990) will repeatedly be addressed.

Looking at the above reasons for government intervention, it can safely be stated that most of them may be relevant for the road transport sector. In this book, mainly external effects will be considered, as well as distributional and equity considerations (in Part III). Imperfect information is considered in Chapter 5, and Chapter 4 pays some attention to market power in the supply of infrastructure.

The other types of market failures mentioned above, as well as some other forms of and reasons for government intervention in transport, will not be discussed. Most of them have been covered elsewhere, and this seems the right place to mention some relevant references. The question of returns to scale in infrastructure provision is, for instance, considered in Small (1992a, ch. 3). Quinet (1993) discusses market power in transport. Next, the public good argument often plays a role in the public supply of infrastructure. An important reason for public provision of transport infrastructure, besides reasons of indivisibility and the sheer size and risks of the projects, is its quasi-collective or mixed character. Nevertheless, (partly) private provision of transport infrastructure increasingly receives attention (see Nijkamp and Rienstra, 1995). Besides the public good argument, the potential impacts of infrastructure on spatio-economic development often play a role in decision making on transport infrastructure investments (see Rietveld, 1989; and Bruinsma, 1994).

In the list of topics that will not explicitly be covered in this book also belongs the energy use by (road) transport. The optimal use of depletable resources requires dynamic modelling approaches which are quite different from the ones employed in this book, and would thus probably deserve a study all of its own. However, the analysis in Chapter 7 does give some ideas of how this issue might be approached.

Narrowly related to the economic regulation of transport is the issue of deregulation in transport, such as the privatization of formerly publicly provided services. This topic is dealt with, for instance, in Button and Pitfield (1991) and Berechman (1993).

A last note concerns the regulation of road transport for other than purely economic reasons, such as traffic rules. Although these regulations may have their impact on the externalities of road transport — consider, for instance, separate truck lanes or take-over interdictions for reducing congestion, or the impact of speed limits on emissions or safety — they will also not be analysed in any depth in this book.

The following chapter is dedicated to the most important form of market failures in road transport considered in this book, namely its external effects.

2 EXTERNAL EFFECTS AND SOCIAL COSTS OF ROAD TRANSPORT: CONCEPTUAL ISSUES AND RECENT EMPIRICAL RESULTS FOR THE NETHERLANDS[1]

2.1 Introduction

The growing social pressures resulting from transport have led to a large body of literature on the external costs of transport. However, the extensive research efforts have not yet been able to initiate the political response that is often hoped for with the publication of the research findings. A number of factors can be mentioned that may contribute to this fact. First of all, governments face a problem of limited social feasibility of regulatory policies (see also Part III). Apart from that, owing to differences in the interpretation of the concept of externalities, and the wide range of techniques and methodologies employed in the estimation of these effects, empirical estimates of external costs of transport may differ by a factor 10 or more, whereas they often intend to measure the same thing. This uncertainty in estimates, of course, renders them a rather disputable and weak basis for policy making. Next, there is still no consensus on the question of whether external benefits of transport might compensate for the external costs. In addition, debates on the implications of the research findings are often further clouded by a mixing up of arguments of an allocative efficiency and of an equity nature.

This chapter deals with these issues. Like in the rest of the book, the focus is on road transport, which is by far the most important transport mode in terms of external costs generation. By discussing the external effects of road transport, the chapter provides some relevant background information to the analysis of the regulation of these externalities in the subsequent chapters. The chapter is organized as follows. Section 2.2 starts with discussing the definition of externalities. This, of course, is also relevant for the following chapters, in which externalities will play a central role. Applying this definition of externalities in Section 2.3, it will be concluded that road transport hardly yields any positive external effects.

---

[1]This chapter is based on an earlier article in *Transportation Research A* (Verhoef, 1994a).

However, considerable negative externalities are involved. Section 2.4 deals with the efficiency and equity impacts of externalities. In Section 2.5, some recent estimates of external costs of transport in The Netherlands are discussed. Section 2.6 concludes this chapter.

2.2 A definition of externalities

Although the concept of external effects is widely used in economics, there seems to be some uncertainty on its exact definition and interpretation, which justifies a short discussion of the concept itself here. It is commonly recognized that externalities are an important form of market failure. Their existence leads to a deviation from the first-best neo-classical world, in which the price mechanism takes care of socially optimal resource allocation (Pareto efficiency). In presence of externalities, market prices do not reflect full social costs (or benefits), and additional taxes (or subsidies) are called for to restore the efficient workings of the market mechanism. Furthermore, it is generally accepted that the source of externalities is typically to be found in the absence of property rights (see Baumol and Oates, 1988, p. 26). Hence, the theory of externalities is often applied in environmental economics. Environmental quality is a typical 'good' for which property rights are not defined and hence no market exists.

These commonplaces may clearly indicate the causes and consequences of external effects, but still leave the definition unclear. However, an exact definition is necessary in order to identify transport's external effects. Such a definition can be as follows: *an external effect exists when an actor's (the receptor's) utility (or production) function contains a real variable whose actual value depends on the behaviour of another actor (the supplier), who does not take this effect of his behaviour into account in his decision making process.* This definition is in line with for instance Mishan (1971). In the terminology proposed by Bator (1958), such externalities concern his concept of 'ownership externalities', as opposed to the 'technical externalities' (increasing returns to scale or indivisibilities in production) and 'public good' externalities he distinguishes. In the terminology of Viner (1931) and Scitovsky (1954), the above definition concerns 'technological' externalities, as opposed to 'pecuniary externalities'.[2] These latter, which are ruled out by considering real variables only (that is, excluding monetary variables), do not lead to shifts of production and utility functions, but merely to movements along these functions. Consequently, in the terminology of Buchanan and Stubblebine (1962), externalities as defined above are potentially 'Pareto-relevant', whereas pecuniary externalities are not (see also Mishan, 1971). The final

---

[2]Note that Bator's 'technical externalities' are completely different from Viner's and Scitovsky's 'technological externalities'.

condition in the definition distinguishes externalities from other types of unpriced interactions such as barter, violence, jealousy, altruism or goodwill-promoting activities. Such phenomena differ fundamentally from external effects, both in a theoretical and in a policy-relevance respect. According to Mishan (1971), "the essential feature of an external effect [is] that the effect produced is not a deliberate creation but an unintended or incidental by-product of some otherwise legitimate activity" (p. 2).

The unresolved tension between the receptor, facing a quantitative constraint on the 'consumption' of the externality, and the supplier, who has no *a priori* interest in the magnitude of the externality, can only persist provided there is no market on which the externality is traded. This stems from a lack of well-defined property rights concerning the externality, which is in turn often related to prohibitive high transaction costs. As pointed out by Coase (1960), in absence of transaction costs, both the supplier and the receptor of the externality can benefit from negotiations on the size of the externality. Corrective Pigouvian taxation would in that case only distort the resulting Pareto efficient outcome (Turvey, 1963).

Externalities comprise both efficiency and equity aspects. The first refer to the fact that, in presence of externalities, the competitive market outcome is not Pareto efficient. The second relate to the fact that the receptors of a negative (positive) externality are clearly worse (better) off at any non-zero level of the effect, unless compensations take place. As will be pointed out in Section 2.4, this distinction is also important when assessing the policy implications of externalities.

The question of whether unpriced external relations are either external effects or other types of unpriced external relations involves important policy consequences. This is demonstrated in Figure 2.1 for a certain activity Q. The normal case in (a) shows the optimal workings of the market mechanism in absence of external effects. In this case, no government intervention is called for: Adam Smith's invisible hand secures social welfare maximization (the bold triangle) at the market equilibrium Q^0 where marginal private cost (MPC) equals marginal private benefits (MPB). MPB and MPC can be interpreted as the benefits and costs as experienced by one actor. They can also be thought of as being the demand and supply curves for a marketed good, in which case P^0 is the market clearing (efficient) price.

The existence of (marginal) external costs (MEC) in (b) drives a wedge between marginal social cost (MSC) and marginal private cost (the fact that both MPC and MEC are equal to 0 at Q=0 and rising afterwards is an arbitrary choice, and does not affect the generality of the discussion). The market outcome Q^0, where private welfare is maximized, is not optimal from a social point of view. The resulting level of the externality $(A+B+C)$ is excessively large. Social welfare maximization requires the activity to be restricted to a level of Q^*, where the marginal social cost is equal to the

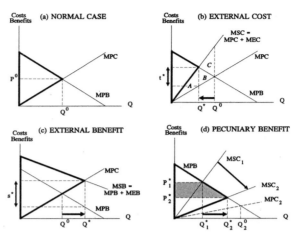

Figure 2.1   Policy implications of external costs, external benefits and pecuniary benefits

marginal benefits and the dead-weight welfare loss C is avoided. This optimum can for instance be accomplished by means of a quantitative restriction (Q^*) or a Pigouvian tax (t^*) on the activity. The triangle A gives the optimal level of the external cost. The bold triangle again represents maximum social welfare.

Quadrant (c) shows the reverse case, where (marginal) external benefits (MEB) exist. Marginal social benefits (MSB) now exceed the marginal private benefits. In this case, social welfare maximization requires encouragement of the activity up to Q^*, for instance by means of Pigouvian subsidization (s^*).

Finally, (d) illustrates the case of pecuniary benefits. Quadrant (b) serves as a starting point, assuming that the activity gives rise to external costs. Suppose the private cost curve shifts downwards, perhaps due to technological developments or lower input prices. Assuming unaltered external costs, MSC will fall as well. A new social optimum Q_2^*, with a higher social welfare arises: the bold triangle is increased in comparison with (b). Moreover, if Q is a traded good and MPB reflects market demand, the consumer surplus increases by the shaded area. This results from the lower market price P_2^* and the larger quantity sold Q_2^*. This benefit, however, is not external but pecuniary: it results from a movement along — not a shift in — the MPB curve. For the attainment of the new social optimum (the move from Q_1^* to Q_2^*), market forces can be relied upon, and there is no reason for stimulating the activity, unlike in case of external benefits. Also, the pecuniary benefits do not 'compensate' for the external costs: social welfare maximization still requires a restriction from

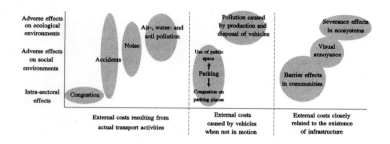

Figure 2.2   A typology of external costs of road transport

the new market outcome Q_2^0 to the new social optimum Q_2^*. Consequently, the question of whether unpriced costs and benefits of road transport are either external or pecuniary in nature, is crucial from a policy point of view. The next section discusses the important question of whether road transport gives rise to external costs and/or benefits.

2.3   External effects of road transport

2.3.1   External costs of road transport

The existence of external costs of road transport is in fact beyond dispute. In Figure 2.2, the main external cost categories are roughly classified along two dimensions. Along the vertical axis, a distinction is made between external costs that road users pose upon each other: intra-sectoral external costs; and external costs which are posed upon the rest of the society: environmental or inter-sectoral externalities. A further distinction is made between environmental externalities in the ecological sense, concerning natural environments, and in a somewhat different sense, namely concerning social environments. On the horizontal axis, the external costs are divided into (1) effects that arise from actual road transport activities; (2) external costs that arise when vehicles are not in motion; and (3) external costs that are closely related (but not solely attributable) to the existence of road infrastructure.

The shaded areas indicate the first-order incidence of the external costs. Some external costs are partly intra-sectoral and partly environmental. For instance, external accident costs are to a certain extent imposed upon fellow car drivers (the intra-sectoral incidence), partly upon people outside this population (the social environmental incidence) and may finally have an ecological environmental incidence when transport of hazardous substances is involved.

		1970	1985	1990	1993	Index 1993 (base 1985)
Road usage[a]		49 260	80 870	97 390	104 380	129
	CO_2	13 340	20 720	23 790	25 400	123
	CO	1 662	923	675	547	59
Emissions[b]	NO_x	143	262	273	259	99
	SO_2	16	11	13	14	127
	VOCs	317	225	191	157	70
Noise[c]			54			
Fatalities[d]		3 382	1 529	1 376	1 252	82
Congestion	# traffic jams		5 635	6 075	11 695	208
	severity[e]		1.92	2.55	3.66	191

[a]   In million vehicle-kilometres
[b]   In million kilograms
[c]   Percentage of population with noise annoyance from road transport of 55 dB(A) or more (1987)
[d]   1986 instead of 1985
[e]   In million kilometre-minutes

Sources: AVV (1995), CBS (1995), Ministerie van Verkeer en Waterstaat (1995), RIVM (1993), OECD (1993)

Table 2.1   Some trends relevant for the external effects of road transport in The Netherlands

The second-order incidence of the externalities can occur at different scale levels. For example, congestion usually increases emissions per vehicle-kilometre, whereas it may reduce the number of fatalities per vehicle-kilometre (Shefer, 1994; Shefer and Rietveld, 1994).

The severeness of these external costs will to a large extent be time and place sensitive, but in a qualitative sense, Figure 2.2 indicates that road traffic indeed causes a wide range of external costs. Table 2.1 gives an impression of the magnitudes of, and trends in, some of the negative externalities associated with road transport in The Netherlands. These trends can be explained by developments in road transport volumes on the one hand, and some other developments, including technological progress, on the other. It is in that respect interesting to see that for most pollutants and accidents, the growth since 1985 has been significantly less strong than the growth in total mobility, and often even negative (see the last column). This reflects, for example, the favourable impacts of improved average vehicle technology on emissions and fatalities. Congestion, on the other hand, rises more than proportionally with road usage. Although these figures are aggregates, this latter finding is in accordance with what one would expect on the basis of the theory.

Finally, one may be tempted to conclude on the basis of Table 2.1 that environmental externalities of road transport can or will be solved on the basis of technological solutions only. Although such solutions are without doubt important, it should not be forgotten that in the longer run, continued growth in mobility is likely to outweigh favourable impacts of improved vehicle technologies. Studies by Acutt (1996) and Dodgson (1996) actually do suggest so. Moreover, it should be stressed that the figures for 1993 still considerably exceed Dutch policy targets for the year 2000 (in million kilograms, 23 000 for CO_2, 112 for NO_x, and 65 for VOCs).

2.3.2 External benefits of road transport?

There seems to be some confusion on the question of whether road transport yields important external benefits. Especially representatives of the automobile industry and related sectors often claim that the external benefits of road transport largely exceed the external costs, thus casting doubt on the necessity to restrict car use. For instance, according to Diekmann (1991), (car-)mobility "contributes towards the quality of life... [and]... the overall growth in prosperity and leisure time since World War II could never have been accomplished without mass-motorization".

However important though the contribution of road transport to general well-being may be, the crucial question is of course whether such benefits are indeed external. If so, Pareto efficiency might require encouragement of road mobility by means of Pigouvian subsidies, or through the creation of Coasian markets where the non-paying profiteers could compensate road users in order to seduce them to increase their mobility. External benefits would, at least to a certain extent, compensate for the external costs of road transport. Therefore, it is important to examine the suggested external benefits of road transport (perhaps needless to say, the arguments in this section also apply to other transport modes).

First, road transport obviously plays a vital role in modern economies. However, the interrelations of the transport sector with other actors and sectors generally take place on well-defined markets. Often claimed 'external benefits' of road transport, like lower production costs and consumer prices, greater variability in product choice, and faster delivery, are actually pecuniary benefits. These benefits (the realization of the increase in the consumer surplus in Figure 2.1(d) due to cheaper and hence more road transport) require no government intervention. As pointed out in Section 2.2, these effects do not compensate for road transport's external costs.

Related to this type of argument are the sort of propositions stating that most modern economies would collapse without road transport. This is obviously true; however, the conclusion that therefore a large share of gross domestic product (GDP) is actually an external benefit of road transport is equally obviously false. The same sort of reasoning could be applied to the food industry, the energy sector, various raw materials sectors, and, in the long run, maternity care; be it commercial, public, or supplied within the household. With such reasoning, one could explain a multiple of GDP as 'external benefits' of various activities. Clearly, these are simply market internal interdependencies.

Secondly, spin-off effects of road transport in terms of value added or employment in related economic sectors, such as vehicle manufacturing and maintenance, or oil industry, do not provide a sound economic reason for not restricting transport to its optimal levels. Insofar as these effects result from excessive road mobility, such general economic goals should preferably be aimed at by means of less distorting instruments.

Third, there is a large group of unpriced external relations associated with road transport which do not qualify as external benefits. Such effects for instance occur when people receiving guests derive benefit from the visit, but do not actually compensate for the associated travel costs. Usually however, this involves either barter behaviour or altruistic behaviour. In the first case, the travelling person expects a counter visit in the future, and therefore both parties − implicitly − agree not to pay for each others' travel costs. Alternatively, the visitor takes the utility of the receiving person into account. Insofar as the receiving person finds that he (or she) is not being paid enough visits, he may be expected to be able to reveal his willingness to pay for more visits directly to the visitor. Neither form of individual utility maximizing behaviour is inconsistent with Pareto optimality, and social welfare can therefore not be increased by encouraging such behaviour.

Furthermore, the benefits of road infrastructure are often mistaken for external benefits of road transport itself. Such benefits concern for instance the effects of infrastructure on (regional) economic development and employment levels. Rietveld (1989) asserts that, according to the theory, the regional economic effects of the building of new infrastructure will be moderately positive (if infrastructure was initially lacking), neutral (if infrastructure already exists) or even negative (redistributional effects between regions). Consideration of such effects may very well play an important role in decisions on infrastructure investments, for instance in cost−benefit analyses, but should be clearly separated from the regulation of the actual usage of the infrastructure. This point can be clarified with Figure 2.1(d). Apart from showing the pecuniary benefits of transport as such, this diagram can also be used to demonstrate lower costs for users resulting from infrastructural investments. The shaded increase in the consumer surplus now reflects the benefits of road infrastructural improvements as enjoyed by road users, for instance in terms of gains in travel times. However, these gains by no means compensate for road transport's external costs. Here, the investment in additional infrastructure is socially desirable only if the increase in the social surplus is large enough to cover the investment's social costs, provided the infrastructure will be used at the socially optimal level. Any investment in road infrastructure will of course only yield maximum net benefits when it is used at, not beyond, the socially optimal level of road transport.

A comparable category of often claimed external benefits of road transport is the increased security resulting from better accessibility for fire-engines, police cars, or ambulances. However, the increased accessibility for such services is to be attributed to the infrastructure only, and certainly not to the actual road transport activities. On the contrary, the higher the mobility, the more such services will suffer from congestion. Consequently, if there is any external effect of road transport in this respect, it is an external cost rather than a benefit.

In summary, it seems hard to identify any significant external benefits of road transport activities; apart, perhaps, from benefits as enjoyed by 'car spotters'. Since, on the other hand, considerable external costs are involved, road transport may be expected to be beyond its socially optimal level. Road transport indeed puts an excessive burden on our societies, and government intervention which aims at reducing the external costs of road transport will therefore generally increase social welfare.

2.4 Efficiency and equity impacts of externalities

As already mentioned before, externalities comprise both equity and allocative efficiency aspects. These two elements are often confused in debates on the regulation of road transport externalities. Unfortunately, there is no straightforward one-to-one mapping between the two goals of efficient allocation and 'equitable distribution', however defined. One can therefore arrive at rather different policy recommendations on the regulation of externalities, depending on the viewpoint taken.

First of all, let us consider the welfare of the receptors of an external cost. It seems reasonable that, from an equity point of view, Pigouvian tax revenues should be used to compensate the receptors of the external cost for the remaining optimal level of the externality. However, this turns out to be problematic as soon as the receptor of an externality is able to protect him- or herself by means of defensive measures (such as double glazing in case of noise annoyance, or relocation in case of localized externalities). In Chapter 8, this problem is investigated in several settings, and a main conclusion is that it is in general not in line with overall efficient allocation to compensate receptors for the external cost suffered, nor for any defensive measures undertaken. In some cases, efficient allocation even requires taxation of receptors in order to secure the optimal number of receptors of an external cost. Compensations would prevent receptors of external costs from undertaking the optimal level of defensive measures. Hence, for the optimal efficient allocation, one might end up in a situation which is not very attractive from the equity point of view, namely where receptors of an external cost not only remain uncompensated for the externality they suffer, but should also be (financially) responsible for their own defensive measures.

Related to this issue is, from a distributional point of view, the unattractive property of externalities that their valuation should be based on the receptors' willingness to pay for their avoidance. It is not difficult to show that this value, apart from being directly related to the marginal disutility of the effect itself, is inversely related to the marginal utility of income. This means that, other things being equal, the same exposure to a negative external effect implies a higher external cost for higher income receptors (see Chapter 8 for a formal derivation). The inequitable implications of this property are evident: an externality generating activity should then, from the efficiency point of view, be located near low income rather than near high income receptors.

Focusing on the generators of externalities now, also in this case there is often a tension between allocative efficiency, and what seems to be just from the equity point of view. For instance, consider the *Polluter Pays Principle*. Taking Figure 2.1(b) as an example, optimal Pigouvian taxation implies a total tax sum $Q^* \cdot t^*$, which is in the sketched case twice as large as the optimal level of the external cost (area A). Hence, the question of whether the polluter should pay the total external cost, or whether marginal tax rules should be used, may often lead to different outcomes in terms of both allocative efficiency and equity – unless of course marginal external costs are constant and therefore equal to average external costs.

Given such tensions between efficiency and equity considerations, it is no surprise that the mixing up of equity and allocative efficiency arguments may often lead to rather fuzzy discussions about the policy implications of research findings on external costs of road transport. Table 2.2 gives an overview of the most important characteristics and implications of taking these two perspectives, demonstrating the absence of a direct mapping between the two, and hence identifying some sources of confusion in the debates.

First of all, the ultimate research goal is different. From the efficiency perspective, one would ultimately like to arrive at an assessment of optimal levels of road transport, preferably to be realized with first-best optimal Pigouvian taxation. This means that each road user should be taxed according to his or her marginal external costs, implying that the appropriate level of analysis is the individual level. Consequently, intra-sectoral externalities (such as congestion) as well as inter-sectoral environmental externalities should play a role, and hence also the full (expected) marginal external costs of accidents call for regulatory taxation.

	Allocative efficiency perspective	Equity perspective ('unpaid bill')
Goal of the analysis	Assessment of 'optimal road mobility' and optimal regulatory taxes	Assessment of the total costs shifted to society at large
Relevant external cost measure	Marginal external cost	Total external cost *plus* induced defensive outlays
Apt level of aggregation	Individual	Sectoral
Relevant external cost categories	Intra-sectoral and inter-sectoral external costs	Inter-sectoral external costs
Relevance of some existing financial transfers:		
Defensive outlays by receptors	Should not be accounted for in optimal taxes	Should be added to 'unpaid bill'
Insurance premiums	Very limited relevance[a]	Limited relevance[b]
Car ownership taxes	Very limited relevance[a]	Relevant[c]
Indirect taxes on fuel	Potential relevance[d]	Potential relevance[e]

[a] These transfers are usually fixed yearly payments, (largely) independent of total kilometres driven. Hence, they have no direct impact on road usage.

[b] A certain share of accident costs (including fatalities) are intra-sectoral, and hence should not play a role in the 'unpaid bill' analysis. Neither therefore should a certain share of the insurance premiums. Moreover, from the perspective of the 'unpaid bill', the relevant question is whether the payments from the insurance companies to society are enough to cover the costs posed on the rest of the society.

[c] These taxes are a relevant coverage for part of the 'unpaid bill' only if they exceed government outlays on infrastructure (depreciation, maintenance, management, police, etc.).

[d] Taxes on fuel will act as a substitute for Pigouvian taxation only when the rate exceeds those of indirect taxes on other goods (forgetting here about the 'optimal taxation' argument for the sake of simplicity).

[e] Also here, only any indirect taxes above average rates can be considered as relevant transfers from road users to society, compensating for part of the unpaid bill.

Table 2.2   *Characteristics and implications of the allocative efficiency versus the equity perspective for studying external costs of road transport*

From the equity point of view on the other hand, road transport's 'unpaid bill' is presumably the relevant research goal, and this is also what people often have in mind when confronted with empirical results on the external costs of transport. This bill amounts to the sum of total external costs plus the induced defensive measures undertaken by the receptors of the external costs. In this case, a sectoral perspective is the most natural one. Intra-sectoral externalities (congestion as well as a certain part of the accident costs) are no part of this burden that road transport poses upon the rest of the society, and therefore need not be included in this 'unpaid bill'.[3]

In the bottom rows of Table 2.2, the relevance of some existing financial transfers for the interpretation of external cost estimates according to both perspectives is indicated. For instance, whereas defensive outlays by receptors of the externalities are part of the 'unpaid bill', they should not be accounted for in optimal Pigouvian taxes. These should simply be based on marginal external costs, given the level of protection chosen by the receptors of the externality.[4]

More important are the following three categories, which are often mentioned as compensating financial outlays by road users, followed by the suggestion that they should therefore be subtracted from external cost estimates before assessing any policy implications. It is especially at this point that allocative efficiency and equity arguments are often mixed up.

As indicated in the table, these financial transfers have only very limited relevance from the allocative efficiency perspective. Insurance premiums and car ownership taxes only have a limited impact on car mobility since they mainly involve fixed yearly payments, often independent of actual mileage driven (insurance premiums, however, are sometimes divided into a number of categories depending on yearly vehicle-kilometres). Although a distributional impact is therefore clearly present, the regulatory impact is limited and strongly distorted, as these payments at best only affect car ownership. But even the impact of fuel taxes as a substitute for optimal Pigouvian taxation should not be overestimated. As allocative efficiency is strongly dependent on relative prices, such an impact of fuel taxes cannot be expected for rates below the average indirect tax rate for other goods. Moreover, taking the purist stance, the theory of optimal taxation (see, for instance, Sandmo, 1976) dictates indirect taxes to be inversely related to demand elasticity. Clearly then, even in absence of externalities, and given the often claimed relative inelasticity of demand for road transport, fuel taxes might have to be relatively high in comparison to other indirect taxes anyway when the goal of allocative efficiency is pursued. However, even without speculation on relative demand elasticities, it will be clear that only a modest part of the

---

[3]An important reason for taking the 'unpaid bill' perspective could be the goal of 'green accounting', for which purpose the unpaid bill is an important input. At the risk of unnecessarily complicating matters, in that case also the total intra-sectoral external cost should be accounted for in the determination of road transport's actual productivity.

[4]However, defensive outlays can be used to *assess* the marginal external costs. The household production function valuation method of externalities is based on this assumption.

three financial transfers discussed above can indeed be interpreted as a substitute for optimal regulatory taxes.

The relevance of these payments for the assessment of the equity issue is larger than for allocative efficiency, but is also not as straightforward as it may seem at first sight. Starting with the insurances for accidents, it can be noted that, as far as the inter-sectoral incidence of external accident costs is concerned, the relevant question is in particular whether the payments from the insurance companies to society are enough to cover the inter-sectoral costs involved (medical care, emergency services, legal costs, repairing damages to buildings, psychological costs of pain and suffering incurred by victims outside the road sector, etc.). Insurance premiums themselves are less relevant from this perspective. Car ownership taxes, insofar as exceeding government outlays on supplying road infrastructure capacity in general (including costs of depreciation, maintenance, management, police, etc.), can indeed be considered as a relevant coverage for part of the 'unpaid bill' of road transport. Finally, any indirect fuel taxes above average rates can also be considered as relevant transfers from road users to society, compensating for part of the unpaid bill.

It will be clear now that estimates of external costs of road transport do not lead to unambiguous policy implications unless a clear goal for regulation is formulated. From the viewpoint of environmental quality, this should be the goal of allocative efficiency. For this goal, one can safely state that additional Pigouvian taxation of road transport is necessary. However, representatives of for instance the road lobby tend to use arguments of an equity nature to point out that road users already pay a lot to society, and that additional economic regulation is 'unfair'. Chapter 9 will point out a number of possibilities to escape from this impasse.

2.5   Some recent empirical research in The Netherlands
2.5.1   The valuation of externalities
For the valuation of external effects (that is, putting a monetary value on external effects which are by definition unpriced), a broad range of techniques have been developed over the last decades. Table 2.3 gives a concise overview of the methods used for especially environmental externalities, including noise annoyance.

On the left-hand side, methods aiming at the assessment of the actual external costs are given. It would take too long to discuss these techniques in great detail here; good discussions can be found in Johansson (1987), Mitchell and Carson (1989), Pearce and Markandya (1989), and Freeman (1993). From a theoretical point of view, behaviourial techniques deserve preference, as they aim at assessing the receptors' valuation of the effect. In contrast, a major drawback of non-behaviourial linkage techniques is that the victims' valuation of the effect is not considered at all. Mitchell and Carson (1989) observe in this respect that there is little theoretical basis for the use of these techniques in welfare economics, since the damage functions are not directly related to the consumers' utility functions. Furthermore, non-behaviourial techniques result in an estimate of the user value of environmental goods at best, and are not capable of inferring non-use values. Still, non-behaviourial techniques receive much support in practice, in particular because the figures produced seem to be 'harder'.

	Valuation approaches		Short-cut approaches	
Behaviourial		**Non-behaviourial**		
Surrogate markets	Hypothetical markets			
* *Hedonic techniques* * *Travel cost methods* * *Household production functions*	* *Contingent valuation methods*	* *Damage costs (buildings, agricultural crops, etc.)* * *Costs of illness*	* *Prevention costs: potential defensive-, abatement- or repair programmes*	* *Actual defensive-, abatement- or repair outlays*

Table 2.3   Some valuation methods and short-cut approaches for the assessment of environmental external costs

Often, however, time or money is lacking to undertake actual valuation studies. Then, short-cut approaches as mentioned on the right-hand side of Table 2.3 are usually applied, in which the costs of actual or potential defensive-, abatement- or repair programmes, instead of the external costs themselves, are assessed. Two such strategies can be distinguished, namely where actual, and where potential outlays are considered. Although these techniques yield results that may be relevant for assessing the equity impacts of external costs, they are not particularly apt for the allocative efficiency type of study (compare Table 2.2).

Consider for instance the most often used short-cut approach, where an external effect is valued at the theoretical cost of prevention programmes, necessary to reduce the externality to a 'reasonable' level. First of all, this approach suffers from circular reasoning, since the 'optimal' level of these programmes and hence also of the remaining externality is more or less arbitrarily chosen, whereas it should actually result from weighing off the costs of such programmes against the benefits in terms of reducing the external costs. Hence, assuming the externality to be not a very serious problem leads to considering relatively moderate programmes at relatively low costs, in turn producing a relatively low 'external cost' estimate. A particular problem for using these figures for the regulation of transport is that Pigouvian fees should be equal to the *remaining* marginal external costs, given the abatement-, defensive- and repair programmes undertaken. Indeed, once carried out, an extremely effective but expensive abatement programme, reducing the remaining marginal external costs to zero, implies zero Pigouvian taxes, and certainly not regulatory taxes based on the excessively high costs of the programme. Clearly however, these remaining external costs are just not measured with such methods. Therefore, only in case the circular reasoning would happen to be undertaken for the optimal level of the external cost, would it produce results that could also be used for the purpose of a marginal analysis, eventually resulting in the assessment of Pigouvian taxes.

In the second approach, actual defensive-, abatement- or repair outlays are interpreted as representing the victims' or social willingness to pay for reducing annoyance to 'acceptable' levels and therefore representing 'the' external cost. Although market data on victims' expenditures on defensive measures may indeed be used for inferring their valuation of an external cost (the household production function approach is based on that notion), this short-cut approach as such only measures the defensive outlays, and again does not say much about the total or marginal level of the remaining external cost. For that purpose, indeed a household production function study is needed, focusing on the *marginal* behaviour of the receptors of the externality.

The measurement of external accident costs yields some additional problems. The cost components associated with traffic accidents usually include physical damage to vehicles, infrastructure, properties and natural environment; legal, police and emergency service costs; costs of injuries and fatalities, such as medical and funeral costs; psychological costs of pain and suffering; values of life; and production losses. In the first place, as outlined in Sections 2.3 and 2.4, these costs are to a certain extent intra-sectoral. The common practice of adding accident costs to costs of air pollution and noise annoyance in order to assess the 'total external costs' of transport is therefore questionable. If anything, this is not correct for analyses from the viewpoint of equity. Secondly, the valuation of life, pain and suffering is of course a very difficult thing. On the one hand, we almost have to put a monetary value on these items, as one would otherwise run the risk of implicitly assuming a zero price. On the other hand, one could argue that for the purpose of Pigouvian taxation based on marginal external costs, it would be sufficient to use *ex ante* valuations of increased risk, rather than to work with 'full' values of life, pain and suffering. These latter are relevant only for the *ex post* assessment of total external costs.

Finally, the valuation of the intra-sectoral congestion externality mainly involves data on time losses due to congestion, and value of time estimates, which can also be based on behaviourial or non-behaviourial techniques (compare Table 2.3). Table 2.4 provides an overview of the value of travel time in The Netherlands according to mode and trip purpose (for further details, see HCG, 1990a, 1990b, 1992).

| | Passengers (1988) | | | Freight (1989, per shipment) |
	Commuters	Business	Other	
Road	18	52	10	65
Train	14	30	8	1500 (train) 60 (wagon)
Bus/tram	9	25	6	
Inland shipping				350

Source: HCG (1990a, 1990b, 1992)

Table 2.4   Average value of time in passenger and freight transport in The Netherlands (DFl⁵/hour)

In conclusion, before turning to empirical estimates of external costs of transport, it is important to realize that the valuation of externalities is a very difficult thing to do, and that one should be very careful in interpreting the results obtained. First of all, the absolute values will be very sensitive to the methods used. Secondly, a translation of these figures into marginal measures, needed in order to study the allocative efficiency implications, is fraught with methodological difficulties, among which the estimation of the external cost *function* is likely to be the most important. Finally, figures obtained with prevention cost methods are in particular suspicious for the purpose of Pigouvian tax derivation.

2.5.2   Empirical estimates of the external costs of transport in The Netherlands

Over the last decade, many studies on the valuation of the external costs of transport have been undertaken. A number of reports, books and articles have subsequently summarized these findings. The estimated external costs of transport may range between a couple of tenths of percents, up to over ten percent of GDP (for OECD countries), depending on coverage of effects and valuation methods applied. Road transport is consistently identified as causing the largest share of these external costs (see also Table 2.5 below). The interested reader may consult, among others, Quinet (1989), Kågeson (1993), Verhoef (1994a), Bleijenberg, Van den Berg and De Wit (1994), Gastaldi, Pradayrol, Quinet and Rega (1996), and

---

⁵The exchange rate of the Dutch guilder (DFl) is DFl 2.06 = 1 ECU.

Maddison, Pearce, Johansson, Calthrop, Litman and Verhoef (1996). This section will discuss two recent empirical studies for The Netherlands.

Empirical work towards the external costs of transport in The Netherlands is relatively scarce. The two most important recent estimates were undertaken by Bonenschansker, Leijsen and De Groot (1995) and Bleijenberg, Van den Berg and De Wit (1994). Their main results are given in Table 2.5.

	Road			Rail			Water (inland)		
Bleijenberg *et al.* **(1994)**	*Low*	*Mid*	*High*	*Low*	*Mid*	*High*	*Low*	*Mid*	*High*
Air pollution									
CO_2	0.95	2.62	11.66		0.01	0.05	0.06	0.17	0.74
NO_x	0.49	2.57	3.28		0.01	0.01	0.04	0.22	0.28
SO_2	0.01	0.03	0.09						0.01
VOCs	0.23	1.80	2.64					0.01	0.01
Noise	0.20	0.64	1.09	0.01	0.02	0.03			
Fatalities	0.73	1.80	2.02					0.01	0.01
Injured	0.48	1.87	4.33						
Total	**3.09**	**11.32**	**25.09**	**0.01**	**0.04**	**0.10**	**0.11**	**0.41**	**1.05**
Bonenschan-sker *et al.* **(1995)**									
Air pollution (excl. CO_2)		0.9 − 1.2			0.0			0.0	
Noise		0.5 − 1.1			0.1			0.0	
Accidents		2.3 − 3.8			0.0			0.0	
Congestion		0.3 − 0.6							
Total		**4.0 − 6.6**			**0.1**			**0.0 - 0.1**	

Table 2.5   *Estimates of external costs of transport in The Netherlands (1990, milliard DFl)*

It would take too long here to discuss both studies in detail. In order to give a short description of the methodologies followed, it can be noted that Bonenschansker *et al.* (1995) have tried to estimate the external costs via assessment of damage costs, whereas Bleijenberg *et al.* (1994) have applied a broad range of external costs estimates from the (international) literature to the Dutch situation. Both approaches obviously have their respective weaknesses; however, any approach would. In any case, the method used by Bonenschansker will certainly only give a lower bound estimate of the external costs of transport; first because many items are left as p.m. entries due to a lack of data (for instance, no estimate of the external costs of greenhouse gas emissions has been made), and secondly because damage costs are by definition only a part of total external costs. It is therefore no surprise that the figures reported by Bonenschansker *et al.*, especially those relating to the costs of environmental externalities, are lower than those reported by Bleijenberg *et al.* Given the more comprehensive measures, the estimates of external costs of air pollution of Bleijenberg *et al.* seem more adequate than the rather low values produced by Bonenschansker *et al.*

To increase the comparability of these figures with those of other studies, Table 2.6 gives the implied valuation of environmental externalities per kilogramme emissions according to the more specified study of Bleijenberg *et al.*

	Low	Mid	High
CO_2	0.04	0.11	0.49
NO_x	1.8	9.4	12.0
SO_2	0.8	2.0	6.9
VOCs	1.2	9.4	12.0

Source: Bleijenberg *et al.* (1994)

Table 2.6   Valuation of environmental external costs for the most important pollutants (1990, DFl/kg)

The most uncertain but also the most important factor in the determination of external accident costs is the value of life. The average value of life calculated by Bonenschansker *et al.*, based on production losses, is DFl 528 thousand. This is also the lower bound estimate used by Bleijenberg *et al.* Both studies use a high variant of DFl 1.5 million, based on international (WTP-)studies.

Finally, concerning noise, Bleijenberg *et al.* extract values per person-kilometre and per tonne-kilometre from the international literature. It is especially for this externality that such a procedure seems questionable, since it does not take into account country-specific characteristics such as the proximity of transport infrastructure to residential areas. Bonenschansker *et al.* calculate external costs of noise annoyance based on value reductions of houses. It is noteworthy that the estimates of external costs of noise annoyance of road transport provided by Bonenschansker *et al.* and Bleijenberg *et al.* are rather close, notwithstanding the different approaches.

The results presented above clearly show that estimates of the external costs of transport strongly depend on the measurement methods adopted, and may therefore indeed vary by a factor 10 or more. An obvious research conclusion is that much more research is needed in order to identify the reliability and applicability of the various valuation techniques. An obvious policy conclusion is that the external costs of transport are high, ranging from 0.6% to 5.1% of Dutch GDP in the low and high estimates of Bleijenberg *et al.*, and that, given the current policy practices, there seems to be room for considerable efficiency improvements by means of proper pricing of road transport.

This point is illustrated in Table 2.7, where for the most important transport modes figures are given that represent the 'social deficit'; calculated as government expenditures, notably on infrastructure supply, maintenance and other services, plus external costs, minus taxes collected from these modes (excluding Value Added Taxes for reasons outlined in Section 2.4). These figures are taken from Bonenschansker *et al.* (1995), where further details on the calculations can be found. Apart from passenger transport by car evaluated according to the low external cost estimate of Bonenschansker *et al.*, all figures are positive, indicating that overall tax revenues categorically fall short of public costs plus external costs. For the more comprehensive valuations provided by Bleijenberg *et al.*, these deficits are of course higher. It is interesting to see that, whereas the external costs of road transport by far exceed those for other modes, other uncovered public costs of these other modes are much higher, leading to a rather balanced picture for the overall 'social subsidization' of the various transport modes, especially for passenger transport.

	Passenger		Freight	
	I	**II**	**I**	**II**
Road	2 423	−2 161	4 046	2 017
Rail	2 446	2 466	140	143
Light rail	3 961	3 212		
Inland shipping			1 075	692

I Based on mid estimates of Bleijenberg *et al.* (1994)
II Based on low estimates of Bonenschansker *et al.* (1995)

Source: Bonenschansker *et al.* (1995)

Table 2.7   Balance of public expenditure, external costs, public revenue and other fiscal measures for various modes (1990, million DFl)

Clearly, figures such as given in Table 2.7 are more related to issues of equity than to issues of allocative efficiency. When considering the fact that for instance for road transport only about 40% of the tax revenues in The Netherlands are variable (that is, related to fuel), and that marginal external costs are likely to be rising, it will be clear that from the viewpoint of allocative efficiency, even higher variable taxes may be called for than is implied by Table 2.7. These higher variable taxes may of course be accompanied with reductions in fixed taxes for reasons of social feasibility (see Part III). Concerning these price policies, on the basis of their results, Bleijenberg *et al.* (1994) recommend an average increase of variable taxes of DFl 1 per litre fuel as a bench-mark for road transport policies in The Netherlands in the near future.

2.6   Conclusion

In this chapter, some conceptual issues concerning external effects of road transport were discussed. Starting with the definition of externalities, it was assessed that transport does not yield any significant external benefits, whereas considerable external costs are involved. These latter have equity as well as allocative efficiency implications. Unfortunately, there is no straightforward one-to-one mapping between the two, which gives rise to uncertainty and fuzzy discussions as far as the policy implications of external cost estimates for transport are concerned. A clear separation of these issues is a prerequisite for a less ambiguous interpretation of research results.

Some issues related to the actual estimation of the external costs of transport were raised, and some recent empirical estimates for The Netherlands were presented, indicating that there is a clear need for further research on the valuation of externalities, as well as a clear need for more stringent policies regarding the external costs of road transport. This latter topic is studied in the remainder of this book, starting with the efficiency of regulation in the following part.

One last remark, however, can be made here. The explicit focus on road transport in this book can be justified by pointing at the sheer size of the external costs of road transport compared to those of other modes (see Table 2.5). One might however argue that with more stringent regulation of road transport, the external costs of other modes may increase owing to modal split effects. This is of course true. It is therefore worth mentioning here that transport regulation in a multi-modal setting with mode specific externalities is not entirely neglected, but is considered in the general model in Chapter 7.

PART II

EFFICIENCY OF REGULATION

3   SECOND-BEST REGULATION OF ROAD TRANSPORT EXTERNALITIES [1]

3.1   Introduction

This is the first in a series of five chapters in which the efficiency of regulating road transport externalities will be studied from various viewpoints, and for various policies, concentrating on a number of second-best situations that are likely to occur in the practice of policy making.

Actually, already back in the 1920s, economists like Pigou (1920) and Knight (1924) recognized that 'road pricing' offers the first-best solution for optimizing congested road traffic flows. Since then, the severity of traffic congestion has dramatically increased, turning it from a matter of academic interest into one of the most serious problems affecting urbanized areas and transport arteries nowadays. In addition, along with the growing levels of road transport, inter-sectoral external costs of road transport such as discussed in Chapter 2 became matters of increasing relevance. After seventy years, economists' answers to such market failures in road transport typically still rely heavily on the concept of Pigouvian taxes. Under the rather stringent assumptions of first-best conditions elsewhere in the economic system and perfectly flexible regulatory policies for coping with road transport externalities, there would indeed not be much scope for improving on the Pigouvian solution to the problem of external costs of road transport, at least not when the aim of the policies is merely to achieve Pareto optimal levels of road usage. Unfortunately however, these assumptions are usually not satisfied in reality. The consequences for the efficiency of regulating road transport externalities are the central topic in this part of the book.

In this chapter, the focus is on second-best alternatives to the first-best Pigouvian 'bench-mark' policy of perfectly differentiated marginal external cost pricing. In principle, various types of road charging do exist. From an economic viewpoint, a refined system of Electronic Road Pricing (ERP) is generally seen as the most preferable technical charging mechanism,

---

[1]This chapter is based on an earlier article in *Journal of Transport Economics and Policy* (Verhoef, Nijkamp and Rietveld, 1995a).

approaching first-best standards as close as possible. With ERP, the regulatory tax can be differentiated according to the various dimensions affecting the marginal external costs of each trip, such as the length of the trip, the time of driving, the route followed and the vehicle used. Hence, individual drivers can be confronted with first-best incentives, inducing optimal behaviourial responses. However, although the well-known Hong Kong experiment has demonstrated that it is technically possible to successfully operate an ERP scheme nowadays (Dawson and Catling, 1986; Hau, 1992), various social and political impediments appear to prevent ERP from being widely introduced and accepted, certainly in the short run (see also Chapter 10). Nevertheless, road pricing schemes in various forms have recently been, or soon will be introduced in a number of cities. Table 3.1, taken from Gomez-Ibañez and Small (1994), and Small and Gomez-Ibañez (1996), gives an overview.

Type of road pricing	Degree of implementation		
	In place	Scheduled	Under study
City centre: congestion pricing	Singapore ('75)		Hong Kong Cambridge, UK
City centre: toll ring	Bergen ('86) Oslo ('90) Trondheim ('91)	Stockholm ('97)	
Single facility: congestion pricing	Autoroute A1, France ('92) Route 91, California ('95)		Route 57, California Oakland Bay Bridge, San Francisco
Area wide: congestion pricing			Randstad London

Sources: Gomez-Ibañez and Small (1994), and Small and Gomez-Ibañez (1996)

Table 3.1   Various road pricing schemes in practice

The present chapter concerns the welfare economic characteristics of second-best alternatives to the bench-mark policy of first-best Pigouvian taxes. In particular, attention is focused on the regulator's incapability of optimal tax differentiation between different types of road users, associated with many 'realistic' pricing schemes. Throughout the chapter, the analyses are restricted to economic instruments only; that is, second-best regulatory user fees. The additional shortcomings of physical restrictions in traffic regulations are discussed in Chapter 6.

Discussions of related second-best topics in transport can be found in Wilson (1983), and d'Ouville and McDonald (1990) on optimal road capacity supply with suboptimal congestion pricing; Braid (1989) and Arnott, De Palma and Lindsey (1990b) on uniform or step wise pricing of a bottleneck; and Arnott (1979), Sullivan (1983), and Fujita (1989, ch. 7.4) on congestion policies through urban land use policies. Two classic examples on second-best regulation in transport are Lévy-Lambert (1968) and Marchand (1968), studying optimal congestion pricing with an untolled alternative. Seminal papers on the theory of road pricing as such are Walters (1961), Vickrey (1969), and Arnott, De Palma and Lindsey (1993). Two recently edited books on this topic are Johansson and Mattsson (1995) and Button and Verhoef (1996). Finally, the issues considered in this chapter bear close resemblance to those discussed in the literature on optimal taxation (see, for instance, Diamond, 1973; Sandmo, 1976; and Atkinson and Stiglitz, 1980). Mayeres and Proost (1995) study optimal taxation in the context of transport externalities.

The structure of this chapter is as follows. In Section 3.2, the optimal undifferentiated fee is derived, and in Section 3.3 its welfare effects are compared with first-best regulation. Section 3.4 discusses some aspects related to demand interdependencies, and Section 3.5 considers a simple form of cost interdependencies, where the regulator is not capable of taxing all road users. Section 3.6 concludes.

3.2   The optimal common regulatory fee

The basic issue considered in this and the following section concerns a road network which is used by different groups of road users, each having their own group-specific level of external costs. One may, for instance, consider vehicle-specific externalities, such as emissions of pollutants, or noise. Efficiency requires regulatory fees to be dependent on such vehicle-specific characteristics. However, it will often be practically impossible to operate such a delicate tax structure when applying second-best regulatory instruments. For instance, regulatory parking fees, meant at regulating road usage, are in general not suitable for adaptation according to the type of vehicle; nor are policies such as peak hour permits. Likewise, many practical pricing instruments are not capable of differentiation according to individual trip lengths. This often holds for regulatory parking policies (see Chapter 6) and also for instruments such as peak hour permits or cordon charging. Marginal external costs of road trips, however, are usually dependent on trip length. Comparable problems may arise with route- or time-specific externalities, such as congestion and noise.

In this section, the optimal regulatory fee for such cases is derived. This is the optimal second-best undifferentiated or 'common' fee, as opposed to optimal first-best differentiated or 'fine' fees. First, an environmental externality is considered; then an intra-sectoral externality (congestion).

3.2.1   The optimal common regulatory fee for an environmental externality

Suppose that M different groups of car drivers (denoted m=1,2,...,M) jointly use a certain road network. Each group has its own specific marginal private cost of driving c_m and its own specific marginal external (environmental) cost $\partial E(N_1,N_2,...,N_M)/\partial N_m$ (conveniently denoted $\varepsilon_m(\cdot)$ hereafter); N_m gives the number of trips made by group m. The groups are ordered according to increasing marginal external costs: $\varepsilon_j(\cdot) > \varepsilon_i(\cdot)$ if j>i, where the very mild assumption is made that, over the relevant ranges, groups do not change order in terms of marginal external costs due to changes in any N. Now suppose that the regulatory body wishes to reduce emissions by means of some second-best undifferentiated regulatory tax policy. More ambitiously, it wishes to find the optimal common regulatory fee. This fee maximizes social welfare under the inherent limitation of the policy, being the impossibility of first-best tax differentiation. Such an optimal common fee can be found by solving the following Lagrangian:

$$\mathcal{L} = \sum_{m=1}^{M} \int_0^{N_m} D_m(n_m)\, dn_m - \sum_{m=1}^{M} c_m \cdot N_m - E(N_1,N_2,...,N_m)$$
$$+ \sum_{m=1}^{M} \lambda_m \cdot (D_m(N_m) - c_m - f) \tag{3.1}$$

The first term defines total benefits in the system as the relevant areas under the inverse demand curves D_m. The next term gives the total private cost of driving, for all groups defined as the average cost of a trip c_m, multiplied by the number of trips. Note that an uncongested road network is assumed here: average private costs are constant, and are therefore equal to marginal private costs. The third term gives the total environmental external cost E. Finally, the restrictions indicate that in any equilibrium, for all groups the inverse demand equals the sum of the marginal private cost c_m and the common regulatory fee (f): for all groups, the marginal driver has a zero net surplus. The first-order conditions[2] are as follows (with a prime denoting the first derivative):

$$\frac{\partial \mathcal{L}}{\partial N_m} = D_m(N_m) - c_m - \varepsilon_m(\cdot) + \lambda_m \cdot D_m'(N_m) = 0 \quad m=1,2,...,M \tag{3.1a}$$

$$\frac{\partial \mathcal{L}}{\partial f} = -\sum_{m=1}^{M} \lambda_m = 0 \tag{3.1b}$$

---

[2] In this and the following chapters, necessary second-order conditions are assumed to be fulfilled and will not be discussed. Also issues of existence and uniqueness of (second-best) optima are ignored. For the sort of problems studied, there is no reason to expect any difficulties in these respects, since non-rising demand functions and non-falling (user and congestion) cost functions are sufficient to satisfy these requirements.

$$\frac{\partial \mathcal{L}}{\partial \lambda_m} = D_m(N_m) - c_m - f = 0 \quad m = 1,2,...,M$$

(3.1c)

The parameters λ_m cause these first-order conditions to differ from the first-best optimal ones. In particular, when in the restrictions in the Lagrangian (3.1) the common fee f is replaced by differentiated fees r_m, the first-order conditions include $\lambda_m = 0$ for all m. Hence, the first-best optimum is given by $r_m = \varepsilon_m(\cdot)$, which are the standard Pigouvian fees equal to marginal external costs. In the second-best case under consideration here however, equations (3.1a) imply the following expressions for λ_m:

$$\lambda_m = -\frac{D_m(N_m) - c_m - \varepsilon_m(\cdot)}{D_m'(N_m)}$$

Therefore, using (3.1b) and (3.1c):

$$\sum_{m=1}^{M} \frac{f - \varepsilon_m(\cdot)}{D_m'(N_m)} = 0$$

which gives the following expression for the optimal common fee:

$$f = \sum_{m=1}^{M} \frac{\dfrac{\varepsilon_m(\cdot)}{D_m'(N_m)}}{\displaystyle\sum_{i=1}^{M} \frac{1}{D_i'(N_i)}}$$

(3.2)

Equation (3.2) shows that the optimal common fee is a weighted average of the marginal environmental costs in the second-best optimum. Hence, with constant marginal external costs, the optimal common fee is a weighted average of the first-best Pigouvian fees (r_m). This is an appealing result, which in fact bears close resemblance to other results obtained in the literature on optimal taxation (Sandmo, 1976; Diamond, 1973, equation (10)). The weight attached to a certain group is inversely related to the slope of the demand curve of that group (D_m') in the second-best optimum. This makes sense: the flatter the demand curve, the more distortive deviations from the individual optimal fee are, and hence the larger the weight should be. The slopes of the demand curves in fact capture both the relative importance of the groups, and their demand elasticities: the larger the group and the more elastic the demand, the flatter the demand curve. In order to disentangle these two effects, the definition of demand elasticity η can be used (dropping the argument N_m):

$$\eta_m = \frac{dN_m}{dD_m} \cdot \frac{D_m}{N_m}$$

where dN_m/dD_m is simply defined as $1/(dD_m/dN_m)$. The weight w_m attached to group m can then be written as:

$$w_m = \frac{\dfrac{1}{D_m'}}{\displaystyle\sum_{i=1}^{M} \dfrac{1}{D_i'}} = \frac{\dfrac{\eta_m \cdot N_m}{D_m}}{\displaystyle\sum_{i=1}^{M} \dfrac{\eta_i \cdot N_i}{D_i}} \qquad (3.3)$$

It may be illustrative to note that, when all demand functions have the following form:

$D_m(N_m) = \alpha \cdot \ln N_m + \beta_m$

(where α has the same negative value for all groups), $dD_m/dN_m = \alpha/N_m$ and therefore $\eta_m/D_m = 1/\alpha$ for all values of N_m. This results in weights which are proportional to the group sizes in the (second-best) optimum.

Finally, the fact that the private costs of driving may differ among the groups does not affect the outcome. Such cost differences are internal, and therefore do not enter the expression for the optimal common fee.

3.2.2   The optimal common congestion fee

The foregoing analysis gives the general results for second-best regulation concerning an environmental (inter-sectoral) externality. We now turn to a special intra-sectoral externality associated with road transport: congestion. In its most basic form, congestion can be introduced by making the private cost of driving within each group dependent on the number of drivers in that group. Hence, for S groups, the following Lagrangian can be formulated:

$$\mathcal{L} = \sum_{s=1}^{S} \int_0^{N_s} D_s(n_s)\, dn_s - \sum_{s=1}^{S} N_s \cdot c_s(N_s) + \sum_{s=1}^{S} \lambda_s \cdot (D_s(N_s) - c_s(N_s) - f) \qquad (3.4)$$

The cost functions (the second term) can be interpreted as follows: total costs within a group s (say, C_s) is defined as the group size (N_s) times the average cost (c_s), which in turn depends on the group size. Furthermore, the restrictions show that the individual road user bases his behaviour on the average cost of driving: average social costs are perceived as marginal private costs. Note that the cost functions are assumed to be independent (that is, groups are defined so as to rule out cost interdependencies). Groups may be thought of as users of different radial access roads to a city centre, served by the same parking space where regulatory parking levies are charged. Alternatively, groups may be different cohorts, sufficiently separated in time so as to avoid interdependencies. Clearly, this is a rather restrictive assumption. However, when allowing for inter-group congestion effects, the expression for the optimal common fee can become quite complicated and difficult to interpret (see Appendix 3.A).

It is easy to show that first-best regulation involves fees r_s which are equal to the marginal external congestion costs:

$r_s = N_s \cdot c_s'(N_s)$

However, the regulatory body has to find the optimal common congestion fee by solving (3.4). The first-order conditions are:

$$\frac{\partial \mathcal{L}}{\partial N_s} = D_s(N_s) - c_s(N_s) - N_s \cdot c_s'(N_s) + \lambda_s \cdot \left(D_s'(N_s) - c_s'(N_s)\right) = 0 \quad s = 1,2,...,S$$

$$\frac{\partial \mathcal{L}}{\partial f} = -\sum_{s=1}^{S} \lambda_s = 0$$

$$\frac{\partial \mathcal{L}}{\partial \lambda_s} = D_s(N_s) - c_s(N_s) - f = 0 \quad s = 1,2,...,S$$

yielding the following optimal common fee:

$$f = \sum_{s=1}^{S} \frac{\dfrac{N_s \cdot c_s'(N_s)}{D_s'(N_s) - c_s'(N_s)}}{\displaystyle\sum_{i=1}^{S} \dfrac{1}{D_i'(N_i) - c_i'(N_i)}} \tag{3.5}$$

Like (3.2), (3.5) gives a weighted average of the marginal external congestion costs in the second-best optimum. However, the weights are somewhat different, having turned into:

$$w_s = \frac{\dfrac{1}{D_s' - c_s'}}{\displaystyle\sum_{i=1}^{S} \dfrac{1}{D_i' - c_i'}} = \frac{\dfrac{1}{d_s' + c_s'}}{\displaystyle\sum_{i=1}^{S} \dfrac{1}{d_i' + c_i'}} \tag{3.6}$$

where d' gives the absolute value of the slope of the demand curve (d'=−D'). A group now receives a larger weight, not only the flatter the demand curve (the smaller d_s'), but also the flatter the average cost function (the smaller c_s') in the second-best optimum. The reason is that the weights should be such that the welfare losses due to deviations of the common fee from the optimal individual fees are minimized. With congestion, such welfare losses not only depend on the slopes of the demand curves, but on those of the average cost functions as well. The steeper both curves, the less responsive the group size to deviations of the optimal common fee from the optimal individual fee, and therefore the smaller the group's weight.

3.3   Evaluating second-best policies
3.3.1   The relative efficiency of second-best policies
A crucial question is of course how second-best policies as described by equations (3.2) and (3.5) relate to the first-best solution. In order to shed

some light on this issue, the following *index of relative welfare improvement* ω is used:

$$\omega = \frac{W_{II} - W_0}{W_I - W_0}$$

where W_{II} is social welfare (social benefits minus social costs) under second-best policies of charging the optimal common fee, W_I is welfare under the first-best policy of differentiated regulation, and W_0 is welfare under non-intervention.[3]

By definition, $W_0 \leq W_{II} \leq W_I$. Welfare under second-best regulation is at least as high as under non-intervention, which can always be realized by setting $f=0$. Likewise, welfare under first-best policies is at least as high as under (optimal) second-best policies, since this latter can be realized setting equal fees for all groups. However, $W_0 < W_{II}$ when $f>0$; and $W_{II} < W_I$ if for any $i \neq j$, $r_i \neq r_j$ (where r_m gives the first-best optimal fee for group m), and $D'_i \neq -\infty$ and $D'_j \neq -\infty$. Finally, to avoid $\omega = 0/0$, it has to be assumed that $W_0 < W_I$: an externality should exist, and not all demands should be perfectly inelastic. Under these conditions ($W_0 \leq W_{II} \leq W_I$ and $W_0 < W_I$), ω may range between zero and one. When $\omega = 0$, it is impossible to increase welfare by using second-best policies. On the other hand, $\omega = 1$ means that second-best regulation yields the same welfare improvement as does first-best regulation, implying that the instruments are perfect substitutes.

In order to develop an expression for ω, first consider a simple two-group model with group-specific marginal environmental external costs $\varepsilon_i(N_i)$ (i=1,2). Consider the non-trivial case where $0 < \varepsilon_1 < \varepsilon_2$ and neither demand curve is perfectly inelastic. Hence, $0 < r_1 < f < r_2$, since f is a weighted average of r_1 and r_2. Let $N_i(c_i)$ give the number of trips made by group i under non-intervention. $N_i(c_i+f)$ and $N_i(c_i+r_i)$ give the number of trips under second-best and first-best policies, respectively; all these values satisfy the inverse demand relations $D_i(N_i)$. The following two inequalities hold: $N_1(c_1+f) < N_1(c_1+r_1) < N_1(c_1)$; and $N_2(c_2+r_2) < N_2(c_2+f) < N_2(c_2)$. Both first-best and second-best policies lead to reductions in participation by both groups, be it that group 1 is more restricted under second-best policies (since $r_1 < f$), while group 2 is more restricted under first-best policies (since $f < r_2$). In this case, ω has the following general form:

$$\omega = \frac{\displaystyle\int_{N_1(c_1+r_1)}^{N_1(c_1)} S_1(n_1)\,dn_1 + \int_{N_1(c_1+f)}^{N_1(c_1+r_1)} S_1(n_1)\,dn_1 + \int_{N_2(c_2+f)}^{N_2(c_2)} S_2(n_2)\,dn_2}{\displaystyle\int_{N_1(c_1+r_1)}^{N_1(c_1)} S_1(n_1)\,dn_1 + \int_{N_2(c_2+f)}^{N_2(c_2)} S_2(n_2)\,dn_2 + \int_{N_2(c_2+r_2)}^{N_2(c_2+f)} S_2(n_2)\,dn_2} \tag{3.7}$$

---

[3]Differences in implementation and intervention costs of second-best versus first-best policies can be considered in ω, but are ignored in this chapter.

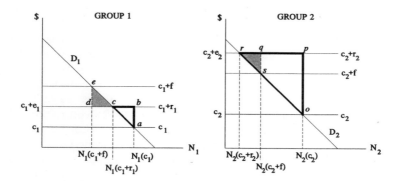

Figure 3.1 *The welfare effects of optimal first-best regulation (bold)
versus optimal second-best regulation (bold minus
shaded) for two groups*

where $S_i(n_i)$ is defined as the marginal private cost plus the marginal
external cost minus the marginal benefit. The first terms in the numerator
and denominator are identical, giving the increase in social welfare that
can be realized by levying group 1 their optimal fee r_1. The second term
in the numerator however, gives the welfare loss due to charging the
higher second-best fee f, rather than r_1. The third term in the numerator,
identical to the second term in the denominator, gives the welfare gain
resulting from charging group 2 the fee f. The third term in the
denominator however, gives the additional welfare gain that may be
realized by charging group 2 the higher fee r_2, rather than f. All terms are
positive, except the second term in the numerator.

Figure 3.1 provides an illustration for the case where both groups have
linear demand curves (D_i), constant marginal private cost (c_i) and constant
marginal external cost (e_i). The maximum possible increase in social
welfare in comparison with non-intervention is given by the sum of the
surfaces of the two bold triangles *abc* and *opr*. This gain can be realized
by charging the first-best fees $r_1=e_1$ and $r_2=e_2$. Under second-best
regulation, equation (3.2) may yield an optimal common fee f ($r_1<f<r_2$). In
comparison with the first-best solution, this policy involves welfare losses
as given by the shaded areas *ced* and *sqr*. Hence, in this case, the
following expression for ω is found:

$$\omega = \frac{abc - ced + opqs}{abc + opqs + sqr}$$

Clearly, the smaller the surface of the shaded areas in comparison with the surface of the bold triangles, the closer to unity ω is. In terms of the more general expression (3.7), ω is closer to unity, the smaller the second term in the numerator and the third in the denominator in comparison to the other terms.

Before turning to the factors determining the value of ω however, (3.7) can be generalized for the M groups' case. For that purpose, a distinction should be made between those groups which are undercharged, and those which are overcharged under second-best policies. The critical (possibly fictive) group μ, which draws the distinction between these two, is determined by that particular value of m for which the optimal first-best fee is equal to the optimal second-best fee. For instance, consider the external cost function to be linear in some physical factor Γ: $E = \varepsilon \cdot \Gamma$, and Γ to be additively separable in group-specific factors γ_m:

$$E = \varepsilon \cdot \Gamma = \varepsilon \cdot \sum_{m=1}^{M} \gamma_m \cdot N_m$$

Groups may for example be classified according to trip length γ_m. The above equation then means that the total distance driven is equal to the summation over all possible trip lengths γ_m times the number of trips of that length, while total external cost depends linearly on total mileage driven. Alternatively, Γ may give total noise emissions over a day, where the different weights γ_m indicate that the severity of noise annoyance varies over the day. In such cases, the marginal external costs can be written as $\varepsilon \cdot \gamma_m$, and μ is that particular group for which:

$$\varepsilon \cdot \gamma_\mu = \varepsilon \cdot \sum_{m=1}^{M} \frac{\dfrac{\gamma_m}{D_m'}}{\displaystyle\sum_{i=1}^{M} \frac{1}{D_i'}} \quad \Rightarrow \quad \gamma_\mu = \sum_{m=1}^{M} (\gamma_m \cdot w_m)$$

At any rate, (3.7) can be generalized as follows:

$$\omega = \frac{\displaystyle\sum_{m=1}^{\mu} \int_{N_m(\bar{c}_m+r_m)}^{N_m(c_m)} S_m(n_m)\,dn_m + \sum_{m=1}^{\mu} \int_{N_m(\bar{c}_m+f)}^{N_m(c_m+r_m)} S_m(n_m)\,dn_m + \sum_{m=\mu}^{M} \int_{N_m(\bar{c}_m+f)}^{N_m(c_m)} S_m(n_m)\,dn_m}{\displaystyle\sum_{m=1}^{\mu} \int_{N_m(\bar{c}_m+r_m)}^{N_m(c_m)} S_m(n_m)\,dn_m + \sum_{m=\mu}^{M} \int_{N_m(\bar{c}_m+f)}^{N_m(c_m)} S_m(n_m)\,dn_m + \sum_{m=\mu}^{M} \int_{N_m(\bar{c}_m+r_m)}^{N_m(c_m+f)} S_m(n_m)\,dn_m} \tag{3.8}$$

Equation (3.8) confirms the intuitive expectation that second-best policies are a better substitute to first-best policies, the more homogeneous the total population of car drivers in terms of external cost generation. Obviously, given the demand structure, ω is closer to 1 the smaller the spread in the terms r_m (that is, the closer the optimal common fee approaches both the minimum and maximum optimal individual fees). In the extreme where $f=r_1=r_2=...=r_M$, $\omega=1$.

The effect of the demand structure on ω is a bit less clear-cut. In absolute terms, deviations of the common fee from the first-best fees are less distortive, and hence absolute welfare losses are smaller, the more inelastic all demands and the smaller all groups. However, since ω is a relative measure, this observation does not get us much further. It may be noted though, that the more concave D_m for groups $m<\mu$, and the more convex D_m for groups $m>\mu$, the smaller the relative welfare losses will be (represented by the two 'distortion terms' in (3.8)), and hence the larger ω (see also Figure 3.1). Furthermore, ω is closer to 1, the steeper the demand curves of the more extreme groups in comparison to those near μ. As indicated in the previous section, these slopes jointly capture the effects of demand elasticities and group sizes. For instance, suppose that in the optimum the distributions of the factors r_m and of the slopes of demand curves are perfectly symmetric, with μ in the centre of both distributions. The optimal second-best fee will then be r_μ. However, the value of ω will be larger, the more inelastic the demands and the smaller the relative importance of the groups in the tails in comparison to those in the centre of the distribution.

When considering the optimal common congestion fee (3.5), the indices m in (3.8) may simply be replaced by s, which also have to be assigned according to increasing optimal individual congestion fees, with σ, like μ, being the group for which the second-best fee equals the first-best congestion fee. Again, ω is closer to 1, the smaller the spread in optimal individual first-best fees and the steeper the demand curves in both tails of the distribution (for groups with either very low or very high congestion levels) as compared with the slopes in the centre. The same holds for the slopes of the average cost functions, which also determine the welfare losses due to uniform taxation in this case. However, one should not ignore the interplay between these slopes and the optimal individual congestion fees, which determine the assignment of the indices s in the first place. In particular, with 'comparable' group sizes, a group with a steep average cost function would never be in the left tail of the distribution.

3.3.2 The effectiveness of second-best environmental policies

From an environmental point of view, it is especially relevant how the absolute reduction in emissions under second-best policies compares to the reduction under a scheme of first-best regulation. Intuition tells that the former is likely to be smaller, since second-best policies involve certain welfare losses. Hence, the cost of reducing the externality is larger, and a lower optimal reduction in total emissions can be expected for any $0\leq\omega<1$. In general, a policy change from second-best to first-best regulation leads to a change in total environmental cost which is equal to:

$$\Delta E = E\big(N_1(c_1+r_1), N_2(c_2+r_2), ..., N_M(c_M+r_M)\big)$$

$$- E\big(N_1(c_1+f), N_2(c_2+f), ..., N_M(c_M+f)\big)$$

In order to keep the analysis manageable, consider a model with linear demand curves and linear, additively separable external cost. The change in total environmental cost due to a change from second-best to first-best policies amounts to:

$$\Delta E = \sum_{m=1}^{M} \Delta N_m \cdot \varepsilon \cdot \gamma_m = \sum_{m=1}^{M} (r_m - f) \cdot \frac{1}{D_m'} \cdot \varepsilon \cdot \gamma_m \tag{3.9}$$

For the relatively low-externality groups ($m<\mu$), $r_m<f$, and the relevant term in (3.9) is positive, indicating the effect of the increase in emissions of these groups due to a higher participation. Reversely, for $m>\mu$, $r_m>f$, and the relevant term in (3.9) is negative, indicating the effect of the decrease in emissions of these groups due to lower participation. The overall effect on total emissions can be found by substitution of the optimal second-best fee f given in (3.2) into (3.9), and using $r_m = \varepsilon \cdot \gamma_m$:

$$\Delta E = \sum_{m=1}^{M} \left[\left[\varepsilon \cdot \gamma_m - \varepsilon \cdot \sum_{i=1}^{M} \frac{\dfrac{\gamma_i}{D_i'}}{\displaystyle\sum_{j=1}^{M} \frac{1}{D_j'}} \right] \cdot \frac{1}{D_m'} \cdot \varepsilon \cdot \gamma_m \right]$$

$$= \varepsilon^2 \cdot \sum_{m=1}^{M} \left[\frac{\gamma_m^2}{D_m'} - \frac{\gamma_m}{D_m'} \cdot \left(\sum_{i=1}^{M} \gamma_i \cdot w_i \right) \right] \tag{3.9'}$$

It is not easy to determine the sign of (3.9') at first sight. After some manipulation however, this expression can be rewritten as:

$$\Delta E = \frac{1}{2} \cdot \varepsilon^2 \cdot \left[\sum_{i=1}^{M} \sum_{j=1}^{M} \left[\frac{(\gamma_i - \gamma_j)^2}{\displaystyle\sum_{k=1}^{M} \frac{D_i' \cdot D_j'}{D_k'}} \right] \right] \tag{3.9''}$$

For instance, for three groups, equation (3.9'') turns into:

$$\Delta E = \varepsilon^2 \cdot \left[\frac{(\gamma_1 - \gamma_2)^2}{D_1' + D_2' + \dfrac{D_1' \cdot D_2'}{D_3'}} + \frac{(\gamma_1 - \gamma_3)^2}{D_1' + D_3' + \dfrac{D_1' \cdot D_3'}{D_2'}} + \frac{(\gamma_2 - \gamma_3)^2}{D_2' + D_3' + \dfrac{D_2' \cdot D_3'}{D_1'}} \right]$$

The expression in (3.9'') is non-positive. Therefore, first-best differentiated regulation usually involves lower total environmental cost, and lower total emissions Γ, than do second-best policies – at least with linear demand and linear, additively separable external cost.

Since congestion is an intra-sectoral external cost, the benefits of optimizing the externality are also to be reaped within the sector. Therefore, it is less useful to consider the consequences of both types of policy on the optimal level of the total external cost. From a welfare point of view, it is sufficient to recognize that, when ω is smaller than 1, the potential welfare gains from second-best instruments are smaller than those resulting from first-best regulation.[4]

3.4 Group choice and modal choice: considering demand interdependencies

Due to the nature of the Lagrangians (3.1) and (3.4), some possibly important behaviourial responses to the kind of regulation applied (that is, first-best versus second-best) are ignored. In particular, the postulated independent, stable demand curves for all groups suggest that car drivers do not consider the possibility of switching group in response to the form of regulation applied. However, this possibility may of course additionally affect the performance of second-best policy instruments.[5] Analytically, the issues of group choice and modal choice, used here as a synonym for overall demand effect, are closely related: whereas the former involves exiting one group and entering another one, the latter merely involves exiting the initial group without entering another.

In transport markets such as those considered here, it seems implausible to specify continuous individual demand functions, including continuous 'cross-relations' between the different groups. Rather, individual behaviour is more adequately described by considering binary choices of whether to make a certain trip, based on the benefits and costs of doing so. Furthermore, the different groups are likely to be mutually exclusive for each individual driver: per trip, he chooses only one route and therewith one trip length, one departure time, and one vehicle. Consequently, when considering the issues of modal- and group choice in relation to the kind of regulation applied, the only assumption concerning individual behaviour that seems generally valid is that the rational individual car driver i chooses that group m where his net surplus (benefits B_m^i, minus group-

---

[4]However, one would intuitively expect the total level of congestion generally to be smaller under first-best policies for the same reason that the cost of reducing congestion is larger under second-best regulation due to the associated welfare losses.

[5]The potential relevance of such behaviourial responses increases, the easier they can be made. For instance, changes in departure times or routes may involve lower costs than changes in trip length (requiring changes in spatial activity patterns), change of mode or change of vehicle. However, such transitional costs will be ignored.

specific private cost c_m, minus any regulatory fee t_m) is maximized, provided it exceeds some threshold money metric indirect utility Q_0^i associated with leaving the road system. This latter depends on the utility associated with the best alternative available, which may be either an alternative mode such as public transport, or refraining from making the trip at all.[6] Therefore, individual behaviour may be characterized as:

$$\text{MAX} \left\{ \text{MAX}_m \left\{ B_m^i - c_m - t_m \right\}; Q_0^i \right\} \qquad (3.10)$$

Via the regulatory fee t_m, which may be either the first-best fee r_m or the optimal common fee f, the prevailing form of regulation to some extent determines the individual net surpluses enjoyed. By definition, under first-best policies, actors face optimal incentives for group and modal choice. They choose a group by maximizing the difference between benefits B_m^i and the generalized costs c_m^g, being the sum of private costs and the regulatory fee. Since under first-best policies these generalized costs are by definition equal to the social costs, individual maximizing behaviour maximizes social welfare, and the optimal distribution of road users over the groups and the optimal group sizes will result. Under second-best regulation however, the incentives given for switching from high-externality groups to low-externality groups are far from optimal.

For the environmental externality, the optimal common fee provides no incentives at all to switch from one group to another, since the factors $t_m = f$ are equal for all groups. This fee reduces the net surpluses achievable in each possible group by equal amounts. Therefore, actors belonging to one group under non-intervention will either remain in that group or leave the system. Hence, the incentive to switch from a 'high externality group' j to a 'low externality group' i misses out on a factor:

$$\varepsilon_j(\cdot) - \varepsilon_i(\cdot)$$

Therefore, second-best uniform taxation not only leads to a larger (smaller) than optimal reduction in the sizes of low (high) externality groups via the direct effect discussed in the foregoing sections. This is the 'modal choice effect' that, in terms of equation (3.8), for $m < \mu$ the excess reduction in the number of trips is $N_m(c_m + r_m) - N_m(c_m + f)$; and for $m > \mu$ the reduction in car use falls short with $N_m(c_m + f) - N_m(c_m + r_m)$. In addition, there is the

---

[6]After the drivers have chosen a group, the discontinuous individual demand functions can still be aggregated to more or less continuous demand functions on the group level, simply by ordering the group members according to decreasing willingness to pay (as was done in Section 3.2). However, within each group, the individual willingnesses to pay to make a trip in one of the other groups may of course very well vary unsystematically among the group members. Therefore, general analyses such as those in Section 3.2, which require continuous functions, are not used here, and the discussion is restricted to a comparison of incentives faced by the actors under first-best and second-best regulation.

more dynamic indirect effect (the 'group choice effect') of actors facing insufficient (that is, no) incentives to change their behaviour in terms of switching towards low externality groups.

For congestion, the modal choice effect is analogous to the effect mentioned above: for $s<\sigma$, the excess reduction in the number of trips is $N_s(c_s+r_s) - N_s(c_s+f)$; and for $s>\sigma$, the reduction in car use falls short with $N_s(c_s+f) - N_s(c_s+r_s)$. However, the group choice effect may actually even be counterproductive for common congestion fees. Again, the uniform tax in the first instance leads to increases in generalized costs which are equal for all groups, suggesting a lack in incentive to switch from a 'high congestion group' j towards a 'low congestion group' i equal to:

$$N_j \cdot c_j'(N_j) - N_i \cdot c_i'(N_i)$$

However, the common fee may very well lead to larger reductions in the average cost c_m for high congestion groups than for low congestion groups. If this is the case, the generalized costs for less congested groups increase stronger than for more congested groups. This may lead to the adverse indirect effect of drivers who initially belonged to low congestion groups switch towards more congested groups (compare (3.10)). Whether this adverse 'group choice effect' can occur depends on the slopes of the demand and average cost curves of the initial groups. Suppose, there are only two groups: a low congestion group i and a high congestion group j. The common fee f by definition leads to reductions in road usage by both groups such that, in terms of the initial demand and average cost curves:

$$\int_{N_i(c_i)}^{N_i(c_i+f)} \left[\frac{dD_i}{dN_i} - \frac{dc_i}{dN_i} \right] dN_i = f = \int_{N_j(c_j)}^{N_j(c_j+f)} \left[\frac{dD_j}{dN_j} - \frac{dc_j}{dN_j} \right] dN_j$$

Since j is the high congestion group, $N_j \cdot dc_j/dN_j > N_i \cdot dc_i/dN_i$, and $dc_j/dN_j > dc_i/dN_i$ if congestion rises progressively with group size. Then, the decrease in c_j exceeds the decrease in c_i unless the absolute value of the average slope (over the relevant range) of the demand curve D_j exceeds that of D_i at least to the same extent as the slope of the average cost curve c_j exceeds that of c_i. This, of course, need not be the case; especially not since high congestion is often associated with large groups, *ceteris paribus* implying a flatter demand curve.

For instance, Figure 3.2 shows a road network used during peak hour by group j and in the off-peak by group i. The curves D give demand, MSC is the marginal social cost and ASC=MPC gives average social cost = marginal private cost. With a common, weighted average congestion fee f, the generalized cost for group i increases more than for group j: $\Delta c_i^g > \Delta c_j^g$. Therefore, some drivers, initially using the network during the off-peak, may actually be attracted to the peak hour, causing an inward shift of D_i and an outward shift of D_j. As a consequence, the reduction in congestion during the peak (the off-peak) may even be further below

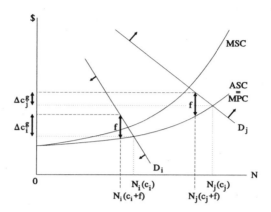

Figure 3.2   Adverse group choice effects resulting from a common congestion fee

(above) the optimal reduction than indicated by the modal choice effect alone. Of course, these shifts will in turn affect the optimal common fee, but this does not affect the general result.

3.5   Second-best charging mechanisms: a simple form of cost interdependencies

A last, somewhat different reason why certain instruments may be an imperfect substitute for optimally differentiated fees occurs when a certain number of actors is not confronted with the fee. Apart from sheer fraud, which may of course also occur under first-best policies, this may happen when second-best fees are levied via second-best charging mechanisms. For instance: road users who use private parking space will not be confronted with a regulatory parking fee.[7] Especially when the aim of the policy is to optimize congestion, the implications are not immediately clear. At first sight, one might argue that those who do park on public space should be taxed more heavily, in order to try and realize the optimal reduction in traffic flows as closely as possible. However, the taxation of the public parkers leads to a reduction in congestion, and therefore to a reduction in the marginal private cost of making trips, thus inducing additional traffic from private parkers. There is clearly a welfare loss associated with this process, as some road users (public parkers) with a

---

[7]The type of problem considered in this section is not specific to parking. Another example would be congestion pricing with the constraint that commercial vehicles be exempted, as in fact happened originally in Singapore.

certain willingness to pay who are 'taxed off the road' will to a certain extent be replaced by others (private parkers) with a necessarily lower willingness to pay. This type of problem introduces a simple cost interdependency into the model; a more complex case of cost interdependencies is discussed in Appendix 3.A.

When tolled road users (group 1) and untolled road users (group 2) jointly use a congested road network, where the average cost of driving depends on the total number of road users $N=N_1+N_2$, implying that the marginal cost of adding an extra road user is equal for both groups, the regulator faces the following Lagrangian:

$$\mathcal{L} = \int_0^{N_1} D_1(n_1)\, dn_1 + \int_0^{N_2} D_2(n_2)\, dn_2 - N{\cdot}c(N)$$
$$+ \lambda_1{\cdot}\big(D_1(N_1)-c(N)-f\big) + \lambda_2{\cdot}\big(D_2(N_2)-c(N)\big) \tag{3.11}$$

with: $N = N_1 + N_2$

The first-order conditions are:

$$\frac{\partial \mathcal{L}}{\partial N_1} = D_1(N_1) - c(N) - N{\cdot}c\,'(N) + \lambda_1{\cdot}\big(D_1'(N_1)-c\,'(N)\big) - \lambda_2{\cdot}c\,'(N) = 0$$

$$\frac{\partial \mathcal{L}}{\partial N_2} = D_2(N_2) - c(N) - N{\cdot}c\,'(N) - \lambda_1{\cdot}c\,'(N) + \lambda_2{\cdot}\big(D_2'(N_2)-c\,'(N)\big) = 0$$

$$\frac{\partial \mathcal{L}}{\partial f} = -\lambda_1 = 0$$

$$\frac{\partial \mathcal{L}}{\partial \lambda_1} = D_1(N_1) - c(N) - f = 0$$

$$\frac{\partial \mathcal{L}}{\partial \lambda_2} = D_2(N_2) - c(N) = 0$$

Using $\lambda_1=0$, we find:

$$f = N{\cdot}c\,'(N) + \lambda_2{\cdot}c\,'(N)$$

Solving for λ_2 yields:

$$\lambda_2 = -\frac{N{\cdot}c\,'(N)}{c\,'(N) - D_2'(N_2)}$$

Substitution of λ_2 then yields the following optimal second-best fee:

$$f = N{\cdot}c\,'(N) \cdot \left[\frac{-D_2'(N_2)}{c\,'(N) - D_2'(N_2)}\right] \tag{3.12}$$

A comparison of $(3.12)^8$ with the standard congestion fee (see Section 3.2) shows how the presence of untolled road users affects the result. The optimal second-best fee now depends on the slope of the demand curve of the untolled users, which in turn depends on their group size and demand elasticities as outlined in Section 3.2.

In the one extreme, where the untolled users have a perfectly elastic demand in the second-best optimum (group 2 is infinitely large and completely homogeneous), the term between the large parentheses in (3.12) is zero, and the optimal second-best fee is zero. Any positive fee will only lead to welfare losses, since any tolled driver that is 'taxed off the road' will be replaced by an untolled driver with a lower willingness to pay for using the road network. Congestion therefore remains unaffected, while the total benefit decreases. Therefore, the best thing the regulator can do is not levy any fee at all. In the other extreme, where the untolled road users have a perfectly inelastic demand in the second-best optimum, the term between the large brackets in (3.12) is equal to 1, and (3.12) reduces to:

$$f = N \cdot c'(N) \tag{3.12'}$$

This optimal fee is similar to the standard congestion fee derived in Section 3.2. In this case, however, the optimal fee for the tolled users depends on the (fixed) number of untolled users. In a sense, the presence of untolled drivers can be thought of as a mere restriction on the road network capacity, *ceteris paribus* leading to a lower optimal number of tolled users and therefore to a higher second-best regulatory fee.

In any situation between these two extreme cases, the optimal fee depends on the joint effects of the slope of the untolled drivers' demand curve (the flatter this curve, the lower the optimal fee) and, of course, on the overall second-best demand in relation to the capacity of the network.

Clearly, the presence of users who are not subject to regulatory policies seriously harms the performance of such policies. In the first place, not every road user responsible for (and subject to) congestion can be reached with such policies. Moreover, and perhaps less obvious, the policy will be frustrated by the fact that the users who are 'taxed off the road' may be replaced by untolled users, representing a lower willingness to pay for road use and consequently representing lower benefits. This process involves welfare losses which have to be weighted against the welfare gains of second-best regulatory policies in terms of reducing congestion.

Figure 3.3 gives a diagrammatic representation of this situation. In the left panel, the demand (D), average social cost (ASC), equal to marginal private cost (MPC), and the marginal social cost (MSC) curves are drawn for the entire population of road users. The middle and right panel give the

---

[8]This result is also found by Glazer and Niskanen (1992, equation (18)).

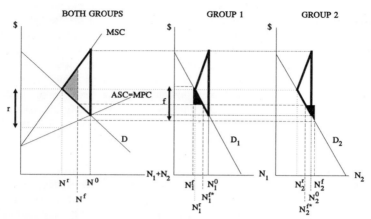

Figure 3.3   *The welfare effects of first-best congestion fees versus the optimal second-best fee in presence of both tolled users (group 1) and untolled users (group 2)*

demand curves for group 1 (the tolled users) and group 2 (the untolled users), respectively. Optimal first-best regulation implies a levy r for both groups, leading to a reduction in the total number of trips from N^0 to N^r and an increase in social welfare equal to the bold triangle in the left panel (or the sum of the two bold triangles in the middle and right panel). However, the use of the optimal second-best fee as given by (3.12) leads to a reduction in the number of trips made by group 1 from N_1^0 to N_1^f (rather than N_1^r) and an increase in the number of trips made by group 2 from N_2^0 to N_2^f (rather than the optimal reduction to N_2^r). The total reduction in number of trips is therefore only from N^0 to N^f, and the use of this policy misses out on the potential welfare gains as given by the shaded triangle in the left panel. Moreover, the reduction from N^0 to N^f is not accomplished in the most efficient way, being reductions to N_1^{f*} and N_2^{f*}, respectively, where the marginal benefits for both groups are equalized. Therefore, the two black triangles give additional welfare losses of optimal second-best regulation in comparison with first-best regulation. The index of relative welfare improvement ω will now be as follows:

$$\omega = \frac{\int_{N^f}^{N^0} S(n)\, dn \; - \int_{N_1^f}^{N_1^{f*}} \left(D_1(n_1) - D_1(N_1^{f*})\right) dn_1 \; - \int_{N_2^{f*}}^{N_2^f} \left(D_2(N_2^{f*}) - D_2(n_2)\right) dn_2}{\int_{N^r}^{N^f} S(n)\, dn \; + \int_{N^r}^{N^0} S(n)\, dn} \tag{3.13}$$

The functions S are as defined before, be it that they are now specified for the entire population of road users. From (3.13), it follows that ω is closer to 1, the steeper the demand curve of group 2, either due to a lower demand elasticity or a smaller group size. This reduces the value of the first term in the denominator, since f in (3.12) approaches r. Furthermore, the second and third term in the numerator then approach zero.

Finally, the total reduction in the number of trips under second-best policies is in this case obviously always smaller than under first-best regulation whenever the demand of group 2 is not perfectly inelastic. First, group 1 is confronted with a lower fee; and secondly, group 2 even enjoys a fall in the cost of driving.

3.6   Conclusion

This chapter investigated the welfare economic characteristics of second-best alternatives to first-best differentiated marginal external cost pricing in the regulation of road transport externalities. Second-best regulation will often suffer from the impossibility of optimal tax differentiation in cases where first-best policies do call for such differentiation; for instance when external costs are trip length-, time-, route- or vehicle-specific.

The optimal common fee is a weighted average of the optimal first-best differentiated fees. For an environmental externality, the optimal weight assigned to a group depends on the inverse of the slope of its demand curve in the optimum, and is therefore positively related to its group size and to its demand elasticity in the second-best optimum. For the optimal common congestion fee, the weight is in addition (inversely) related to the slope of the average cost function in the second-best optimum.

By application of an index of relative welfare improvement, the welfare effects of second-best policies can be compared to those resulting from first-best policies. It turned out that second-best instruments become a less favourable substitute, the larger the differences in marginal external costs, and the larger the relative importance and the demand elasticities of the groups in the extremes. It was also shown that the optimal reduction in the externality is usually smaller when second-best instruments are used, than under first-best regulation.

A second-best common fee results in non-optimal incentives in terms of modal choice in that low externality groups are overcharged and high externality groups are undercharged. In terms of group choice, a common fee completely fails to provide incentives to switch from high externality to low externality groups for an environmental externality. A common congestion fee may even create adverse incentives for group choice.

In the last section, it was shown that the performance of a second-best congestion fee, suffering from the incapability of charging all road users on a network, critically depends on the relative size and the demand elasticity of the group which remains unaffected by the policy.

Appendix 3.A The optimal common fee with cost interdependencies

In equations 3.4 and 3.5 (Section 3.2), the optimal common congestion fee is derived for S different groups having their own level of intra-group congestion, ignoring the possibility of inter-group congestion effects. When allowing for congestion effects not only within, but also between groups (such as congestion at road crossings when considering route-specific congestion, or groups with different trip lengths using one joint network), the Lagrangian in (3.4) may be rewritten as follows:

$$\mathscr{L} = \sum_{s=1}^{S} \int_{0}^{N_s} D_s(n_s)\, dn_s - \sum_{s=1}^{S} N_s \cdot c_s(N_1, N_2, ..., N_S) + \sum_{s=1}^{S} \lambda_s \cdot (D_s(N_s) - c_s(N_1, N_2, ..., N_S) - f) \quad (3.A1)$$

The cost functions (in the second term) have changed so as to allow the average cost of group s (c_s) to depend not only on the size of the group itself, but (possibly) on all group sizes. Consequently, optimal discriminatory road pricing involves road prices r_s equal to:

$$r_s = \sum_{t=1}^{S} N_t \cdot \frac{\partial c_t(\cdot)}{\partial N_s}$$

The optimal common fee can be found by solving the set of first-order conditions to (3.A1):

$$\frac{\partial \mathscr{L}}{\partial N_s} = D_s(N_s) - c_s(\cdot) - \sum_{t=1}^{S} N_t \cdot \frac{\partial c_t(\cdot)}{\partial N_s} + \lambda_s \cdot \frac{dD_s(N_s)}{dN_s} - \sum_{t=1}^{S} \lambda_t \cdot \frac{\partial c_t(\cdot)}{\partial N_s} = 0 \quad s=1,2,...,S \quad (3.A2)$$

$$\frac{\partial \mathscr{L}}{\partial f} = -\sum_{s=1}^{S} \lambda_s = 0 \quad (3.A3)$$

$$\frac{\partial \mathscr{L}}{\partial \lambda_s} = D_s(N_s) - c_s(\cdot) - f = 0 \quad s=1,2,...,S \quad (3.A4)$$

Contrary to the problem in (3.4), it is not possible to solve for each λ_s in terms of $\partial D_s/\partial N_s$ and $\partial c_s/\partial N_s$ only. In matrix notation, the set of first-order conditions can be represented as follows:

$$\begin{bmatrix} \frac{dD_1}{dN_1} - \frac{\partial c_1}{\partial N_1} & -\frac{\partial c_2}{\partial N_1} & \cdots & -\frac{\partial c_S}{\partial N_1} \\ -\frac{\partial c_1}{\partial N_2} & \frac{dD_2}{dN_2} - \frac{\partial c_2}{\partial N_2} & \cdots & -\frac{\partial c_S}{\partial N_2} \\ \vdots & \vdots & \ddots & \vdots \\ -\frac{\partial c_1}{\partial N_S} & -\frac{\partial c_2}{\partial N_S} & \cdots & \frac{dD_S}{dN_S} - \frac{\partial c_S}{\partial N_S} \\ -1 & -1 & \cdots & -1 \end{bmatrix} \begin{bmatrix} \lambda_1 \\ \lambda_2 \\ \vdots \\ \lambda_S \end{bmatrix} = - \begin{bmatrix} f - \sum_{t=1}^{S} N_t \cdot \frac{\partial c_t}{\partial N_1} \\ f - \sum_{t=1}^{S} N_t \cdot \frac{\partial c_t}{\partial N_2} \\ \vdots \\ f - \sum_{t=1}^{S} N_t \cdot \frac{\partial c_t}{\partial N_S} \\ 0 \end{bmatrix} \quad (3.A5)$$

By leaving out the bottom row of the matrix and of the vector to the right of the equal sign, Cramer's rule can be used to solve for each λ_s in terms of the remaining elements of the vector on the right and elements of the matrix. Next, using (3.A3), one of the conditions (3.A2) can be rewritten as:

$$f - \sum_{t=1}^{S} N_t \cdot \frac{\partial c_t}{\partial N_s} - \sum_{t \neq s} \lambda_t \cdot \left[\frac{dD_s}{dN_s} - \frac{\partial c_s}{\partial N_s} + \frac{\partial c_t}{\partial N_s} \right] = 0 \quad (3.A6)$$

It is then a matter of substitution of the expressions found for the terms λ_s and rewriting (3.A6) to find the expression for the optimal common fee. For two groups, the expression for the optimal common fee is still quite straightforward:

$$f = \left[N_1 \cdot \frac{\partial c_1}{\partial N_1} + N_2 \cdot \frac{\partial c_2}{\partial N_1} \right] \cdot \frac{\dfrac{1}{\dfrac{dD_1}{dN_1} - \dfrac{\partial c_1}{\partial N_1} + \dfrac{\partial c_2}{\partial N_1}}}{\dfrac{1}{\dfrac{dD_1}{dN_1} - \dfrac{\partial c_1}{\partial N_1} + \dfrac{\partial c_2}{\partial N_1}} + \dfrac{1}{\dfrac{dD_2}{dN_2} - \dfrac{\partial c_2}{\partial N_2} + \dfrac{\partial c_1}{\partial N_2}}}$$

$$+ \left[N_1 \cdot \frac{\partial c_1}{\partial N_2} + N_2 \cdot \frac{\partial c_2}{\partial N_2} \right] \cdot \frac{\dfrac{1}{\dfrac{dD_2}{dN_2} - \dfrac{\partial c_2}{\partial N_2} + \dfrac{\partial c_1}{\partial N_2}}}{\dfrac{1}{\dfrac{dD_1}{dN_1} - \dfrac{\partial c_1}{\partial N_1} + \dfrac{\partial c_2}{\partial N_1}} + \dfrac{1}{\dfrac{dD_2}{dN_2} - \dfrac{\partial c_2}{\partial N_2} + \dfrac{\partial c_1}{\partial N_2}}}$$

(3.A7)

For more than two cohorts, the expression for the optimal common fee becomes increasingly complicated, due to the appearance of an increasing number of cross-effects. For instance, for three cohorts, it can be shown that:

$$f = \frac{\displaystyle\sum_{s=1}^{3} \frac{\displaystyle\sum_{i=1}^{3} N_i \cdot \frac{\partial c_i}{\partial N_s}}{\displaystyle\prod_{u,v \neq s; u \neq v} \left[\left[\frac{dD_s}{dN_s} - \frac{\partial c_s}{\partial N_s} \right] \cdot \left[\frac{dD_u}{dN_u} - \frac{\partial c_u}{\partial N_u} + \frac{\partial c_v}{\partial N_u} \right] + \frac{\partial c_v}{\partial N_u} \cdot \left[\frac{dD_u}{dN_u} - \frac{\partial c_u}{\partial N_u} + \frac{\partial c_s}{\partial N_u} \right] + \frac{\partial c_u}{\partial N_s} \cdot \left[\frac{\partial c_v}{\partial N_s} - \frac{\partial c_s}{\partial N_u} \right] \right]}}{\displaystyle\sum_{s=1}^{3} \frac{1}{\displaystyle\prod_{u,v \neq s; u \neq v} \left[\left[\frac{dD_s}{dN_s} - \frac{\partial c_s}{\partial N_s} \right] \cdot \left[\frac{dD_u}{dN_u} - \frac{\partial c_u}{\partial N_u} + \frac{\partial c_v}{\partial N_u} \right] + \frac{\partial c_v}{\partial N_u} \cdot \left[\frac{dD_u}{dN_u} - \frac{\partial c_u}{\partial N_u} + \frac{\partial c_s}{\partial N_u} \right] + \frac{\partial c_u}{\partial N_s} \cdot \left[\frac{\partial c_v}{\partial N_s} - \frac{\partial c_s}{\partial N_u} \right] \right]}}$$

(3.A8)

Comparison of (3.A7) and (3.A8) with (3.5) shows how the cross-effects associated with inter-group congestion effects affect the weights in the optimal common fee. In Section 3.2, it was concluded that a group receives a larger weight, both the flatter its demand curve and its average cost curve. The reason was that the optimal weights should be such that the welfare losses due to deviations of the common fee from the optimal individual fees are minimized. In presence of inter-group congestion effects, the welfare losses due to such deviations obviously also depend on the extent to which a group influences congestion (and therefore welfare) in other groups. For two groups, a group's weight decreases, the stronger the cross-effect it has on the other group; the terms reflecting the cross-effects have a sign opposite to those reflecting own-welfare effects. This is easy to understand once it is realized that the decrease of a group's weight simply implies a relative increase of the other group's weight. In fact, (3.A7) says that the regulator's concern with welfare losses in a certain group A due to second-best intervention should be reduced, and his concern with losses in group B should be increased, (1) the smaller the welfare losses within group A itself due to such second best intervention, and (2) the stronger group A influences welfare in group B compared to the opposite effect. Equation (3.A8) reflects a comparable message, though it is even more difficult to put the content of (3.A8) into words, due to the appearance of all possible cross-effects in the expression.

4

SECOND-BEST CONGESTION PRICING WITH AN UNTOLLED ALTERNATIVE [1]

4.1 Introduction

This chapter studies the relative efficiency of second-best congestion pricing in the case where road users can choose between a tolled and an untolled route. It thus investigates some peculiarities in the regulation of road transport externalities that are due to the fact that road transport takes place in a network environment. Clearly, as people will generally prefer free (or at least cheap) alternatives, the resulting choice processes are particularly interesting when considering congestion.

There are various reasons why untolled alternatives may be present in practice. First, the regulator may leave a route untolled for equity reasons; for instance to protect low-income groups from having to pay fees, or to increase the social feasibility of road pricing (Starkie, 1986). Alternatively, untolled alternatives may be present when (electronic) toll experiments are being undertaken. Furthermore, the same type of situation prevails with the occurrence of so-called 'rat-running': drivers using escape routes in order to avoid certain toll-points. On the other hand, the cost of toll collection may actually justify the choice of not regulating an entire road network, but only some of its major links instead. Finally, part of the road infrastructure may be privately owned and tolled, with a publicly provided alternative offered for free. In what follows, the efficiency sides to one-route tolling are discussed, and the analysis therefore concerns the latter four types of reason for untolled alternatives to exist.

Pigou (1920) and Knight (1924) were probably the first to discuss congestion pricing with two routes (one of which, in their case, was assumed to be uncongested). Later on, Lévy-Lambert (1968) and Marchand (1968) were the first to derive the optimal one-route toll with an untolled congested alternative. Recent discussions of two-route problems in the context of the dynamic bottleneck model with inelastic demand can be found in Arnott, De Palma and Lindsey (1990a, 1992) and Bernstein and

---

[1]This chapter is based on an article that will appear in *Journal of Urban Economics* (Verhoef, Nijkamp and Rietveld, 1996a).

El Sanhouri (1994) – although the latter actually also do consider elastic demand, but not with the second-best optimal one-route toll. In the present analysis, elasticity of demand, for instance resulting from the presence of alternative transport modes, can easily be considered, and will actually turn out to be of crucial importance for the efficiency of one-route tolling. However, dynamic departure time decisions are ignored, which renders the present models supplementary to the latter three mentioned above. In addition, also (private) revenue maximizing tolling will be considered here.

The plan of the chapter is as follows. Section 4.2 starts off with investigating the optimal one-route toll and its welfare economic properties. By comparing these to first-best regulation, the relative performance of one-route tolling will be evaluated in Section 4.3. Also the question of whether the cost of congestion charging itself may be a reason for leaving some alternatives untolled will be considered. Section 4.4 discusses the case where tolling occurs for the purpose of revenue raising by some private operator. Section 4.5 contains the conclusions.

4.2   Optimal second-best congestion pricing with an untolled alternative: some basic welfare economic properties

This section discusses some basic welfare economic properties of congestion pricing with an untolled alternative. A simple network is considered, with two competing, congested routes: one tolled (T), and one untolled (U). It is assumed that the regulator wishes to set the fee on the tolled route so as to maximize efficiency under the inherent limitation of not tolling the other route. In doing so, some sub-goals related to overall efficiency have to be traded off. These are (1) an overall demand ('modal split') effect, being the extent to which road users efficiently leave the road system altogether due to congestion pricing; and (2) a route split effect, being the extent to which the remaining road users divide themselves efficiently among both routes. Generally, as one of the routes remains untolled, it will be impossible to realize the first-best situation where both effects are optimized (see also Bernstein and El Sanhouri, 1994).

When considering congestion pricing with an untolled alternative, one has to take account of both demand and cost interdependencies between the two routes (compare Chapter 3). In the problem's purest form, the public regards the two alternative routes as perfect substitutes. The model therefore contains one single demand function D(N), where N denotes the total number of road users (on both routes); and two average user cost functions $c_T(N_T)$ and $c_U(N_U)$, where naturally $N=N_T+N_U$, and where average user cost and also the value of time are assumed to be equal for all road users. In line with Wardrop's first principle (Wardrop, 1952), at any equilibrium should then the average cost on route U be equal to the average cost on route T plus the one-route fee f; otherwise people would shift from the one route to the other. Furthermore, both should be equal to marginal benefits D(N). The optimal one-route toll in this setting has originally been derived by Lévy-Lambert (1968) and Marchand (1968). The reason for presenting an alternative derivation in this chapter is that it is more transparent and easy to follow than the two earlier mentioned.

The optimal one-route toll f, maximizing total benefits minus total costs, can be found by solving the following Lagrangian:

$$\mathcal{L} = \int_0^N D(n) \, dn - N_T \cdot c_T(N_T) - N_U \cdot c_U(N_U)$$
$$+ \lambda_T \cdot (D(N) - c_T(N_T) - f) + \lambda_U \cdot (D(N) - c_U(N_U)) \tag{4.1}$$

with: $N = N_T + N_U$

The first-order conditions are:

$$\frac{\partial \mathcal{L}}{\partial N_T} = D(N) - c_T(N_T) - N_T \cdot c_T'(N_T) + \lambda_T \cdot \left(D'(N) - c_T'(N_T)\right) + \lambda_U \cdot D'(N) = 0$$

$$\frac{\partial \mathcal{L}}{\partial N_U} = D(N) - c_U(N_U) - N_U \cdot c_U'(N_U) + \lambda_T \cdot D'(N) + \lambda_U \cdot \left(D'(N) - c_U'(N_U)\right) = 0$$

$$\frac{\partial \mathcal{L}}{\partial f} = -\lambda_T = 0$$

$$\frac{\partial \mathcal{L}}{\partial \lambda_T} = D(N) - c_T(N_T) - f = 0$$

$$\frac{\partial \mathcal{L}}{\partial \lambda_U} = D(N) - c_U(N_U) = 0$$

Using $\lambda_T = 0$, we find:

$$f = N_T \cdot c_T'(N_T) - \lambda_U \cdot D'(N)$$

Solving for λ_U yields:

$$\lambda_U = \frac{N_U \cdot c_U'(N_U)}{D'(N) - c_U'(N_U)}$$

Substitution of λ_U then yields the following optimal second-best fee:

$$f = N_T \cdot c_T'(N_T) - N_U \cdot c_U'(N_U) \cdot \left[\frac{-D'(N)}{c_U'(N_U) - D'(N)}\right] \tag{4.2}$$

while the first-best road price r_i on route i (i=T,U) would be:

$$r_i = N_i \cdot c_i'(N_i) \tag{4.3}$$

The first term in (4.2), equal to the marginal external congestion costs on route T in the second-best optimum, captures the direct impact of the fee on congestion on the tolled route. The second term reflects that one should also take account of the 'spill-over' effects on the untolled route by subtracting some non-negative term, which is a fraction of the marginal external congestion costs on the untolled route in the second-best optimum. This fraction, which may range between 0 and 1, is given by the term between the large parentheses, and depends on the (relative) values of $D'(N)$ and $c_U'(N_U)$; that is, on the slopes of the demand curve and the average cost curve on the untolled route in the second-best optimum.

The actual impact of D' and c_U' on the expression for f is a bit hard to trace at once, as both appear twice in the second term. However, some insight can be obtained by considering some extreme values of D' and c_U'. For instance, if overall demand is perfectly inelastic ($D'=-\infty$) in the second-best optimum, the term between the large parentheses in (4.2) approaches 1, and (4.2) reduces to:

$$f = N_T \cdot c_T'(N_T) - N_U \cdot c_U'(N_U) \tag{4.2'}$$

As there is no effect of the policy on overall demand, but solely on route split, the best thing the regulator can do is to concentrate on achieving the optimal route split. Hence, the fee should be set at the difference between the marginal external congestion costs on both routes in the second-best optimum, in order to attain the efficient distribution of road users over both routes. Note that, particularly when approaching this extreme case, one cannot tell in advance whether (4.2) yields a positive tax. It may well be negative, implying an optimal subsidy on using route T. In the extreme case of completely inelastic overall demand, this is the case whenever marginal external congestion costs are higher on the untolled route than on the tolled route in the second-best optimum. Another possibility in this case would of course be taxation of route U, leaving T untolled.

Alternatively, if overall demand is perfectly elastic ($D'=0$) in the second-best optimum, (4.2) reduces to the following extreme expression:

$$f = N_T \cdot c_T'(N_T) \tag{4.2''}$$

The regulator may now ignore spill-over effects from route T to route U since road usage on route U remains unaffected anyway: due to the completely homogeneous and sufficiently large group of potential road users, they will keep on entering route U up to a level where (constant) marginal benefits are equal to marginal private cost, regardless of the type of regulation on route T. Therefore, the best thing the regulator can do in this case is to optimize usage of route T, ignoring the unavoidable welfare loss on route U. In contrast to the former case, overall demand effects of regulation (be it solely on route T), rather than route split impacts, now receive full attention.

The same expression (4.2'') for the optimal one-route toll is found in the case considered by Knight (1924), where route U is completely

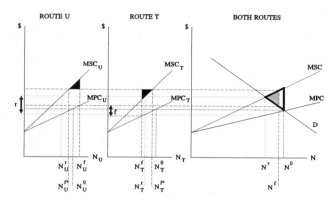

Figure 4.1   The welfare effects of first-best two-route (bold) versus second-best one-route (bold minus shaded and black) congestion pricing

uncongested ($c_U'=0$) in the second-best optimum. Since regulation on route T then apparently causes no 'spill-over cost' in terms of increasing congestion externalities on route U (there is no congestion on route U in the second-best optimum), the regulator may just optimize road use on route T as if first-best conditions would apply.

The fourth extreme case, where route U is completely congested in the second-best optimum ($c_U'=\infty$), is not discussed here, as this is of course a highly unrealistic one. It is hard to imagine how, given the extreme congestion on route U, the average user costs on route U and route T can still be equal, as they should be in such an equilibrium. It is perhaps worth underlining here that road usage is not measured in flows (in which case, because of the backward-bending cost curve, its derivative will indeed be infinite at some relevant point), but in numbers of road users instead (see also Alan Evans, 1992).

Generally then, it can be concluded that the second-best one-route congestion fee in its optimal use trades off a number of 'sub-goals' contributing to the overall goal of efficient allocation. These sub-goals are related to usage and congestion on both routes, and therefore comprise overall demand and route split effects.

Figure 4.1 gives a diagrammatic sketch of the situation discussed above. In the right panel, the demand (D), marginal private cost (MPC), and the marginal social cost (MSC) curves are drawn for the entire group of road users using two identical alternatives U and T (identical routes are used for ease of diagrammatic presentation). The middle and left panel give the cost curves for both routes. Optimal first-best regulation implies a levy r on both routes, leading to a reduction in usage from N^0 to N^r, composed of reductions from N_T^0 to N_T^r and from N_U^0 to N_U^r. The increase in social welfare is given by the surface of the bold triangle in the right panel.

However, the use of the optimal second-best fee f on route T alone, as given by (4.2), leads to a reduction in the number of trips made on route T from N_T^0 to N_T^f, and an increase in the number of trips made on route U from N_U^0 to N_U^f because of route switching (note that switching occurs so that marginal benefits on both routes remain equalized). The reduction in total usage is therefore only from N^0 to N^f, and the use of this policy misses out on the potential welfare gains as given by the shaded triangle in the right panel. Moreover, the reduction from N^0 to N^f is not accomplished in its most efficient way, which would have been reductions to N_T^{f*} and N_U^{f*}, respectively, where the marginal social costs on both routes are equalized. Therefore, the two black triangles give additional welfare losses of one-route tolling in comparison with first-best regulation. Obviously, the total welfare gain of optimal one-route tolling will be non-negative; otherwise the optimal second-best fee would simply be zero.

In Chapter 3, the index of relative welfare improvement ω was used, defined as the ratio of the overall welfare gain under second-best regulation compared to non-intervention, and the overall welfare gain under first-best regulation compared to non-intervention. This index will in this case be as follows:

$$\omega = \frac{\displaystyle\int_{N^r}^{N^0} S(n)\,dn - \int_{N_U^{f*}}^{N_U^f} \left(k_U(n_U) - k_U(N_U^{f*})\right)\,dn_U - \int_{N_T^r}^{N_T^{f*}} \left(k_T(N_T^f) - k_T(n_T)\right)\,dn_T}{\displaystyle\int_{N^r}^{N^r} S(n)\,dn + \int_{N^r}^{N^0} S(n)\,dn} \quad (4.4)$$

where the function S is defined as the difference between marginal social cost minus marginal benefits, and k_i denotes marginal social cost for group i. The denominator of (4.4) represents the bold triangle in the right panel of Figure 4.1. The first term in the numerator gives the surface of this triangle minus the shaded area, and the second and third term represent the two black triangles in the left and middle panel, respectively. The various factors determining the value of ω will be considered in the next section.

4.3 Factors determining the relative performance of one-route tolling

This section discusses the outcomes of some simulations that were performed in order to arrive at some more explicit results than the general specification in the foregoing section allows. When switching towards explicit functions, one is soon confronted with very tedious expressions, depending of course on the functional forms chosen for the demand and cost functions. As there is no theoretical reason to prefer any of the functional forms possible, and in order to keep the analysis manageable and the outcomes tractable, the simulation model is kept as simple as possible by assuming that these functions are linear over the relevant ranges considered (that is, the range containing the non-intervention, second-best, and first-best levels of usage). Although the use of linear functions may be criticized, they are in any case sufficient to serve the general goal of the simulations, being the assessment of the influence of some key factors related to demand and cost structures on the relative performance of one-route tolling. Also, it is worth mentioning here that Arnott, De Palma and Lindsey (1990a, 1992) have pointed out at several occasions that the linear congestion cost function is not necessarily unreasonable, since it can be interpreted as a reduced form representation of the Vickrey (1969) bottleneck model.

4.3.1 The model

The model then consists of one joint linear demand function, characterized by slope α and intersection δ:

$$D = \delta - \alpha \cdot (N_T + N_U) \tag{4.5}$$

Next, for both routes ($i=T,U$), the marginal private cost MPC, equal to average social cost ASC, consists of a free-flow cost component κ_i, and a congestion cost component which is assumed to be proportional to total usage N_i with a factor β_i:

$$MPC_i = ASC_i = \kappa_i + \beta_i \cdot N_i; \quad i = T,U \tag{4.6}$$

All parameters are non-negative; and only 'regular' networks will be considered, where both routes are at least marginally used under non-intervention, first-best, and second-best regulation. Apart from the explicit functions, the model is further identical to the one presented in Section 4.2. Under the three different regulatory regimes of non-intervention, second-best one-route tolling, and first-best two-route tolling, equilibrium usage on both routes will be as given in Table 4.1.

For the 'base case' of the model, the following parameter values were chosen: $\alpha=0.01$; $\delta=50$; $\kappa_T=\kappa_U=20$; and $\beta_T=\beta_U=0.02$. So, both routes are assumed to be identical in the base case. No surprise then, that equilibrium usage under non-intervention is equal on both routes: $N_T=N_U=750$. Marginal private cost amounts to 35.00 on both routes; marginal social cost to 50.00. Under first-best regulation, optimal road prices of $r_T=r_U=10.00$ are found for both routes, with marginal private cost then amounting to 30.00, and marginal social cost to 40.00 on both routes. The optimal road prices for both routes are therefore equal to the difference between these two, as theory dictates. Optimal usage is 500 on both routes.

	Non-intervention	Two-route tolling	One-route tolling
N_T	$\dfrac{\delta - \dfrac{\alpha\cdot(\kappa_T-\kappa_U)}{\beta_U} - \kappa_T}{\dfrac{\alpha\cdot\beta_T}{\beta_U}+\alpha+\beta_T}$	$\dfrac{\delta - \dfrac{\alpha\cdot(\kappa_T-\kappa_U)}{2\cdot\beta_U} - \kappa_T}{\dfrac{\alpha\cdot\beta_T}{\beta_U}+\alpha+2\cdot\beta_T}$	$\dfrac{\delta - \dfrac{\alpha\cdot\dfrac{\alpha}{\alpha+\beta_U}\cdot(\kappa_T-\kappa_U)}{\left[1+\dfrac{\alpha}{\alpha+\beta_U}\right]\cdot\beta_U} - \kappa_T}{\dfrac{\alpha\cdot\dfrac{\alpha}{\alpha+\beta_U}\cdot 2\cdot\beta_T}{\left[1+\dfrac{\alpha}{\alpha+\beta_U}\right]\cdot\beta_U}+\alpha+2\cdot\beta_T}$
N_U	$\dfrac{\delta - \dfrac{\alpha\cdot(\kappa_U-\kappa_T)}{\beta_T} - \kappa_U}{\dfrac{\alpha\cdot\beta_U}{\beta_T}+\alpha+\beta_U}$	$\dfrac{\delta - \dfrac{\alpha\cdot(\kappa_U-\kappa_T)}{2\cdot\beta_T} - \kappa_U}{\dfrac{\alpha\cdot\beta_U}{\beta_T}+\alpha+2\cdot\beta_U}$	$\dfrac{\delta - \dfrac{\alpha\cdot(\kappa_U-\kappa_T)}{2\cdot\beta_T} - \kappa_U}{\dfrac{\alpha\cdot\left[1+\dfrac{\alpha}{\alpha+\beta_U}\right]\cdot\beta_U}{2\cdot\beta_T}+\alpha+\beta_U}$

Table 4.1   Equilibrium usage on both routes under non-intervention, first-best and second-best regulatory policies

Under second-best one-route tolling, the second-best optimal fee for route T is 5.45. Marginal private cost is 30.91 on route T, and 36.36 on route U; the difference is exactly equal to the additional fee on route T, so that user equilibrium is indeed guaranteed. Marginal social cost is 41.82 on route T, and 52.73 on route U, readily demonstrating a non-optimal route split: road usage is 545 on route T and 818 on route U. Finally, the index of relative welfare improvement ω is equal to 0.273 in this base case, indicating that 27.3% of the potential efficiency gains under two-route tolling will be realized with one-route tolling.

By varying the model's respective parameters, it is possible to gain insight into the conditions under which one-route tolling is a relatively (un)attractive option. The results are presented below. Obviously, with this type of modelling exercises, there are many more possibilities than just the ones reported below. Many of these have been studied; the ones discussed below are those that were found to be the most interesting.

4.3.2   Varying cost parameters

First, consider the free-flow cost parameters, for instance reflecting the length of the links. Figure 4.2 gives the course of ω, and of the optimal first-best and second-best fees, for an increasing difference between these parameters. Instead of varying just one of the parameters, κ_T was raised while simultaneously lowering κ_U; both by 1.5 each step, the base case of

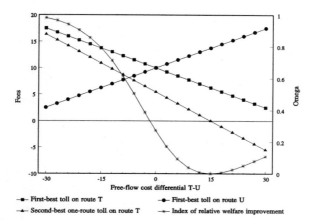

Figure 4.2 Varying free-flow costs: optimal fees and index of relative welfare improvement

$\kappa_T = \kappa_U = 20$ being in the centre. First of all, although the congestion parameters are equal for both routes, first-best tolls on both routes do not coincide. This may be surprising at first sight, as one might expect the level of free-flow cost to be a purely 'internal' cost component, without any impact on optimal fees. However, due to the fact that road users distribute themselves among the two routes such that marginal private cost, including the internal congestion cost component, are equalized, there is a direct effect of differences in free-flow costs on the optimal tolls. Generally speaking, the lower the free-flow cost, the higher the internal congestion cost, and hence also the higher the external congestion cost will be. This is illustrated in Figure 4.2 by the courses of the first-best fees.

Due to this effect, also the optimal one-route toll and the index of relative welfare improvement show an interesting pattern in Figure 4.2. When the free-flow costs on route T grow sufficiently high compared to those on route U, on the right-hand side of the figure, the optimal one-route toll may actually turn into a subsidy: f is negative. Marginal social costs on route U are then so much higher than those on route T that it is even worthwhile attracting some new traffic as a negative side-effect to the main aim of diverting traffic from route U to route T. For obvious reasons, first-best congestion tolls will never be negative. At the turning point, where f changes sign and is equal to zero, the index of relative welfare improvement therefore reaches its theoretical minimum of zero. Sticking to the range where the optimal one-route toll is a tax, it is clear that second-best regulation becomes more attractive the lower the free-flow costs on route T compared to those on route U. This is due to the fact that the regulator then controls that route which is in the first place more important in terms of usage, and secondly, where market forces tend to give rise to the largest congestion externalities. The first of these two reasons is illustrated by the fact that the optimal one-route toll approaches the optimal first-best toll on route T in these cases.

Also for varying differences in the congestion cost parameters $ß_i$ while keeping $\kappa_T=\kappa_U=20$ (not presented graphically here, but the interested reader is referred to Verhoef, Nijkamp and Rietveld (1994)), one-route tolling is more efficient, the higher $ß_U$ in comparison to $ß_T$. Apart from the fact that the regulator then again controls the more important route, route U then becomes an increasingly unattractive alternative for route T because of the internal part of the congestion cost, which makes the occurrence of adverse spill-overs due to regulation on route T less likely. In contrast with Figure 4.2, for any difference in the congestion cost parameters, the first-best fees will be equal for both routes. The reason for this again perhaps counter-intuitive result becomes clear after considering the equilibrating effects of user behaviour. In the first-best optimum, marginal social cost should be equalized between the two routes. Given the fact that road users distribute themselves over both links such that average social costs are equalized, and given the equality of free-flow costs and the linear form of the marginal cost functions, the result follows. Finally, with equal free-flow costs, f will not fall below zero.

In conclusion, for both types of cost parameter, the regulator should preferably perform one-route tolling on the lower cost route.

4.3.3 *Varying demand characteristics*

Next, the demand parameters will be considered. Figure 4.3 shows what happens when 'tilting' the demand curve around the original non-intervention equilibrium, doubling the slope at each step. Both the slope α and intersection δ therefore change simultaneously, in order to avoid ending up with very large (small) markets when demand approaches perfect (in-) elasticity. Both routes are again assumed to be identical in terms of cost functions, and it should therefore be no surprise that the optimal first-best tolls are equal for both routes in all cases.

On the left-hand side of Figure 4.3, low values for α are found, indicating high demand elasticities. As noted in Section 4.2, the regulator may in the extreme of a flat demand curve ignore spill-over effects from route T to route U, as road use on route U remains unaffected by changes in f due to the completely homogeneous and sufficiently large group of potential road users. The best thing to do in this case is to optimize usage of route T. This is also reflected by the fact that the optimal one-route fee on route T is equal to the first-best optimal fee. Logically, the index of relative welfare improvement is 0.5 in this case. In the same section however, it was asserted that as demand approaches complete inelasticity,

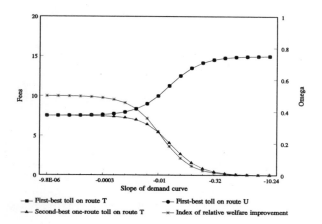

Figure 4.3   Varying demand characteristics: optimal fees and index of relative welfare improvement

regulation should more and more concentrate on route split effects than on overall demand, suggesting increasing scope for one-route tolling. It may in that light seem odd that ω decreases when moving towards more inelastic demand. The reason, however, is that with identical routes, the market itself will take care of optimal route split. Since, in this case, any one-route toll will therefore only act distortionary in this respect, its beneficial effects in terms of overall demand reduction are largely eroded. Put differently, the property of one-route tolling affecting route split is only useful in those cases where the market itself does not lead to efficient route splits, which it actually does when both routes are identical.

As a matter of fact, it is not even enough to introduce a difference in the congestion cost parameter to make one-route tolling only slightly efficient at inelastic demand. As already noted, differentials in congestion cost parameters do not affect the efficiency of market based route split. However, when free-flow user costs differ between the two routes, the effect suggested in Section 4.2 is obtained, where one-route tolling at inelastic demand yields the same welfare improvement as does two-route tolling. In Figure 4.4 the tolled route is assumed to have the higher free-flow costs (this case could correspond to two highways between two cities, with the tolled highway being longer than the untolled highway). The optimal one-route toll at perfectly inelastic demand is a subsidy, exactly equal to the difference between the two first-best tolls, and yielding exactly the same welfare improvement: ω=1. As in Figure 4.2, the turning point where the optimal one-route toll turns into a subsidy, so that f=0 and ω=0, marks that specific unfavourable combination of parameters where the sub-

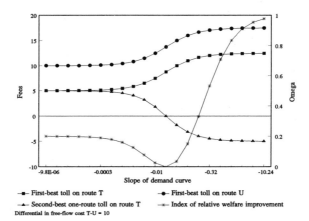

Figure 4.4   Varying demand characteristics with a free-flow cost differential: optimal fees and index of relative welfare improvement

goals of route split and overall demand are equally important for overall efficiency, but require opposite incentives.

When setting $\kappa_T - \kappa_U = -10$ instead of 10 (that is the case corresponding to the reasonable real-world situation where an arterial road parallel to a toll-road is not priced), optimal one-route taxes (no subsidies), and higher values of ω result throughout. The optimal one-route toll again equals the first-best toll on the tolled route in the limit of completely elastic demand, and equals the difference between the two first-best tolls in the limit of perfectly inelastic demand, with again $\omega=1$. For reasons of space, the corresponding graph is not presented here.

4.3.4   Considering the cost of congestion charging

Obviously, if regulation were costless, there would not be much that could be said in favour of one-route tolling, at least not from an efficiency point of view. In the foregoing sub-sections, values of ω generally smaller than 1 were reported, indicating a general inferiority of one-route tolling. However, tolling is not costless in practice, and the cost of congestion charging might indeed be such that it is actually preferable to leave one route untolled, as the losses in terms of smaller welfare gains from regulation may be offset by savings in terms of the cost of tolling. The simulations presented in the previous section may give an idea of when this could be the case; in other words, when 'rat-running' should be allowed from an efficiency point of view. One could distinguish various sorts of costs of congestion charging. One useful distinction may be into

(1) fixed costs, depending on the question of whether to regulate at all (for instance, the costs of having a regulatory agency); (2) route-specific fixed costs (for instance, costs of installing electronic devices when using electronic road pricing); and (3) variable costs (the cost per regulated user, such as administration costs). As it is in particular these latter two that may eventually determine the choice of whether to leave the option of an untolled alternative, the first one is ignored in what follows.

When considering the cost of tolling within the framework of the simulation model used above, it is not particularly insightful to engage in a 'cost−benefit of regulation' type of analysis, in which the policy yielding the highest net benefits would be the most favourable: when dealing with simulated data, one could make any assumption about the costs of regulation. In order then to obtain some insight into the impacts of such costs, let us assume that the same technology is used for both types of regulation, so that the fixed costs of regulation are twice as high for two-route tolling than they are for one-route tolling, and that the (per vehicle) variable costs of tolling are the same for both policies. At least some general observations can then be made on the relative 'cost-effectiveness of regulation' of one-route and two route tolling.

For instance, consider fixed (route-specific) cost of tolling, assuming that the variable (per vehicle) costs of tolling are equal to zero. It can then be asserted that one-route tolling cannot be 'overall efficient' (that is, when also taking account of such fixed costs of tolling) when $\omega<\frac{1}{2}$. If $\omega<\frac{1}{2}$, two-route tolling will yield more than double net benefits, at only double investment costs. Hence, either two-route tolling, or no tolling at all will eventually be the most 'overall efficient' option. With $\omega\geq\frac{1}{2}$, it is not clear beforehand which type of regulation is optimal: although the investment in regulation on the second route yields smaller net benefits than does the investment on the first route, these additional benefits may or may not exceed the additional cost. A first conclusion then is that, with identical routes, fixed cost of tolling cannot be a reason for choosing one-route tolling: ω for the simulation in Figure 4.3 is always smaller than $\frac{1}{2}$, and only approaches $\frac{1}{2}$ when demand tends towards complete elasticity. However, cost differentials between the routes may indeed cause one-route tolling to be more overall efficient than two-route tolling; in particular when the cost parameters for the tolled route are lower than those for the untolled route so that it is the more important one (see Figure 4.2). These are the ranges where it may be inefficient to prevent all rat-running. However, when the cost parameters on the tolled route are higher than on the untolled route, one-route tolling can only be more overall efficient than two-route tolling at relatively inelastic demand (see Figure 4.4).

The question of whether also the variable (per vehicle) cost of tolling may affect the relative performance of both types of policy in such a way that one-route tolling may eventually be the more efficient option is not as easy to consider with the simulations presented above, as the inclusion of such variable costs of regulation would actually lead to a new optimization problem, different from (4.1). Still, a first impression can be obtained by observing that in the simulations, apart from situations with rather inelastic demand in combination with free-flow cost differentials, high values of ω are only found when the tolled route is the relatively attractive one. However, calculations have shown that the welfare improvement per regulated vehicle with one-route tolling then at best only mildly exceed (and often fall short of) the welfare improvement per regulated vehicle with two-route tolling; this again implies that two-route tolling will often be more overall efficient than one-route tolling, also when accounting for variable cost of regulation. The exception, again, is at inelastic demand with free-flow cost differentials.

In conclusion, the simulations suggest that one-route tolling can in some cases be more 'overall efficient' than two-route tolling; that is, when considering also the costs of regulation. This might particularly occur in situations of inelastic demand in combination with free-flow cost differentials between the two routes, and — especially for fixed (route-specific) costs of regulation — when the cost parameters for the untolled route exceed those for the tolled route. Finally, fixed costs of regulation seem to be more of a reason to apply one-route tolling for efficiency reasons than are variable costs of regulation.

4.4 Revenue maximizing tolling under private control

A quite different reason for one-route tolling to occur in practice could be private ownership, with revenue maximizing tolling on a part of the network. In this section, this possibility is discussed. Investment decisions of such a private owner are not considered (these were also ignored with public tolling). The analysis concentrates on the pricing behaviour of a revenue maximizing operator, controlling either a part of the infrastructure, or the entire network. Only revenue maximizing non-discriminatory fees are considered: the operator sets one fee for all users on a route.

4.4.1 Revenue maximizing fees

The revenue maximizing one-route fee ϕ can be found by solving the following Lagrangian:

$$\mathcal{L} = \phi \cdot N_T + \lambda_T \cdot \left(D(N) - c_T(N_T) - \phi\right) + \lambda_U \cdot \left(D(N) - c_U(N_U)\right)$$

(4.7)

with: $N = N_T + N_U$

The first-order conditions are:

$$\frac{\partial \mathcal{L}}{\partial N_T} = \phi + \lambda_T \cdot \left(D'(N) - c_T'(N_T)\right) + \lambda_U \cdot D'(N) = 0$$

$$\frac{\partial \mathscr{L}}{\partial N_U} = \lambda_T \cdot D'(N) + \lambda_U \cdot \big(D'(N) - c_U'(N_U)\big) = 0$$

$$\frac{\partial \mathscr{L}}{\partial \phi} = N_T - \lambda_T = 0$$

$$\frac{\partial \mathscr{L}}{\partial \lambda_T} = D(N) - c_T(N_T) - \phi = 0$$

$$\frac{\partial \mathscr{L}}{\partial \lambda_U} = D(N) - c_U(N_U) = 0$$

Using $\lambda_T = N_T$, we find:

$$\phi = N_T \cdot \big(c_T'(N_T) - D'(N)\big) - \lambda_U \cdot D'(N)$$

Solving for λ_U yields:

$$\lambda_U = \frac{-N_T \cdot D'(N)}{D'(N) - c_U'(N_U)}$$

Substitution of λ_U yields the following revenue maximizing one-route fee:

$$\phi = N_T \cdot c_T'(N_T) - N_T \cdot D'(N) \cdot \left[\frac{c_U'(N_U)}{c_U'(N_U) - D'(N)}\right] \tag{4.8}$$

whereas it can be shown that revenue maximizing two-route tolling implies a toll ρ_i on route i (i=T,U) equal to:

$$\rho_i = N_i \cdot c_i'(N_i) - N \cdot D'(N) \tag{4.9}$$

A first remark is that a monopolistic supplier is inclined to internalize the congestion externality. Especially in (4.9) this is clear: the revenue maximizing two-route toll consists of the marginal external congestion costs plus a demand related monopolistic mark-up (see also Rouwendal and Rietveld, 1989). Also a comparison of (4.8) with (4.2) shows a similarity between f and ϕ: the first term, giving the first-best congestion fee on the tolled route, appears in both expressions. However, whereas for the optimal one-route toll some non-negative term has to be subtracted, for the revenue maximizing one-route toll some non-positive term has to be subtracted. Clearly, the revenue maximizing toll will never be a subsidy. This second term is a variation on the monopolistic mark-up — N in (4.9) is replaced by N_T in (4.8) — weighted by a factor depending on the slopes of the cost function on the untolled route and of the demand curve. One could trace through these effects in the same way as was done in Section 4.2 for the optimal one-route toll. However, for the sake of space, we turn immediately to the relative efficiency of revenue maximizing tolling.

	Revenue maximizing two-route tolling	Revenue maximizing one-route tolling
N_T	$\dfrac{\delta - \dfrac{\alpha \cdot (\kappa_T - \kappa_U)}{\beta_U} - \kappa_T}{\dfrac{2 \cdot \alpha \cdot \beta_T}{\beta_U} + 2 \cdot \alpha + 2 \cdot \beta_T}$	$\dfrac{\delta - \dfrac{\alpha \cdot (\kappa_T - \kappa_U)}{\beta_U} - \kappa_T}{\alpha \cdot \left[\dfrac{2 \cdot \beta_T + \dfrac{\alpha \cdot \beta_U}{\alpha + \beta_U}}{\beta_U} \right] + \alpha + 2 \cdot \beta_T + \dfrac{\alpha \cdot \beta_U}{\alpha + \beta_U}}$
N_U	$\dfrac{\delta - \dfrac{\alpha \cdot (\kappa_U - \kappa_T)}{\beta_T} - \kappa_U}{\dfrac{2 \cdot \alpha \cdot \beta_U}{\beta_T} + 2 \cdot \alpha + 2 \cdot \beta_U}$	$\dfrac{\delta - \dfrac{\alpha \cdot (\kappa_U - \kappa_T)}{2 \cdot \beta_T + \dfrac{\alpha \cdot \beta_U}{\alpha + \beta_U}} - \kappa_U}{\dfrac{\alpha \cdot \beta_U}{2 \cdot \beta_T + \dfrac{\alpha \cdot \beta_U}{\alpha + \beta_U}} + \alpha + \beta_U}$

Table 4.2   Equilibrium usage on both routes under revenue maximizing one-route and two-route tolling

The same basic simulations as in Section 4.3 are considered, and the index of relative welfare improvement not only for revenue maximizing tolling on one, but also on both routes will be discussed (see Table 4.2 for equilibrium usage in both cases). The reason is that one might suspect that private ownership of both routes can in some instances be preferable to private ownership of one route, due to adverse route split effects in the latter case. Such adverse route split effects may indeed be considerable with revenue maximizing tolling on one route, as can be seen from the difference between equations (4.2) and (4.8): whereas the second term is negative in the former, reflecting the public regulator's concern with spill-over effects, it is positive in the latter, reflecting complete neglect of such effects by a revenue maximizing operator.

4.4.2   Varying cost parameters

Figure 4.5 shows, for the same free-flow cost parameter differentials as in Figure 4.2, the optimal second-best and the revenue maximizing one-route tolls, as well as the index of relative welfare improvement for these two regimes and for private tolling of both routes. As may be expected, both intuitively and from the expressions for f and ϕ in equations (4.2) and (4.8) respectively, the revenue maximizing one-route toll ϕ exceeds the optimal one-route fee f throughout. The difference between the revenue maximizing one-route toll ϕ and the optimal one-route fee f turns out to be quite stable, slightly increasing with higher free-flow costs on the tolled route in comparison to those on the untolled route. In the extreme on the

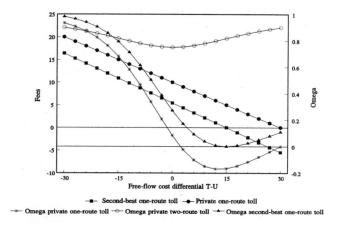

Figure 4.5 *Varying free-flow costs: optimal and revenue maximizing one-route fees and indices of relative welfare improvement*

right-hand side, where optimal one-route tolling is in terms of subsidizing usage of route T, the private owner still applies positive tolls. The private toll only falls to zero when non-intervention usage on route T falls to zero, in the most extreme case considered.

Given the relative closeness of the two fees, it is not surprising that the index of relative welfare improvement for revenue maximizing one-route tolling, denoted ω_p, remains relatively close to ω over the entire range considered, with ω naturally exceeding ω_p throughout. It should also be noted that ω_p may of course fall below zero when welfare under revenue maximizing regulation is below welfare under non-intervention. For almost the entire right-hand side of Figure 4.5, where free-flow costs on the tolled route exceed those on the untolled route, this is indeed the case.

Next, it is remarkable that the index of relative welfare improvement for revenue maximizing two-route tolling, denoted ω_{p2}, exceeds ω_p over a considerable range. Apparently, in many cases it is preferable from an efficiency point of view to have a private owner tolling the entire network rather than just a part of it, because in the former case he will have an incentive to avoid adverse route split effects which are not in line with overall revenue maximization. Therefore, the intuitive expectation that it is 'good' for overall economic efficiency to restrict monopolistic market power does certainly not necessarily hold for the control of congested road networks. Here, it may often be more efficient to have a monopolist controlling the entire network rather than just a part of it, as route split may become seriously distorted in the latter case.

Perhaps even more surprising, private two-route tolling even outperforms optimal one-route tolling over a considerable range: whenever the free-flow costs on the tolled route exceed those on the untolled route, and also if the free-flow costs on the untolled route only moderately exceed those on the tolled route. Distortions caused by adverse route split effects, even with optimal one-route tolling, then exceed distortions from monopolistic pricing on both routes. However, a large part of the potential efficiency gain due to monopolistic pricing will of course accrue to the private regulator. Hence, although the effect of monopolistic two-route pricing on overall efficiency of road usage may be attractive, the distribution of these welfare benefits needs not be.

For congestion cost parameter differentials (not presented graphically here) ω_p also consistently falls short of ω, the difference increasing the smaller β_T in comparison to β_U (recall from Section 4.3.2 that these are the ranges where public one-route tolling is relatively attractive). Also, ω_p may again fall below zero, in particular for more extreme congestion cost parameter differentials. Finally, ω_{p2} was again found to exceed both ω_p and ω over significant ranges (this latter especially when the two routes are more comparable in terms of congestion cost parameters).

4.4.3   Varying demand characteristics
Finally, Figure 4.6 shows what happens when demand characteristics vary. Only the case with identical routes is presented, as the courses of ϕ, ω_p, and ω_{p2} over the range of slopes of the demand curve studied turned out to be hardly influenced by the occurrence of cost differentials on both routes (unlike f and ω; see Section 4.3.3).

When comparing equations (4.8) and (4.2), it can be seen that the two types of one-route tolling will yield a more similar fee, the flatter the demand curve, as then the second terms approach zero and the identical first terms remain. Likewise, when comparing (4.9) and (4.3), the same turns out to hold for the two types of two-route fees. This explains the equivalence between f and ϕ, and between ω and ω_p on the left-hand side of Figure 4.6, as well as the fact that ω_{p2} is practically equal to 1.

On the other hand, when demand becomes more inelastic, the one-route fees f and ϕ rapidly diverge, leading to a fast growing gap between ω and ω_p, with the latter becoming negative due to the fact that it is especially route split, neglected by the revenue maximizer, that becomes important for overall efficiency. The pattern of ω_{p2} is roughly the same, but more extreme. In general, at more inelastic demand, revenue maximizing tolling tends to become more inefficient due to extremely high road prices charged. Hence, for the relative performance of revenue maximizing tolling, be it one-route or two-route, the prevailing demand structure is a crucial factor.

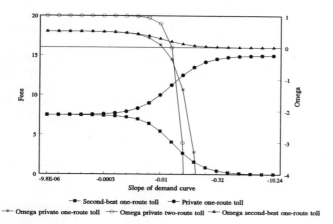

Figure 4.6 Varying demand characteristics: optimal and revenue maximizing one-route fees and indices of relative welfare improvement

4.5 Conclusion

This chapter studied second-best congestion pricing in presence of an untolled alternative. For the various reasons outlined in the introduction, this is certainly not an issue of mere academic interest, but one that may be encountered nowadays and in the (near) future in numerous instances. The findings reported may therefore be highly relevant for the design of congestion policies.

A two-link network was considered, with one route tolled and one untolled, and with elastic demand; taking completely inelastic demand as a limiting case. The second-best one-route congestion toll in its optimal use trades off a number of 'sub-goals' contributing to the overall goal of efficient usage of road infrastructure capacity. These sub-goals are related to usage and congestion on both routes, and therefore comprise overall demand and route split effects.

Using a simulation model, the effects of several parameters relating to the cost and the demand structure on the relative efficiency of one route tolling were investigated. It was found that the lower the two cost parameters considered (a free-flow cost parameter and a congestion cost parameter) on the tolled route, the less unattractive one-route tolling becomes from an efficiency point of view. With identical routes, one-route tolling becomes less unattractive the more elastic the demand; when free-flow costs differ between the two routes however, one-route tolling also becomes attractive at inelastic demand, as it is then route split that determines the efficiency of regulation. Concerning the costs of regulation, with fixed (per route) cost of regulation it may indeed be efficient not to toll both routes, in particular if the cost parameters for the untolled route exceed those for the tolled route. Variable (per vehicle) cost of regulation are less of a reason to allow rat-running for efficiency reasons.

Finally, revenue maximizing tolling on one or on both routes was considered. Revenue maximizing one-route tolling can by definition never be more efficient than optimal one-route tolling. However, revenue maximizing two-route tolling may actually lead to a more efficient usage of road space than does optimal one-route tolling. The intuitive expectation that it is 'good' for overall economic efficiency to restrict monopolistic power does certainly not necessarily hold for the control of congested road networks. Here, it may often be more efficient to have a monopolist controlling the entire network rather than just a part of it, as route split may become seriously distorted in the latter case.[2] However, when demand gets more inelastic, revenue maximizing tolling tends to get more inefficient due to extremely high road prices charged. Furthermore, a large part of the potential efficiency gain due to monopolistic pricing will of course accrue to the private regulator. Hence, although the effect of monopolistic two-route pricing on overall efficiency of road usage may be attractive, the distribution of these welfare benefits needs not be.

---

[2]Perhaps it should be stressed here that the case of two private controllers, each pricing one route, was not considered here. Depending on the degree of cooperation between the two, the index of relative welfare improvement may then exceed the one for monopolistic control of both routes. It may prove worthwhile to address this matter in future work.

5   Information Provision, Flat and Fine Congestion Pricing in Regulating Stochastic Congestion[1]

5.1   Introduction

Many societies face a problem of steadily growing levels of road traffic congestion on the one hand, and a declining scope for dealing with this problem by means of road capacity expansion on the other. As a consequence, transportation research is nowadays increasingly directed towards the identification of feasible ways of dealing with congestion by improving the efficiency of road network usage. Two main classes of instruments for congestion regulation are the so to speak 'traditional' congestion tolls, essentially based on the works of Pigou (1920) and Knight (1924); and 'modern' telematics solutions, using relatively new, user-oriented information technologies. Some issues related to the first group of instruments have already been dealt with in the previous two chapters; now the second group of instruments is added to the analysis.

Clearly, if it were not for its limited political and social feasibility (see also Part III), a system such as Electronic Road Pricing (ERP), where the actual tolls depend on the prevailing levels of congestion, would be the ideal 'first-best' instrument for coping with road transport congestion, resulting in efficient usage of road infrastructure (see also Chapter 3). Information provision on the other hand, is often seen as a user-friendly instrument, especially when the information is given for free. By providing information on prevailing levels of congestion, (potential) road users can adjust their behaviour in terms of, for instance, trip timing, route choice, and modal choice (see for example Ben-Akiva, De Palma and Kaysi, 1991; and Bonsall, 1992). Apart from benefiting themselves from such behavioural responses, which are voluntary, this will often have a positive effect on the overall efficiency of road use (see also Appendix 5.A.1), because individuals will generally prefer to avoid congested situations. This in itself will, *ceteris paribus*, relieve that same congestion to a certain

---

[1]This chapter is based on an article that will appear in *Regional Science and Urban Economics* (Verhoef, Emmerink, Nijkamp and Rietveld, 1996).

extent.[2] Obviously, information provision will only have merits when the information provided adds to the knowledge (potential) road users already possess. In other words, information provision will be particularly relevant when dealing with stochastic congestion; that is, congestion prevailing with limited predictability, such as 'non-recurrent' congestion resulting from accidents or road works.[3]

Pricing and information provision do in fact bear a close similarity. As first-best congestion charges depend on the actual level of congestion, they clearly contain quite some information, and even imply perfect information provided road users are perfectly aware of their private costs. At the same time, fluctuating congestion tolling without proper pre-trip and on-route information provision is likely to have only a limited impact on user behaviour, as many choices (modal choice, departure time, route choice) will then be based on expected rather than actual tolls and congestion levels. In addition, such information provision to a considerable extent determines the social acceptability of fluctuating road pricing (imagine the emotions of a commuter not only ending up in unexpectedly severe congestion, but facing an unexpectedly high toll on top of that). As is the case for any market, efficient pricing of road usage only yields its desired optimal effects if individual choices are based on perfect knowledge of the prevailing price and quality of the 'good' to be purchased.

In response to the apparent social and political reluctance to introducing first-best pricing systems like ERP, second-best alternatives such as cordon pricing, regulatory parking policies, or fuel taxes have recently received much political and academic attention. These second-best alternatives often suffer from the impossibility of perfect fee differentiation (see Chapter 3). In such cases, regulatory taxes do not reflect perfect information. It is, on the other hand, evident that non-fluctuating tolls do bear some specific advantages, especially in terms of user-friendliness (transparency, predictability) and costs of toll collection.

Therefore, both with perfect and with imperfect tolling, information provision and tolling may be expected to be complementary measures on theoretical grounds. In addition, one may envisage technical complementarity of pricing and information systems. Nevertheless, most

---

[2]On the other hand, Arnott, De Palma and Lindsey (1991b), Ben-Akiva, De Palma and Kaysi (1991) and Mahmassani and Jayakrishnan (1991) mention a number of reasons why information may have adverse effects, such as overreaction, saturation, and concentration.

[3]Empirical evidence suggests that a considerable share of traffic congestion results from more or less unpredictable events. No less than 44% of traffic jams in The Netherlands (both unweighted and weighted for severity) directly results from events such as road works, accidents or lost cargo (AVV, 1995).

of the literature addresses the implications of congestion pricing and information provision in isolation (see, for the first topic, Chapters 3, 4 and 6 and the references therein; and for the second: Boyce (1988), Arnott, De Palma and Lindsey (1991b), Mahmassani and Jayakrishnan (1991), and Watling and Van Vuren (1993)). The present chapter aims at investigating the relative efficiency of, and interactions between, these two types of instruments, which is particularly important now that both the introduction of high quality information systems and the application of road pricing schemes may become reality in the foreseeable future. Analytical studies of this topic are rare; only De Palma and Lindsey (1992, 1995) and El Sanhouri (1994) study these matters in the context of the bottleneck model.

In the following analysis, five regulatory 'regimes' will be considered. The first one is no tolling/imperfect information (I), where road users base their behaviour on expected private costs only. The second regime is no tolling/perfect information (II), where road users base their behaviour on actual private costs. The third is non-fluctuating ('flat') tolling/imperfect information (III), where behaviour is based on expected social costs. The fourth regime is a combination of II and III: flat tolling/perfect information (IV). Here, the regulator provides perfect information on prevailing levels of congestion, but charges only one single flat toll in all circumstances, the level of which is determined so as to maximize expected efficiency of road use given the fact that drivers are fully informed. Finally, there is the first-best case of fluctuating ('fine') tolling, implying perfect information (V). Although the mere equilibrium tolls as such need not reflect all information, the fact that these tolls may be adapted when necessary secures that they indeed do imply perfect information, at least in the equilibrium approach to be used below (see Appendix 5.A.2 for further details). Therefore, the combination of fine tolling and imperfect information will not be analysed explicitly. Still, this combination is actually described by regime III, since it can be shown that the expected value of the optimal fine fees with imperfect information should be equal to the optimal flat fee with imperfect information, rendering the two regimes identical in terms of user behaviour and welfare effects.

Some important points need to be addressed before proceeding. First, only 'public' information will be dealt with: either no driver or each driver has perfect information. In practical terms, this means that, for information without fine tolling, information is given through, for instance, public message signs or radio information (assuming that everybody listens to the radio). The case of 'club' information, associated with for example on-board information systems, is considered in a series of other papers (Emmerink, Verhoef, Nijkamp and Rietveld, 1995, 1996a–d).

Secondly, a static equilibrium approach with elastic demand and a two-link road network is used. In this respect, the analysis is supplementary to the work of El Sanhouri (1994), in which dynamic bottleneck models with inelastic demand are considered. Also De Palma and Lindsey (1992) mainly consider models with inelastic demand, focusing on route split and departure time effects. In a more recent paper, De Palma and Lindsey (1995) do consider elastic demand, but only in the context of a single congestible facility such as a one-link network. In the present approach, elasticity of demand, for instance resulting from the presence of alternative transport modes, can easily be considered, and will actually turn out to be of great importance for the efficiency of the various regulatory regimes. Perfect information then, is provided 'on time', and can thus be seen as pre-trip information, possibly affecting overall demand and route choice in the time period considered.

Furthermore, as noted before, the issue of perfect versus imperfect information becomes relevant when the actual level of congestion cannot be predicted with certainty. Uncertainty is introduced by considering stochastic cost functions, where link capacities may be either relatively high or low, with given probabilities. Imperfectly informed drivers then use the probabilities to determine expected costs, while perfectly informed drivers base their behaviour on actually prevailing costs. Therefore, imperfectly informed drivers are certainly not completely uninformed.

Finally, it may be of interest to the reader to know that this chapter is part of a larger set of research efforts on the topic of information in road networks, the results of which can be found in Emmerink, Verhoef, Nijkamp and Rietveld (1995, 1996a-d).

The structure of the chapter is as follows. The next section discusses the optimal tolls for the three pricing regimes (III−V) mentioned above. Section 5.3 presents various simulation results, providing insight into the influence of some key parameters on the relative efficiency of the various regulatory regimes (I−V). Finally, Section 5.4 contains the conclusions.

5.2   Optimal congestion pricing under various regulatory regimes

This section discusses some basic welfare economic properties of congestion pricing under the three 'pricing regimes' distinguished above. A simple road network is considered, with two alternative routes, denoted by subscripts 1 and 2, between one origin and one destination. On the basis of this network, both 'modal split' effects, related to overall demand, and route split effects can be studied. In the problem's purest form, the public regards the two alternative routes to be perfect substitutes. Therefore, one single inverse demand function $D(N)$ is introduced, where N denotes the total number of road users (on both routes). Furthermore, there are two by two average user cost functions giving the private cost of road use: for either route one representing high capacity, denoted by superscript 0, and one representing low capacity, denoted with superscript 1: $c_1^0(N_1)$, $c_2^0(N_2)$, $c_1^1(N_1)$ and $c_2^1(N_2)$. Naturally, $N=N_1+N_2$ for each of the four possible combinations of cost functions. The probability of low capacity on route i is denoted by p_i, which may run from 0 to 1. For notational ease, the following probabilities are introduced for the four possible states s^{jk} ($j=0,1$; $k=0,1$): $\rho^{00}=(1-p_1)\cdot(1-p_2)$ to denote the probability of state s^{00} with high capacity on both routes; $\rho^{10}=p_1\cdot(1-p_2)$ and $\rho^{01}=(1-p_1)\cdot p_2$ to denote the probability of low capacity only on route 1 (s^{10}) and route 2 (s^{01}), respectively; and $\rho^{11}=p_1\cdot p_2$ to denote the probability of simultaneous low capacity on both routes (s^{11}). The probabilities for both routes are therefore assumed to be independent (in Section 5.3.5, dependent probabilities are considered). Average user cost and the value of time are assumed to be equal for all road users. The social welfare measure W to be applied below is given by total benefits, represented by the area under the demand curve, minus total costs.

In line with Wardrop's first principle (Wardrop, 1952), at any user equilibrium, depending on the availability of perfect information and on whether tolls are charged, the sum of either the actual or the expected average cost plus the contingent fee should be equal for both routes; otherwise people would shift from the one route to the other. Furthermore, in line with individual optimizing behaviour, this sum should be equal to the benefits $D(N)$ of the marginal road user N.

We now turn to the derivation of the optimal fees in the three pricing regimes that were distinguished. First, consider regime V, with fine tolling and perfect information. In this case, the regulator can set first-best fees in each of the four states s^{jk}. For instance, in s^{00}, the optimal fees r_1^{00} and r_2^{00} follow from maximizing social welfare W subject to individual maximizing behaviour based on perfect information:

$$\underset{r_1^{00},r_2^{00}}{\text{MAX}}\ W\ =\ \int_0^N D(n)\ dn\ -\ N_1\cdot c_1^0(N_1)\ -\ N_2\cdot c_2^0(N_2)$$

$$\text{s.t.: } D(N)-c_1^0(N_1)-r_1^{00}\ =\ 0 \tag{5.1}$$
$$D(N)-c_2^0(N_2)-r_2^{00}\ =\ 0$$
$$\text{with: } N\ =\ N_1\ +\ N_2$$

Problem (5.1) indicates that both demand and cost interdependencies are present between both routes. Consequently, the optimal level of road use on the one route not only depends on the prevailing cost function on that route itself, but also on the prevailing cost function on the other route. For the expressions for the optimal fees on both routes however, these interdependencies cancel out, as the first-order conditions for problem (5.1) are (with primes denoting derivatives):

$$\frac{\partial W}{\partial N_i}\ =\ D(N)\ -\ c_i^0(N_i)\ -\ N_i\cdot c_i^{0\prime}(N_i)\ =\ 0;\quad i=1,2$$

implying optimal fees for both routes i in state s^{00} of:

$$r_i^{00} = N_i \cdot c_i^{0\prime}(N_i); \quad i=1,2 \tag{5.2}$$

For the other states, the optimal road prices are found by replacing the appropriate superscripts. Therefore, with fine fees and perfect information, the regulator should apply marginal external cost pricing in each state.

In regime III, with flat tolling and imperfect information, the regulator finds the optimal flat tolls f_1 and f_2 by maximizing expected welfare subject to individual maximizing behaviour under imperfect information:

$$\text{MAX}_{f_1,f_2} \; E(W) = \sum_{j=0}^{1} \sum_{k=0}^{1} \rho^{jk} \cdot \left[\int_0^N D(n) \, dn - N_1 \cdot c_1^j(N_1) - N_2 \cdot c_2^k(N_2) \right]$$

$$\text{s.t.:} \; D(N) - (1-p_1) \cdot c_1^0(N_1) - p_1 \cdot c_1^1(N_1) - f_1 = 0 \tag{5.3}$$

$$D(N) - (1-p_2) \cdot c_2^0(N_2) - p_2 \cdot c_2^1(N_2) - f_2 = 0$$

with: $N = N_1 + N_2$

The first-order conditions to problem (5.3) are:

$$\frac{\partial E(W)}{\partial N_i} = D(N) - (1-p_i) \cdot \left(c_i^0(N_i) + N_i \cdot c_i^{0\prime}(N_i) \right) - p_i \cdot \left(c_i^1(N_i) + N_i \cdot c_i^{1\prime}(N_i) \right) = 0;$$
$$i=1,2$$

which lead to the following flat tolls:

$$f_i = (1-p_i) \cdot N_i \cdot c_i^{0\prime}(N_i) + p_i \cdot N_i \cdot c_i^{1\prime}(N_i); \quad i=1,2 \tag{5.4}$$

Therefore, with flat fees and imperfect information, the flat tolls are for both routes equal to the expected marginal external costs. It may be stressed here that the total and per route levels of road usage are state-independent due to imperfect information.

Finally, in regime IV with flat tolling and perfect information, road usage will be different according to the prevailing state due to the information. However, in setting the optimal flat toll, the regulator can do no better than maximizing expected welfare. The optimal flat fees f_i then follow from the solution of the following Lagrangian:

$$\mathcal{L} = \sum_{j=0}^{1} \sum_{k=0}^{1} \rho^{jk} \cdot \left[\int_0^{N^{jk}} D(n) \, dn - N_1^{jk} \cdot c_1^j(N_1^{jk}) - N_2^{jk} \cdot c_2^k(N_2^{jk}) \right]$$

$$+ \sum_{j=0}^{1} \sum_{k=0}^{1} \lambda_1^{jk} \cdot \left(D(N^{jk}) - c_1^j(N_1^{jk}) - f_1 \right)$$

$$+ \sum_{j=0}^{1} \sum_{k=0}^{1} \lambda_2^{jk} \cdot \left(D(N^{jk}) - c_2^k(N_2^{jk}) - f_2 \right) \tag{5.5}$$

with: $N^{jk} = N_1^{jk} + N_2^{jk}; \quad j=0,1 \; k=0,1$

where the variables N_i^{jk} denote road usage on route i in state s^{jk}. The following equations give the eighteen first-order conditions:

$$\frac{\partial \mathcal{L}}{\partial N_1^{jk}} = \rho^{jk} \cdot \left(D(N^{jk}) - c_1^{j}(N_1^{jk}) - N_1^{jk} \cdot c_1^{j'}(N_1^{jk}) \right)$$

$$+ \lambda_1^{jk} \cdot \left(D'(N^{jk}) - c_1^{j'}(N_1^{jk}) \right) + \lambda_2^{jk} \cdot D'(N^{jk}) = 0 \quad j=0,1 \ k=0,1$$

$$\frac{\partial \mathcal{L}}{\partial N_2^{jk}} = \rho^{jk} \cdot \left(D(N^{jk}) - c_2^{k}(N_2^{jk}) - N_2^{jk} \cdot c_2^{k'}(N_2^{jk}) \right)$$

$$+ \lambda_2^{jk} \cdot \left(D'(N^{jk}) - c_2^{k'}(N_2^{jk}) \right) + \lambda_1^{jk} \cdot D'(N^{jk}) = 0 \quad j=0,1 \ k=0,1$$

$$\frac{\partial \mathcal{L}}{\partial f_i} = -\sum_{j=0}^{1} \sum_{k=0}^{1} \lambda_i^{jk} = 0 \quad i=1,2$$

$$\frac{\partial \mathcal{L}}{\partial \lambda_1^{jk}} = D(N^{jk}) - c_1^{j}(N_1^{jk}) - f_1 = 0 \quad j=0,1 \ k=0,1$$

$$\frac{\partial \mathcal{L}}{\partial \lambda_2^{jk}} = D(N^{jk}) - c_2^{k}(N_2^{jk}) - f_2 = 0 \quad j=0,1 \ k=0,1$$

This set of first-order conditions can then be solved to yield the following optimal flat fee for perfectly informed road users on route 1:

$$f_1 = \frac{\displaystyle\sum_{j=0}^{1} \sum_{k=0}^{1} \frac{\rho^{jk} \cdot \left[N_1^{jk} \cdot c_1^{j'}(N_1^{jk}) - \dfrac{D'(N^{jk}) \cdot \delta_1^{jk}}{c_2^{k'}(N_2^{jk})} \right]}{c_1^{j'}(N_1^{jk}) - D'(N^{jk}) \cdot \left[1 + \dfrac{c_1^{j'}(N_1^{jk})}{c_2^{k'}(N_2^{jk})} \right]}}{\displaystyle\sum_{j=0}^{1} \sum_{k=0}^{1} \frac{\rho^{jk}}{c_1^{j'}(N_1^{jk}) - D'(N^{jk}) \cdot \left[1 + \dfrac{c_1^{j'}(N_1^{jk})}{c_2^{k'}(N_2^{jk})} \right]}} \tag{5.6}$$

with: $\delta_1^{jk} = \left(c_1^{j}(N_1^{jk}) + N_1^{jk} \cdot c_1^{j'}(N_1^{jk}) \right) - \left(c_2^{k}(N_2^{jk}) + N_2^{jk} \cdot c_2^{k'}(N_2^{jk}) \right)$

A symmetric expression can be found for the optimal flat fee on route 2 in this regime. Although (5.6) is a tedious expression, its interpretation becomes easier when noticing that it is a weighted summation (over all states) of the terms in the large parentheses in the numerator's numerator. These terms consist of the marginal external congestion cost on the particular route in that state, to which a term is added which represents the extent to which marginal social cost on that route exceeds marginal social cost on the other route, multiplied by the slope of the demand curve and divided by the slope of the average cost function on the other route. This latter part represents the extent to which the flat toll on a certain route should take account of possible distortions resulting from inefficiencies in route split in that particular state.

The weights are in the first place positively related to the probability of the state, which seems plausible. In addition, the weights are positively related to the responsiveness of total usage on that route in that state in equilibrium: the flatter the demand and the cost curve (the latter also compared to the cost curve on the other route) the larger the weight. This reflects that deviations from optimal fluctuating tolls are less distortive when usage is less responsive.

5.3   The relative performance of the various regulatory regimes

It is clear that the results derived in Section 5.2 do not lead to straightforward analytical or manageable solutions. Nevertheless, it is important to investigate the properties of the various regulatory regimes. Therefore, as in the previous chapter, simulation experiments were undertaken in order to gain more insight into the relative performance of the various regulatory regimes. Again, it is assumed that all demand and cost functions are linear over the relevant ranges (that is, the ranges containing the levels of usage in each of the possible states and in each of the possible regulatory regimes). As outlined in the previous chapter, these are sufficient to serve the general goal of the simulations, being the assessment of the influence of some key factors related to demand and cost structures on the relative efficiency of non-optimal regulation. Moreover, as already noted, the linear congestion cost function is a reduced form representation of Vickrey's (1969) bottleneck model of road traffic congestion (Arnott, De Palma and Lindsey, 1992).

5.3.1   The model

The two-link model for non-recurrent congestion caused by shocks in cost functions contains one joint linear demand function, characterized by slope α and intercept δ:

$$D(N_1 + N_2) = \delta - \alpha \cdot (N_1 + N_2) \tag{5.7}$$

Next, for both routes (i=1,2), there is a cost function for both high (j=0, k=0) and low capacity (j=1, k=1). The marginal private cost MPC_1^j (MPC_2^k), which is equal to average social cost ASC_1^j (ASC_2^k), consists of a free-flow cost component κ_1^j (κ_2^k) and a congestion cost component, which is assumed to be proportional to total usage N_1 (N_2) with a factor β_1^j (β_2^k):

$$MPC_1(N_1) = ASC_1(N_1) = \kappa_1^j + \beta_1^j \cdot N_1; \quad j = 0,1 \tag{5.8a}$$

$$MPC_2(N_2) = ASC_2(N_2) = \kappa_2^k + \beta_2^k \cdot N_2; \quad k = 0,1 \tag{5.8b}$$

	Imperfect information[a,b]	Perfect information[a,c]
No tolling	I: $\quad N_1 = \dfrac{\delta - \dfrac{\alpha\cdot(\bar{\kappa}_1 - \bar{\kappa}_2)}{\bar{\beta}_2} - \bar{\kappa}_1}{\dfrac{\alpha\cdot\bar{\beta}_1}{\bar{\beta}_2} + \alpha + \bar{\beta}_1}$	II: $\quad N_1^{00} = \dfrac{\delta - \dfrac{\alpha\cdot(\kappa_1^0 - \kappa_2^0)}{\beta_2^0} - \kappa_1^0}{\dfrac{\alpha\cdot\beta_1^0}{\beta_2^0} + \alpha + \beta_1^0}$
Flat tolling	III: $\quad N_1 = \dfrac{\delta - \dfrac{\alpha\cdot(\bar{\kappa}_1 - \bar{\kappa}_2)}{2\cdot\bar{\beta}_2} - \bar{\kappa}_1}{\dfrac{\alpha\cdot\bar{\beta}_1}{\bar{\beta}_2} + \alpha + 2\cdot\bar{\beta}_1}$	IV: $\quad -$[d]
Fine tolling	$-$[e]	V: $\quad N_1^{00} = \dfrac{\delta - \dfrac{\alpha\cdot(\kappa_1^0 - \kappa_2^0)}{2\cdot\beta_2^0} - \kappa_1^0}{\dfrac{\alpha\cdot\beta_1^0}{\beta_2^0} + \alpha + 2\cdot\beta_1^0}$

[a] Usage on route 1. Symmetric expressions are found for usage on route 2.
[b] A bar denotes expected values.
[c] Levels for state s^{00}. For other states, where low capacity actually does occur, the correct expressions can be found by replacing the relevant superscripts.
[d] For this case, a nice analytical expression cannot be obtained. For the simulations conducted, equilibrium usage was computed by matrix inversion.
[e] Irrelevant alternative.

Table 5.1   Equilibrium road usage under each of the five regulatory regimes

All parameters are non-negative; and only 'regular' networks are considered, where both routes are at least marginally used under each regime. Apart from the explicit functions, the model is further identical to the one presented in Section 5.2. Under each regime, equilibrium usage is as given in Table 5.1.

For the 'base case' of the simulations, the following parameter values were chosen: $\alpha=0.015$; $\delta=100$; $\kappa_1^0=\kappa_2^0=\kappa_1^1=\kappa_2^1=20$; $\beta_1^0=\beta_2^0=0.015$ and $\beta_1^1=\beta_2^1=0.04$; and $p_1=p_2=0.25$.[4] So, both routes are assumed to be identical

---

[4]To give an idea of the quantities and prices generated in this base case, equilibrium usage under regime I is 1561 on both routes in each state, with expected marginal private cost of 53.17, and an expected total net welfare of 73099. Expected usage under the optimal regime V is 1203 on both routes, with expected marginal private costs of 41.96 and expected fine fees of 21.96 on both routes, and an expected total net welfare of 96229.

in the base case. The cost shock is assumed to affect link capacity, leaving free-flow costs unaffected.

By varying the model's parameters, insight can be obtained into their impact on the relative efficiency of the five regulatory regimes. The results are discussed below. The performance of regimes II−IV will be expressed in the 'index of relative welfare improvement' ω (see Chapter 3), which is for instance for regime II defined as:

$$\omega^{II} = \frac{\overline{W}^{II} - \overline{W}^{I}}{\overline{W}^{V} - \overline{W}^{I}}$$ (5.9a)

where $\overline{W}^r$ denotes expected welfare in regime r. Therefore, ω gives for a regime the achievable welfare gains as a proportion of the theoretically possible or optimal efficiency gains. For comparing regimes I and V, the following index of potential relative welfare improvement ω^V is used:

$$\omega^V = \frac{\overline{W}^{V} - \overline{W}^{I}}{\overline{W}^{V}}$$ (5.9b)

Note that the index ω^V is not directly comparable to the other indices ω; the reason for including ω^V is that it enables a better interpretation of the other ω's. In the base case, $\omega^{II}=0.41$; $\omega^{III}=0.66$; $\omega^{IV}=0.99$ and $\omega^V=0.24$.

Obviously, by means of this type of modelling exercises, one may generate a great variety of simulation possibilities. Many of these have been studied; the ones presented below are those that were found to be particularly interesting and the most suitable for discussing the general properties of the various regulatory regimes.

5.3.2 Varying probabilities

The first parameters studied are the probabilities of cost shocks. Figure 5.1 shows the various ω's when p_1 and p_2 are simultaneously raised from 0 to 1. Clearly, information provision without tolling only makes sense if there is uncertainty: ω^{II} falls to 0 at $p_1=p_2=0$ and $p_1=p_2=1$; that is, when two of the four cost functions apply with certainty. On the other hand, ω^{III} is equal to 1 in these cases: flat tolling is as efficient as fine tolling when the fine fees would always be set at the same levels anyway.

For intermediate values of the p_i's, ω^{II} and ω^{III} show opposite patterns. This is also found in the simulations reported below, and it indicates that flat tolling and information provision are highly complementary instruments. This is underpinned by the fact that ω^{IV} is close to unity throughout, indicating that the combination of flat tolling and perfect information provision yields an expected welfare almost as high as under first-best fine tolling. Finally, also the sum of ω^{II} and ω^{III} is shown, to examine whether the efficiency gains of flat tolling and information provision are sub- or super-additive. In Figure 5.1, sub-additivity appears to hold throughout; except, of course, for the two extreme cases.

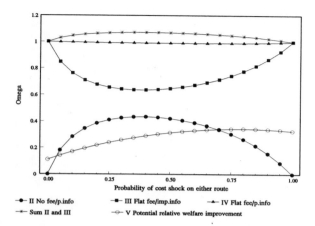

Figure 5.1   Varying probabilities of cost shocks: indices of relative welfare improvement

5.3.3 Varying congestion cost parameter volatility

Next, in Figure 5.2, the volatility of the congestion cost parameters is considered, expressed in the difference between the congestion cost parameters in the different states. On the left-hand side of this figure, the parameters β are all identical, while β_1^1 and β_2^1 simultaneously increase when moving to the right. Therefore, on the extreme left-hand side, there is complete certainty, and in accordance with Figure 5.1, $\omega^{II}=0$ and $\omega^{III}=1$. When volatility increases however, the relative efficiency of information provision (without tolling) increases, due to the increasing value of information (both from a private and from a social point of view). In contrast, flat tolling becomes less efficient due to the increasingly important shortcoming of fee adaptation. At sufficiently high levels of volatility then, ω^{II} may exceed ω^{III}. As shown by ω^V, this happens in situations where potential efficiency gains are relatively large.

Again, flat tolling and information provision are highly complementary, as reflected by the rather constant and high (close to unity) value of ω^{IV}. Over a large range, the efficiency gains of the instruments are sub-additive; only at extremely high volatility does super-additivity occur.

5.3.4 Varying demand characteristics

Next, demand characteristics are considered in Figures 5.3 and 5.4. In these figures, the demand curve is 'tilted' around the original intersection in regime I, varying from high elasticities on the left-hand side to almost perfect inelasticity on the right-hand side. The reason for changing both α and δ simultaneously is to avoid very (small) large levels of road usage

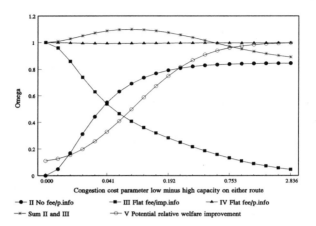

Figure 5.2   Varying congestion cost parameter volatility: indices of relative welfare improvement

when demand approaches complete (in-) elasticity. In general, misallocations due to imperfect pricing become more serious with more elastic demand. Hence, in Figure 5.3, ω^V approaches unity in these cases: W^I decreases rapidly. For the same reason, ω^{II} is low when demand becomes more elastic: the large majority of the potential efficiency gains can only be obtained by means of tolling. Moreover, when demand is perfectly elastic (implying that marginal benefits are equal to average benefits) and no tolling takes place, expected welfare is zero both in states I and II: with imperfect information, marginal and average benefits are equal to expected average costs on both routes; with perfect information, marginal and average benefits are equal to average costs on both routes in all states. In contrast, flat tolling without information provision already yields considerable efficiency gains (see ω^{III}).

When moving to more inelastic demand however, route split rather than modal split decisions become increasingly important for overall efficiency, simply because overall demand becomes more sticky. Such route split decisions are, with otherwise equal routes, especially relevant in states s^{10} and s^{01}, when a shock occurs on one of the two routes only. As flat tolling without information provision will then have no effect on route split decisions, ω^{III} falls to zero when approaching completely inelastic demand. Information provision on the other hand does affect route split, and ω^{II} increases accordingly. The reason that ω^{II} even approaches unity in Figure 5.3 is that with inelastic demand and identical routes, equalization of marginal private costs on both routes (user equilibrium) implies equalization of marginal social costs (optimal route split) because of the

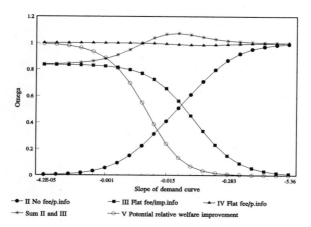

*Figure 5.3   Varying demand characteristics: indices of relative
            welfare improvement*

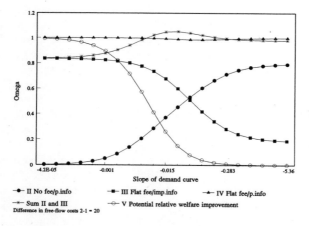

*Figure 5.4   Varying demand characteristics with a free-flow cost
            differential: indices of relative welfare improvement*

linear cost functions. Hence, individual optimizing behaviour based on
perfect information then results in optimal usage of the network. In Figure
5.4, it is assumed that free-flow costs differ between the two routes ($\kappa_2=30$
and $\kappa_1=10$). Then, this property does no longer hold, and ω^{II} reaches a
maximum below unity, whereas ω^{III} remains larger than zero because the

(route-specific) flat tolls can to some extent correct for the expected inefficiency in route split.

Finally, the fact that ω^V is practically zero at inelastic demand suggests that information provision without tolling becomes efficient only when potential efficiency gains become very small. These low values for ω^V however, are also caused by the fact that total benefits, measured as the area under the demand curve, are extremely large in all regimes due to the extreme steepness of this curve. It is therefore noteworthy that fine tolling, compared with no tolling/imperfect information, still yields a cost advantage of 6.5% on the right-hand side of Figure 5.3 (at $\alpha=5.36$).

The almost perfect complementarity of flat tolling and information provision is again clearly demonstrated by the curvature of ω^{IV}. It can finally be noticed that, in Figure 5.3, the efficiency gains exhibit super-additivity at more elastic demand, whereas sub-additivity prevails at more inelastic demand.

5.3.5   Separating out route split and modal split effects

The welfare gains of the various regimes as discussed in the foregoing three sub-sections are in general a combination of route split and modal split (or overall demand) effects. By comparing these gains to those arising on a one-link network, these two effects can be separated. For this purpose, the same simulations were run for a one-link network of comparable capacity as the two-link network considered above. This was accomplished technically by assuming that the probabilities p_1 and p_2 are perfectly dependent, so that $p_1=p_2=\rho^{11}=(1-\rho^{00})$, and $\rho^{10}=\rho^{01}=0$.

For the simulations discussed in Sections 5.3.2 and 5.3.3, the implications were found to be modest, suggesting that for the combinations of parameters considered there, most potential welfare gains are to be attributed to modal split rather than route split effects. The results are therefore presented only textually, not graphically.

For varying probabilities (Figure 5.1), ω^{II} is a bit lower throughout when for a one-link instead of a two-link network; except, of course, for the two polar cases. This reflects that efficiency gains due to voluntary route split adaptation with perfect information, in case of a cost shock on one of the two links, can obviously not occur on a one-link network. Likewise, ω^{III} is a bit higher throughout, reflecting that the impossibility of flat tolling to affect route split in such cases is no longer a relevant shortcoming. Finally, ω^{IV} remains practically unaffected; it is only slightly lower for a one-link than for a two-link network of the same capacity.

When re-running the simulations reported in Figure 5.2 for a one-link network, again ω^{III} is a bit higher, and for modest cost shocks ω^{II} again is a bit lower. The explanation is the same as above. For more extreme cost shocks however, ω^{II} for a one-link network slightly exceeds ω^{II} for a two-link network of comparable capacity. This can be explained by noting that

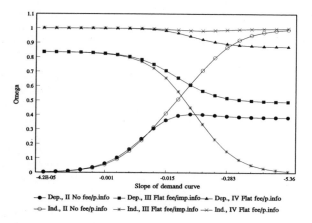

Figure 5.5   Varying demand characteristics: indices of relative welfare improvement on a one-link (Dep. probabilities) and a two-link network (Ind. probabilities)

with an extreme cost shock on one of the routes of a two-link network, information provision without tolling will lead to serious congestion on the other route as well. This effect cannot occur on a one-link network, where, in case of severe congestion, it will be rational for many informed drivers to abstain from using the network altogether. Again, ω^{IV} is slightly lower for a one-link than for a two-link network of the same capacity.

For the simulations discussed in Section 5.3.4, the implications of considering one link instead of a two-link network are more serious. Figure 5.5 illustrates this by comparing ω^{II}, ω^{III} and ω^{IV} for the one-link network with those given in Figure 5.3 for a two-link network. For elastic demand, things remain practically the same; for inelastic demand however, the various ω's diverge quite drastically. In the discussion in Section 5.3.4, it was pointed out that for the case of a relatively inelastic demand, it is actually route split that determines overall efficiency. Obviously, on a one-link network, this is no longer an issue. Therefore, when demand becomes more inelastic, it is still only the effect on total demand that determines the relative efficiency of the various regimes. For regime II this depends on the number of users kept out of the system when being informed on the occurrence of low capacity, and for regime III this depends on the number of people kept out of the system due to the flat toll in both states. Apparently, these effects are such that ω^{II} and ω^{III} tend to some maximum and minimum value, respectively. Furthermore, ω^{IV} is here seen to fall significantly below unity for the first time. However, it is important to stress that when approaching a completely inelastic demand in the case of a one-link network, ω^V itself becomes zero, simply because neither tolling nor information provision will affect road usage on the single link anyway. Therefore, ω^V approaches zero not only because of the extremely large benefits as outlined in the previous section; in addition, for the one-link network it was found that the maximum achievable cost advantage at $\alpha=5.36$ is 0.4%, as opposed to 6.5% for the two-link network. Hence, ω^{II}, ω^{III} and ω^{IV}, being then proportions of practically zero, are not very meaningful measures in this case.

5.3.6   Comparing the fees

Finally, the equilibrium values of the (expected) fees in the various pricing regimes will now be briefly discussed. It is of course hard to give an entirely satisfactory explanation of the equilibrium values of the fees found, as this requires tracing through the entire model. Some interpretation, however, remains possible. The general picture emerging in practically all simulations is as follows.

First, the flat fee with imperfect information was found to exceed both the expected value of the fine fee and the flat fee with perfect information. Without information, more users will use a link when low capacity occurs. The resulting welfare losses are then considerable, and make it apparently worthwhile to set the flat fee relatively high. Consequently, drivers not only benefit from information because of its informational value; a secondary benefit is that tolls will be lower. Secondly, perhaps counter-intuitively, the expected value of the fluctuating fee was found to exceed the value of the flat fee with perfect information. This can to some extent be explained by the fact that the latter is a weighted average of marginal external congestion costs, where the weight decreases with a steeper cost curve; see equation (5.6). Therefore, this fee is biased towards the low congestion value. Figure 5.6 illustrates the findings mentioned above for the simulations related to varying probabilities; where the fees for both routes are identical throughout because the routes were assumed to be identical.

5.4   Conclusion

This chapter studied the relative efficiency of, and the interaction between various information and pricing instruments for the regulation of stochastic road traffic congestion. Five regulatory regimes were considered: no tolling/imperfect information, no tolling/perfect information, non-fluctuating ('flat') tolling/imperfect information, flat tolling/perfect information, and fluctuating ('fine') tolling implying perfect information. By considering elastic demand and a two-link network, both modal split and route split effects could be studied. A simulation model was used to gain insight into the influence of some key parameters on the relative efficiency of the various regulatory regimes.

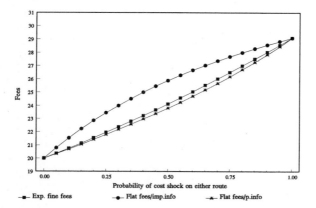

Figure 5.6 *Varying probabilities of cost shocks: flat fees and expected fine fees*

When dealing with stochastic congestion, information provision and flat tolling are found to be highly complementary. The combination of these two instruments performs in practically all cases almost as good as the theoretical first-best option of fine tolling. Given the psychological advantages of flat tolling, related to issues of predictability and transparency, it seems plausible that such a combination of instruments might be more attractive than the use of fine tolls. As long as expected congestion remains the same, the regulator might use the same tolls for certain links at certain times of the day, regardless of the actual level of congestion. Moreover, as outlined in the introduction, for a smooth usage of fine tolls, one could not do without proper pre-trip and on-route information provision, which means that in both cases the same sort of information technologies would be required anyway.

As far as the performance of flat tolling and information provision in isolation is concerned, the relative efficiency of these two was, in line with the above mentioned complementarity, found to behave in an opposite way. Flat tolling with imperfect information performs relatively well with relatively elastic demand, with modest volatility of congestion and with the more extreme probabilities of shocks (that is, with more certainty). Perfect information provision without tolling was found to behave well in the opposite cases. The efficiency gains of the two instruments were most often found to be sub-additive. Super-additivity was only found with relatively elastic demand and high volatility.

Appendix 5.A.1   Is information provision without tolling always efficiency improving?

This appendix discusses whether information provision without tolling is efficiency improving. The simulations in this chapter actually do suggest so. Figure 5.A1 provides a diagrammatic sketch of this issue for a one-link network. D gives demand, MPC marginal private (=average social) cost, and MSC marginal social cost. Superscripts denote states, and subscripts denote information regimes: P (I) denotes (im)perfect information. In state 0 (1), optimal usage is N^{0*} (N^{1*}), where marginal benefits are equal to marginal social costs. Equilibrium usage with perfect information is N_P^0 (N_P^1), where marginal benefits are equal to marginal private costs. With imperfect information, marginal benefits are equated to expected marginal private cost. Assuming for graphical convenience that the states occur with equal probabilities ($p=(1-p)=\frac{1}{2}$) (this does not affect the generality of the discussion), this is seen to hold true only at N_I, where the two arrows are of equal length. N_I is therefore equilibrium usage with imperfect information.

Hence, in the left-hand panel, when switching from imperfect to perfect information, net welfare in state 1 increases by the areas $b+c$, which represent reductions in external and internal costs respectively, in excess of benefits foregone. In state 0, usage increases, yielding net welfare gains d up to N^{0*} and net welfare losses e from N^{0*} to N_P^0. Expected net welfare therefore increases with area $\frac{1}{2}\cdot(b+c+d-e)$, which is positive in the sketched case (the general proof is given below). With perfect information, expected net welfare of course still falls short of the optimal level by $\frac{1}{2}\cdot(a+e)$.

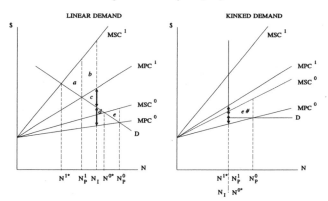

Figure 5.A1   *Information provision without tolling: positive efficiency effects with linear demand and negative efficiency effects with kinked demand*

However, it is not difficult to construct a case where welfare decreases with information provision. In the right-hand panel, it is assumed that demand is extremely convex, namely kinked. This is less absurd than it may seem at first sight, as this would occur if there are two types of drivers: one group with perfectly inelastic demand; and one completely homogeneous, sufficiently large group, with therefore perfectly elastic demand. The various equilibrium values of usage can be derived in the same way as before, and we find that $N_P^0 > N^{1*} = N_P^1 = N^{0*} = N_I$. In comparison to the left-hand panel, the only welfare effect that remains is the loss $\frac{1}{2}\cdot e$, $\frac{1}{2}\cdot e^{\#}$ in this case. Information provision is welfare reducing in this case, as is it only provokes unwarranted usage in state 0.

Clearly then, there are instances where information leads to a less efficient usage of road infrastructure, and it is therefore not possible to give a general answer to the question raised in the title of this appendix. However, for the case of linear demand and cost functions, it can be proven that information provision is never efficiency reducing on a one-link network as long as $(\beta^1 - \beta^0) \cdot (\kappa^1 - \kappa^0) \geq 0$: the 'high capacity' cost function should nowhere exceed the 'low capacity' cost function. The main steps of the proof are as follows. First of all, the single demand function and the cost functions are given by:

$$D(N) = \delta - \alpha \cdot N \tag{5.A1}$$

$$MPC(N) = ASC(N) = \kappa^j + \beta^j \cdot N; \quad j=0,1 \tag{5.A2}$$

It can then be shown that the change in expected welfare when going from imperfect information to perfect information is equal to (where $E(X)$ denotes the expectation of X):

$$\Delta E(W) = \tfrac{1}{2} \cdot \alpha \cdot \left[(1-p) \cdot \left(N_P^0\right)^2 + p \cdot \left(N_P^1\right)^2 - (N_I)^2 \right] = \tfrac{1}{2} \cdot \alpha \cdot \left[E\left((N_P)^2\right) - (N_I)^2 \right] \tag{5.A3}$$

From (5.A3), it can be seen that for extreme demand elasticities, $\Delta E(W)=0$: the two regimes yield the same expected welfare. With perfectly inelastic demand, usage is in all cases the same and the term between the large brackets is equal to zero. With perfectly elastic demand, α is equal to zero. There is no efficiency gain because expected welfare is zero in both regimes: with imperfect information, marginal and average benefits are equal to expected average costs; with perfect information, marginal and average benefits are equal to average costs in both states.

For finitely negative demand elasticities ($0<\alpha<\infty$), the sign of (5.A3) depends on the sign of the terms between the large brackets. For a random variable X, it is generally true that $E(X^2) \geq E^2(X)$. Therefore, when expected usage under both regimes is larger than 1, it only has to be shown that $E(N_P)>N_I$, to be able to infer that the value of (5.A3) is generally positive. The following expression for $E(N_P)-N_I$ can be derived:

$$E(N_P)-N_I = \frac{[p \cdot (1-p)] \cdot [\beta^1 - \beta^0] \cdot [\delta \cdot (\beta^1 - \beta^0) + \alpha \cdot (\kappa^1 - \kappa^0) + (\beta^0 \cdot \kappa^1 - \beta^1 \cdot \kappa^0)]}{[\alpha + \beta^0] \cdot [\alpha + \beta^1] \cdot [\alpha + \overline{\beta}]} \tag{5.A4}$$

The three terms in the denominator are all positive. The first two terms in the numerator are both non-negative, but do show that information provision yields no efficiency gains if there is complete certainty: either when p is equal to 0 or 1, or if the slope of the cost function remains unaffected by the cost shock. The third term in the numerator consists of a summation of three parts, the first two of which are also non-negative. The third part may be negative, but its absolute value can never exceed the value of the first part. Therefore, also the third term in the numerator is larger than zero. Consequently, (5.A4) is non-negative with finite elasticities, and therefore (5.A3) is proven to be non-negative. Information provision on a one-link network with linear demand and cost is never welfare reducing; in addition, it has been shown to be strictly welfare improving if demand elasticity is finitely negative and if there is uncertainty. From (5.A4), it can be seen why the condition $(\beta^1 - \beta^0) \cdot (\kappa^1 - \kappa^0) \geq 0$ is necessary. Then, the low (high) capacity state can be labelled 1 (0), and the proof holds.

The same can be proven to hold true for a two-link network. The proof runs along the same lines as the one discussed above. Expression (5.A3) then looks as follows:

$$\Delta E(W) = \tfrac{1}{2} \cdot \alpha \cdot \left[E\left((N_{1,P}+N_{2,P})^2\right) - (N_{1,I}+N_{2,I})^2 \right] \tag{5.A3'}$$

where the first of the two subscripts refers to the route. Again, it is sufficient to prove that expected usage does not decrease with perfect information. A convenient expression such as (5.A4) cannot be derived for a two-link network, but the proof has been completed (and is available from the author upon request).

Appendix 5.A.2   Why equilibrium values of fine fees do not contain perfect information

This appendix elaborates on the perhaps slightly cryptic remark in the introduction that equilibrium values of fine fees need not reflect perfect information. In Figure 5.A2, a two-link network such as discussed in the chapter is considered, where non-recurrent congestion originates from a possible shock in one of the two cost curves. Consider state s^{01}, where such a shock occurs on route 2. For ease of diagrammatic presentation, demand is assumed to be perfectly elastic, represented by the flat curve D (this does not affect the generality of the discussion). The routes are assumed to be identical, with linear cost functions. On route 1 then, the prevailing marginal private and social cost curves are given by MPC_1^0 and MSC_1^0 respectively. On route 2, a cost shock occurs (affecting route capacity, or the congestion cost parameter β), and MPC_2^1 and MSC_2^1 prevail.

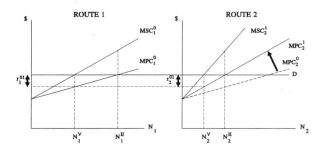

Figure 5.A2   Why equilibrium values of fine fees do not contain perfect information

In regime II, with perfect information and no tolling, equilibrium usage will be N_1^{II} and N_2^{II} respectively, where marginal benefits are equal to marginal private costs on both routes. Optimal route usage is given by N_1^V and N_2^V respectively, where marginal benefits are equal to marginal social costs on both routes. It is however easy to see that the equilibrium fine fees r_1^{01} and r_2^{01} that would yield this outcome are equal, owing to the linear cost functions and the fact that free-flow costs are equal for both routes. Hence, if only equilibrium fine fees are charged, road users are not able to infer on which of the two routes low capacity occurs. Fine fees do clearly not reflect perfect information. However, fine fees of course will be adapted according to marginal congestion costs on both routes. That means that, if operating out of equilibrium, the fine fees certainly need not be identical. In theory, if the 'one-but-marginal' driver (the driver who is, with the ordering along the horizontal axis according to the demand curve, positioned just to the left of the marginal driver) decides to choose the heavily congested route because the fine fees at that time happen to be identical, the marginal driver will notice that the fine fee for that route rapidly increases, and he or she would choose the other route. So, by continuous fee adaptation according to prevailing marginal external congestion cost, the optimum can be reached, and the fact that then the two tolls are identical does not imply that the road users were not perfectly informed when deciding if, and on which route to drive. In the context of this static equilibrium model, this 'continuous fee adaptation' should of course be interpreted as a 'Walrasian tâtonnement' process.

6   THE ECONOMICS OF REGULATORY PARKING POLICIES [1]

6.1   Introduction

In response to the apparent social and political reluctance to apply road pricing schemes for the regulation of road transport, there has been an increasing interest in all sorts of alternatives. One of these, namely parking policies, is studied in some greater depth in this chapter. Regulatory parking policies are one of the most often mentioned means of regulating road transport externalities by affecting the demand for a complementary good (Glazer and Niskanen, 1992; Arnott, De Palma and Lindsey, 1991a) (another example is fuel taxation; see Mohring (1989)). According to the Dutch government, regulatory parking policies are an "indispensable part of an integral transport policy aimed at reducing the growth of road traffic" (Tweede Kamer der Staten-Generaal, 1991−92). In many Dutch cities, more stringent parking policies have been pursued over the last years.

This chapter contains an economic analysis of the ins and outs of regulatory parking policies. In Section 6.2, the scope for parking policies in road transport regulation is discussed. Section 6.3 contains a diagrammatic model, discussing the specific form that regulatory parking policies would preferably take. It includes command-and-control measures in addition to the economic instruments that were considered in the foregoing chapters. Next, Section 6.4 provides a spatial analysis of regulatory parking policies along the lines of the types of models usually applied in urban economics. This section is therewith the first in the book to recognize explicitly the spatial dimension of road transport, and to investigate some of the consequences for the regulation of its externalities. Finally, Section 6.5 contains the conclusions.

6.2   The scope for regulatory parking policies

In the following sections, it will be evaluated how regulatory parking policies may be used in the regulation of road transport externalities. Since

---

[1]This chapter is based on an earlier article in *Transportation Research A* (Verhoef, Nijkamp and Rietveld, 1995b).

virtually every car has to be parked at the end of a trip, parking policies may offer a potentially strong instrument for influencing traffic flows. A first important matter in the evaluation of regulatory parking policies is the question of to what extent regulatory parking policies may serve as a satisfactory substitute for first-best regulation. In general, regulatory parking policies are only apt for influencing numbers of trips, and cannot differentiate according to trip lengths and routes followed, simply because the policy is implemented at the end of each trip (see, however, Section 6.4 for a notable exception to this rule). Therefore, using regulatory parking policies for affecting external costs which are to a large extent dependent on trip length or route followed is not optimal, and may in some derived respects even be counterproductive (see also Chapter 3).

In general, regulatory policies lose more of their signal function, the more they are used for affecting external costs depending on dimensions according to which they cannot differentiate (see Chapter 3). In order to determine the scope for regulatory parking policies, it is therefore necessary to map out the dimensions determining the external costs per trip and the dimensions along which effective differentiation can take place using such policies.

	Total length of trip	Time of driving	Route followed		Vehicle used
			Roads followed	Area of driving	
External costs (X = strong dependence; · = less strong dependence)					
Emissions (air pollution)	X	·	·	·	X
Noise annoyance	X	X	X	X	X
Safety	X	X	X	X	·
Congestion (on highways)	X	X	X	X	·
Congestion (on urban road networks)	X	X	·	X	·
Differentiation possible using regulatory parking policies (X = easily possible; · = hardly possible)	·	X	·	X	·

Table 6.1   Dependence of various marginal external costs of automobile trips on various trip characteristics, and the capability of regulatory parking policies for effective differentiation

In Table 6.1, the main external cost categories of automobile trips are roughly classified according to some relevant dimensions, where the dimension of route followed is hierarchically split into roads followed and area of driving: an X in 'Roads followed' necessarily implies an X in 'Area of driving', whereas the opposite does not hold. Of course, the table is certainly not unambiguous, and only serves to provide a first impression. For instance, external costs of some forms of air pollution actually do depend on the area and/or the time of driving, such as NO_x emissions, contributing to the formation of photochemical smog.

As stated earlier, parking policies can generally not be used for differentiation according to trip length. As the first column in Table 6.1 is further filled with X-es, indicating that in fact all external costs of an automobile trip depend on its length, this may underline the second-best character of regulatory parking policies. Therefore, we have to use the other four columns for determining the scope of regulatory parking policies, given the inherent limitations concerning trip lengths.

First, parking policies can be differentiated according to the time of driving, provided time-dependent parking fees are used. Furthermore, parking policies will only differentiate to a limited extent according to the route followed. That is, parking policies will by definition differentiate according to the area of driving, namely the area around the parking place. On the other hand, parking policies cannot be differentiated according to the actual roads followed. Finally, parking policies seem hardly suitable for adaption according to the type of vehicle parked; except, perhaps, for a rough distinction into private cars, vans, buses and trucks.

Clearly then, regulatory parking policies are not likely to offer a means of controlling road transport's external costs of air pollution, noise annoyance and accidents in a very efficient way. It seems that the scope for regulatory parking policies is limited to the regulation of congestion on urban road networks, insofar as it indeed satisfies the criteria mentioned in Table 6.1. Quite simply, the less these criteria are met, the more regulatory parking policies lose their applicability. For the sake of the argument however, in the following section it is assumed that these criteria are indeed met.

Furthermore, a reasonable requirement for parking policies is of course that the actual activity of parking should be properly priced. Parking markets, let alone efficient parking markets, often do not exist. In many cases, parked vehicles cause annoyance and use public space without any efficient price being charged. Clearly, efficiency requires the parkers to be confronted with such costs of parking. This could be the second goal of regulatory parking policies.[2]

---

[2]It has been calculated that the total value of land used for parking in The Netherlands amounts to 47 billion Dutch guilders, while only a small proportion of this sum is actually paid for by the parkers. For every Dutch car, on average three parking spots are available, which means 190 million square meters for the Dutch vehicle stock (Tweede Kamer der Staten-Generaal, 1991−92). Assuming that only one-third of all parking takes

All in all, the scope for regulatory parking policies is limited, considering the wide range of external costs resulting from road transport. In accordance with the foregoing, it will be assumed that the regulatory parking policy to be analysed in the remainder of this chapter serves the following two goals: (1) optimizing the level of congestion on an urban road network and (2) optimizing the activity of parking itself. In a more comprehensive setting, regulatory parking policies would preferably be supported by supplementary instruments such as fuel taxes.

6.3 A basic diagrammatic analysis of regulatory parking policies: regulatory fees versus physical restrictions

This section contains a comparison of two basic forms that regulatory parking policies might take: regulatory parking fees versus physical restrictions on parking space supply. The basic model of regulatory parking policies is set in a simplified world. It is assumed that (1) each individual car driver uses an equal amount of urban road kilometres for his trip, (2) congestion is equally spread over the urban road network, and (3) the government has full control over all parking space available. Under these assumptions, which are particularly favourable for the potential effectiveness of regulatory parking policies, we can concentrate on the fundamental relations that exist between parking and mobility and, in particular, on the performance of both types of parking policies, without worrying about other second-best aspects as discussed in Chapter 3.

Figure 6.1 serves as the basis for the discussion. Panel (a) considers commuters arriving on the urban road network during the morning peak. Ranking the potential commuters according to descending willingness to pay to make a trip yields the aggregate marginal private benefit or demand curve (D=MPB). The horizontal part of the marginal private cost (MPC) curve indicates the private cost of a trip under free driving conditions. With a growing inflow, the MPC will rise due to congestion. Without government intervention and with free supply of parking space, N^0 trips will be made. As before, MPC is set equal to the average social cost (ASC). The reason is that an individual car driver will experience the average social costs (including congestion costs) as his or her marginal private cost. It is then straightforward to derive the marginal social cost (MSC) curve. The vertical difference between MPC and MSC gives the external congestion costs; N^1 gives the optimal inflow after correcting for

---

place for free on public land, and assuming a 5% interest rate, a yearly social cost of 785 million Dutch guilders (approximately 0.2% of GDP) can be inferred.

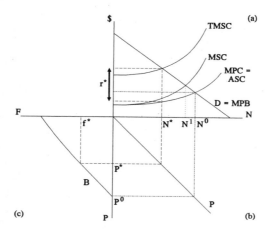

Figure 6.1   A basic model of regulatory parking policies

congestion.[3] Finally, the total marginal social cost (TMSC) curve includes the (social) cost of occupying a parking space during a working day. In this graphical approach, it has to be assumed that all commuters have equal parking duration. The TMSC curve can then be found by shifting the MSC curve upward by the social cost of parking. Hence, the socially optimal number of trips in the morning peak is N^*, where the net social surplus (the area between MPB and TMSC) is at its maximum.[4]

This optimum can in the first place be accomplished by means of road pricing, where r^* is the optimal road price. Furthermore, one may try to accomplish N^* by posing some sort of a quantitative restriction on the inflow. A practical application of such a policy can be found in cities like Athens, where cars with even (odd) number plates are allowed to drive on

---

[3]It should be noted that on the horizontal axis of Figure 6.1(a), traffic inflow per fixed unit of time is measured rather than the 'traditional' variable traffic flow. By doing so, theoretical problems (backward bending cost curves and inconsistent aggregate demand curves) can be avoided. See, among many others, Else (1981, 1982); Nash (1982); Hau (1991); and Alan Evans (1992) for recent contributions to the ongoing discussion on the diagrammatic and mathematical analysis of congestion.

[4]In this stylized setting, the costs and benefits associated with the outflow during the evening peak are equal to those associated with the inflow during the morning peak. Car drivers can be assumed to be aware of the costs of outflow. Therefore, the MPB- and MSC-curves in fact describe the benefits and costs associated with round trips. This has no serious implications for the analysis; shifting all curves simultaneously downwards by a factor two in order to divide all costs and benefits over both trips does not affect the outcomes.

even (odd) days only. However, a somewhat closer inspection of the demand curve reveals that, if such a policy indeed leads to a number of trips equal to the optimal number in terms of volume, this does not imply that the socially optimal outcome, where the social surplus is maximized, is realized. There is simply no guarantee that the most efficient trips, representing the highest utility in terms of willingness to pay, to be found on the demand curve between 0 and N^*, will remain. In the worst case, the trips roughly between $N^0 - N^*$ and N^0 are left over, yielding much smaller benefits. It is therefore conceivable that such a policy involves social costs which largely exceed the potential benefits, and consequently leads to an outcome inferior to the non-intervention outcome. Clearly, the formal equivalence which exists between economic and non-economic instruments for optimizing external costs in textbook single-actor analyses of externality regulation breaks down when the number of actors, rather than the level of the activity (per actor), becomes the optimization variable. As mentioned above, this is the case for regulatory parking policies, where not the trip length per actor but merely the number of trips can be affected. Hence, a reduction in the number of trips to N^* by means of quantitative measures involves merely a *quasi optimum*.[5]

The lower half of Figure 6.1 demonstrates the workings of regulatory parking policies. The vertical axis depicts parking space occupation. The relationship between the number of trips and the number of parking spaces occupied is 1:1 by assumption, as every car is assumed to get parked on publicly managed parking space. This is reflected by the physical parking function (P) in panel (b), which has a 45° angle with the horizontal axis. The government may now conduct regulatory parking policies consisting of a reduction parking space supply to P^*, consistent with the optimal inflow N^*. Two fundamental flaws of such a scheme are immediately apparent in this simple model, which is in fact particularly favourable for the efficiency of parking policies because of the assumptions made.

First, there is an information problem, comparable to the sort of problems studied in the previous chapter. Before deciding whether to make the trip by car, the potential car drivers should know whether there will be a parking space available to them. Otherwise, one runs the risk of not realizing the intended reduction in trips. Moreover, an acute shortage of parking spaces may then occur. This may give rise to more instead of less congestion, caused by car drivers driving around in search of a parking

---

[5]Under such a scheme, a market in 'driving rights' might develop, which will eventually secure that the most efficient trips indeed remain. In that case, the associated transaction costs are the additional social costs of the system. Other possible forms of induced inefficiencies of the odd—even policy include the purchase of extra cars; the choice of different, longer routes, such as ring roads, in order to get as close as possible to the point of destination, avoiding the zone where the policy is conducted; etc.

space. Such situations indeed occur in cities where physically restrictive parking policies are conducted (see Vleugel, Van Gent and Nijkamp, 1990). Secondly, the efficiency problem discussed above applies here. There is no guarantee that the most efficient trips will remain. Even if the information problem were overcome, a quasi optimum may still result.

Panel (c) shows the workings of regulatory parking fees. The B curve depicts the derived demand for parking spaces. Since it may be expected that no direct utility is derived from parking as such, the B curve is derived by projecting the vertical distance between the MPB-curve and the MPC curve in panel (a), via the 'geometrical mirror' of panel (b), into Figure 6.1(c). The parking fee[6] F, depicted along the horizontal axis, determines the number of parkers according to the B curve, and hence the number of trips via the P curve. With free parking place supply (F = 0), P^0 parking spaces will be occupied and an inflow of N^0 cars takes place. Any positive value of F will result in lower values of P and N, since the marginal bid of a certain number of car drivers will be exceeded. The optimal inflow N^* can thus be realized through a parking fee equal to f^*.

In this stylized setting, the optimal parking fee is equivalent to the optimal road price. Both the optimal fees are equal and the revenues will be the same, simply because every car is assumed to get parked and to be subject to the parking policy: $f^* \cdot P^* = r^* \cdot N^*$. In this setting, these instruments only differ in the time of levying: during or after the trip.

The use of parking fees overcomes the two shortcomings of mere restrictions on parking space supply. First, the use of parking fees involves far less stringent information requirements. The existence and level of the fee is static information, requiring a 'once-and-for-all' information flow to potential car drivers in order to secure the optimal inflow (assuming stable traffic demand). On the other hand, a physical restriction on parking space supply requires dynamic information on the actual occupation of the parking space. Secondly, a parking fee will discriminate according to willingness to pay, which overcomes the efficiency problem.

The aforementioned information and efficiency arguments get a different meaning if commuters, when subject to a scheme of a physical restriction on parking space supply, are allowed to make their trips earlier in order to increase their chances of getting a parking space. Such a rescheduling implies a loss in the car drivers' utilities, and in that way serves as a substitute for the price mechanism. In the first place, the process of departure time adaptation may to a certain extent take care of an efficient allocation. The car drivers with the highest utility may, *ceteris paribus*, be expected to be prepared to make the largest adaptations in

---

[6]The parking fee F is *not* defined as an hourly tariff, but as a total fee for the total parking time.

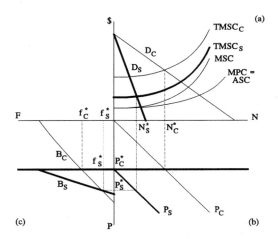

Figure 6.2   Regulatory parking policies for two successive groups of car drivers

departure times. Furthermore, the information argument may to a certain extent be overcome if car drivers know an expected chance of getting a parking space given the time of departure. However, it is important to note that this mechanism of departure time adaptation involves important welfare losses. Whereas the revenues of parking levies can be used for whichever purpose, the implicit price paid by leaving before the preferred time of departure is bygone.

As a matter of fact, a closer consideration of dynamic aspects reveals a third fundamental flaw of physical restrictions on parking space supply as opposed to regulatory parking fees. In Figure 6.2, a second successive cohort of road users is added. These may be shoppers, using the urban road network and parking facilities in period S, just after the commuters as considered in Figure 6.1 have done so in period C. The new bold demand curve D_S gives the demand for this second kind of trips. The MPC and MSC curves do not change; their positions depend on the technical characteristics of the network and the vehicles used. Assuming equal parking durations for all shoppers, which are assumed to be shorter than the commuters' parking duration, $TMSC_S$ can be postulated. N_S^* is the optimal inflow for shoppers.

If the inflow of commuters has indeed been restricted to N_C^* by levying the optimal parking fee f_C^*, the second (bold) horizontal axis describes the initial situation for the shoppers: P_C^* parking spaces are already occupied by the commuters' vehicles. Analogous to the analysis in Figure 6.1, the bold P_S and B_S curves can now be derived, as well as the optimal parking fee f_s^*. This levy guarantees the optimal inflow N_s^* and results in an additional occupation of the parking space of $(P_s^* - P_c^*)$. The sketched result that f_s^* is smaller than f_c^* can be explained by the general observation that the optimal parking levy for a certain cohort will be higher if the parking duration time is longer, and if the optimal congestion costs during the time of driving are higher. Consequently, for the sake of efficiency, regulatory parking policies require fees which are allowed to vary during the day, in particular in accordance with variations in congestion costs during times of inflow and outflow.

A third fundamental flaw of a physical policy that becomes apparent now is that, if the commuters' inflow is restricted to N_c^* by means of a restriction on parking space supply P_c^*, there is no parking space left for the shoppers. This problem might be overcome by distinguishing between parking space for commuters and parking space for shoppers. However, since the group of shoppers also consists of successive cohorts, this does not really solve the problem. Because of the cumulative nature of parking, physical restrictions on parking space supply, aiming at reducing congestion at certain times of day, will in general lead to inefficiently strict restrictions on parking space supply to successive cohorts.

A comparable problem arises when the total capacity of the parking space is not sufficient to provide the necessary parking space to the, otherwise optimal, traffic flows. For instance, in Figure 6.2, the capacity might be somewhere between P_c^* and P_s^*. It is then not optimal to allow P_c^* to get parked. Rather, an inter-temporal optimum requires an extra mark-up on both fees in order to divide the capacity constraint efficiently among both cohorts. The associated Lagrangian can be set up in the same way as for the problems studied in Chapter 3.

Thus, the cumulative nature of parking gives rise to a particular form of inter-temporal external costs, again due to a usual incompleteness of parking markets. When early parkers are not confronted with the implicit search costs they pose upon successive cohorts, the 'first-come-first-serve' rationing principle will lead to inefficient patterns of parking space occupation over the day. This is, in turn, accompanied by a non-optimal distribution of traffic flows over the day.

Consequently, apart from the aforementioned information argument and the temporal efficiency argument, the inter-temporal efficiency argument can be mentioned as a third reason why regulatory parking policies have the largest potential efficiency if time-variable parking fees, rather than physical restrictions, are used. Of course, parking fees and physical restrictions are not mutually exclusive instruments, but rather complementary measures. The use of parking fees will make restrictions on parking space supply possible and even desirable with regard to efficiency in urban land use. On the other hand, physical restrictions on parking space supply will most likely lead to chaotic situations unless accompanied with an appropriate pricing policy. Undoubtedly, the use of diagrams in the foregoing analyses poses some serious limitations on the model. However, the aim of this section was merely to demonstrate that, in a setting in which regulatory parking fees are equivalent to the first-best policy of road pricing, mere physical restrictions on parking space supply certainly are not.

6.4 A spatial model of regulatory parking policies

The foregoing analysis was non-spatial. However, one of the potentially strong features of parking policies is that the fees may be differentiated spatially. This section will elaborate on this option. In particular, it will be shown that, under certain circumstances, it may be possible to overcome the difficulty of regulatory parking policies not being capable of differentiation according to distance driven.

As a matter of fact, congestion is often spatially differentiated. Especially near and in CBD's (Central Business Districts), roads tend to become increasingly congested due to relatively high densities, for instance in terms of capital — land and labour — land ratios. The relationship between spatial patterns of urban land use and traffic congestion has accordingly received ample attention in models of urban economics (see for instance Fujita, 1989; and Kanemoto, 1980). Usually, the trade-off between land use in terms of residential use versus use for transportation is considered in such models, as well as optimal versus market-based locations and lot sizes of households. All of these issues, however, are in fact of a long run nature, and the optimal tax and investment policies derived from these general equilibrium models are in practice bound to be severely hampered by various rigidities. In particular, changes in patterns of land use, such as achieving optimal lot sizes and the optimal distribution of land use for various purposes, may take at least decades to materialize. In this section, the aim is to develop a short run counterpart to these models, in which parking locations are studied. Instead of focusing on location taxes, the optimal spatial distribution of parking fees will be investigated — taking residential and business locations as well as existing infrastructures as given, taking account of space capacity effects in terms of interactions between parking and road use, and allowing for an alternative mode.

Following Fujita (1989) and Kanemoto (1980), let us consider commuters in a monocentric city, with the CBD in the centre and the residential area around it. By taking the distance to the edge of the CBD as the only relevant spatial characteristic of each location, this urban space can be treated as if it were one-dimensional. Let $N(r)$ denote the number of households located beyond a distance r from the edge of the CBD, where $r=0$. Intra-CBD traffic is ignored by taking the CBD as a spaceless point. Assuming one commuter per household, and all employment to be concentrated in the CBD, $N(r)$ equals the number of commuters passing through the tangent at distance r during the morning peak. Commuters are assumed to have two modes of transport at their disposal: car use, denoted by C, and a 'general' alternative mode A. Having started their trip by car, they can switch towards the alternative mode wherever they like, but of course not after having parked their car.[7] While road usage suffers from congestion, the alternative mode is assumed not to be congested, and therefore operates at constant marginal transport cost per unit of distance. The tariff charged for using the alternative mode is equal among all individuals and is fixed in terms of price per unit of distance. All commuters are assumed to be identical, except for their location and the psychological cost they attach to using the alternative mode. Finally, it is assumed that regulation of transport does not affect the overall demand for transportation: no commuter quits his or her job as a result of these policies. Hence, such policies only affect the modal split, and thus the point at which the individual car driver switches towards the alternative mode.[8] Under these assumptions, the individual commuter's optimization problem can be characterized as the minimization of his or her transport cost, given his or her location:

$$\underset{r_A^i}{\text{MIN}}\ T_r^i(r_A^i) = r_A^i \cdot (t_A + c_A^i) + \int_{r_A^i}^{r^i} c_c(N_c(x), \frac{dN_A(x)}{dx}) dx + f_p(r_A^i) + \delta^i \cdot c_p(\frac{dN_A(r_A^i)}{dr_A^i})$$

subject to $\quad r_A^i \geq 0$ $\hspace{4cm}$ (6.1)

$\hspace{2.5cm} r^i - r_A^i \geq 0$

with $\delta^i = 1$ if $r^i - r_A^i > 0$; and $\delta^i = 0$ if $r^i - r_A^i = 0$

T_r^i gives the individual transport cost from the residential location r^i to the CBD; r_A^i gives the point where the individual takes the alternative mode; t_A gives the per unit of distance (p.u.d.) tariff charged for using the alternative mode; c_A^i gives the p.u.d. individual cost associated with using the alternative mode in excess of the tariff and therefore reflects individual tastes; c_C gives the p.u.d. private cost of road transport, which depends on the number of road users at that distance $N_C(r)$, and possibly on the number of cars parked at r, which equals the number of commuters taking the alternative mode at r: $dN_A(r)/dr$. This latter term includes both commuters who switch mode at r, and commuters who reside at r and start their trip by the alternative mode. This effect reflects the extent to which

---

[7]The reverse of starting the trip by the alternative mode and subsequently switching towards car use is assumed not to be possible, nor relevant.

[8]Given the interest in parking policies, N(r) merely includes commuters who *possess* a car that might be used for commuting. Other commuters by definition travel by the uncongested alternative mode, and are therefore not of any relevance to this model.

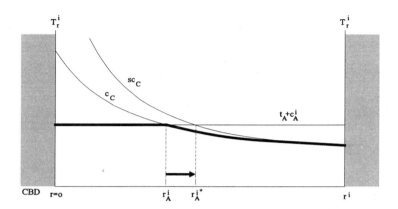

Figure 6.3   The privately and socially optimal point of modal change

parked cars alongside roads may hinder ongoing traffic. Furthermore, $f_p(r)$ denotes the (daily) parking fee at distance r; and the final term c_p indicates search cost for finding a parking space, which also depends on the number of parkers at r and on a 'road use dummy' δ^i: if the commuter travels all the way by the alternative mode (δ^i=0), he or she can leave the car where it is and therefore faces no search costs. The restrictions indicate that the optimal point of modal change is naturally bounded by r_A^i=0 when the commuter travels all the way up to the CBD by car, and r_A^i=r^i when the commuter merely uses the alternative mode.

It may be noted that problem 1 may easily be extended to include evening peak transport costs by assuming that travel patterns during the two peaks are (reversed) replicas. The p.u.d. terms t_A, c_A^i and c_C then simply have to be doubled, while the other terms remain the same. Search costs for a parking space when returning home at night may then simply be incorporated by adding a term very much like the one already included. However, as the analytics remain essentially the same for both models, only the one-peak model will be discussed.

Road usage may be expected to be increasingly congested towards the CBD. This is due both to an increasing potential number of commuters using the road, and to decreasing overall space and hence presumably also decreasing road space towards the CBD. For instance, road space decreases quadratically towards the CBD in a circular city with a fixed share of infrastructure in total land use.

Figure 6.3 illustrates the resulting trade-off that a commuter located at r^i will make, as opposed to the socially optimal choice. Ignoring parking

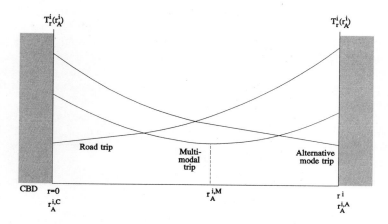

Figure 6.4   Total individual transport costs as a function of the point of modal change for three types of commuters

costs for a moment, the commuter will change mode at $r_A{}^i$. Since he or she causes an external congestion cost him- or herself however, the social cost of driving an additional unit of distance by car, denoted sc_C, are larger than the private cost c_C, and $r_A{}^{i*}$ gives the socially optimal point of modal change, assuming optimal pricing for the alternative mode.

More insight into the individual optimization problem can be obtained by solving the Lagrangian implied by problem (6.1):

$$\mathscr{L}^i = T_r^i(r_A^i) - \lambda^i \cdot (r^i - r_A^i) \tag{6.2}$$

The Kuhn–Tucker conditions to this Lagrangian are:

$$\frac{\partial \mathscr{L}^i}{\partial r_A^i} = t_A + c_A^i - c_C(r_A^i) + \frac{df_P(r_A^i)}{dr_A^i} + \delta^i \cdot \frac{dc_P(r_A^i)}{dr_A^i} + \lambda^i \geq 0;$$

$$r_A^i \geq 0 \quad \text{and} \quad r_A^i \cdot \frac{\partial \mathscr{L}^i}{\partial r_A^i} = 0 \tag{6.3}$$

$$\frac{\partial \mathscr{L}^i}{\partial \lambda^i} = r^i - r_A^i \geq 0; \quad \lambda^i \geq 0 \quad \text{and} \quad \lambda^i \cdot \frac{\partial \mathscr{L}^i}{\partial \lambda^i} = 0 \tag{6.4}$$

with $\delta^i = 1$ if $\lambda^i = 0$; and $\delta^i = 0$ otherwise $\tag{6.5}$

Figure 6.4 illustrates the possible outcomes implied by these conditions. There are three regimes in which the commuter can find himself or herself. First, if $\lambda^i = 0$ (and hence $\delta^i = 1$) and $r_A^i > 0$, the relevant T_r^i curve is the one labelled 'Multi-modal trip': the commuter makes a multi-modal trip and finds the optimal point of modal change by putting the first inequality in (6.3) equal to zero. The result will be an optimal point of modal change shown by $r_A^{i,M}$. Secondly, if $\lambda^i = 0$ and $r_A^i = 0$, the relevant T_r^i curve is the one labelled 'Road trip': the commuter makes the trip entirely by car and consequently has $r_A^{i,C}$ as the optimal point of modal change. Finally, if $\lambda^i > 0$, the T_r^i curve is decreasing in r_A^i, as indicated by the one labelled 'Alternative mode trip': $r_A^{i,A}$ is the optimal point of modal change and the commuter makes the trip entirely by the alternative mode.

To find the optimal spatial distribution of parking fees, the features of individual optimization as implied by equations (6.3)−(6.5) should be compared to the conditions for minimization of the social transport cost T. This problem can be formulated as follows:

$$
\operatorname*{MIN}_{r_A^1, r_A^2, \ldots, r_A^P} T(r_A^1, r_A^2, \ldots, r_A^P) =
$$

$$
\operatorname*{MIN}_{r_A^1, r_A^2, \ldots, r_A^P} \int_0^{r_f} \tau(x)\,dx =
$$

$$
\operatorname*{MIN}_{r_A^1, r_A^2, \ldots, r_A^P} \int_0^{r_f} \left[N_A(x) \cdot c_A + \sum_{i \in N_A(x)} c_A^i + (N(x) - N_A(x)) \cdot c_C(N(x) - N_A(x), n_A(x)) \right. \tag{6.6}
$$

$$
\left. + \gamma(x) \cdot n_A(x) + \sum_{i \in n_A(x)} \delta^i \cdot c_p(n_A(x)) \right] dx
$$

$$
\text{subject to} \quad \frac{dN_A(r)}{dr} \equiv \dot{N}_A(r) = -n_A(r)
$$

$$
N(0) = P = N_A(0)
$$

$$
N(r_f) = 0 = N_A(r_f)
$$

The objective function indicates that the aim is to minimize total transport cost over the total urban area, which ranges from the CBD (r=0) to the urban fringe (r=r_f); $\tau(r)$ represents the p.u.d. social transport cost at each distance r. Furthermore, c_A gives the p.u.d. marginal cost of the alternative mode, and $\gamma(r)$ represents the social land cost associated with occupying a parking spot during the day. Strictly speaking, through the assumption of given patterns of land use, and by explicitly taking account of the congestion costs of parked cars in terms of both hindering ongoing traffic and increasing search costs, one might argue that this residual marginal opportunity cost of parking a vehicle would be zero. Still, $\gamma(r)$ may be interpreted as a reflection of any additional cost caused by parked cars, such as visual annoyance, or as an 'exogenous shadow price' reflecting that, in the long run, any acre of land used for parking actually does imply that it is not to be available for alternative purposes. However, $\gamma(r)$ does not play a crucial role in the subsequent analysis and may therefore be omitted without loss of generality. Finally, note that the identity equating the total number of commuters to the sum of road users and users of the alternative mode is substituted into the objective.

The first constraint defines the number of cars parked at r as $n_A(r)$, being the 'spatial growth' or change in the number of users of the alternative mode: $dN_A(r)/dr = \dot{N}_A(r)$. Furthermore, the first boundary condition specifies that all commuters ($N(0)=P$) are travelling at the edge of the CBD; but since n_A represents the parking of cars, and all cars have to be parked before the spaceless CBD is reached, we also have $N_A(0)=P$. The second boundary condition simply states that no commuters live beyond the city fringe r_f.

Analogous to methods applied in continuous-time optimization problems, the continuous-space Hamiltonian can be defined as:

$$H(N_A(r),n_A(r),\eta(r)) = \tau(N_A(r),n_A(r)) + \eta(r)\cdot(-n_A(r)) \tag{6.7}$$

and the following Lagrangian can be set up:

$$\mathcal{L} = \int_0^{r_f} [H(\cdot) + \dot{\eta}\cdot N_A(x)]dx - [\eta(r_f)\cdot N_A(r_f) - \eta(0)\cdot N_A(0)] \tag{6.8}$$

N_A is the state variable, n_A is the control variable, and η is the adjoint (or costate) variable. The necessary first-order conditions for a minimum are:

$$\frac{\partial H(\cdot)}{\partial n_A(r)} = (N(r)-N_A(r))\cdot\frac{\partial c_c(\cdot)}{\partial n_A(r)} + \gamma(r) + \delta^i \cdot c_p(\cdot)$$

$$+ \sum_{i \in n_A(r)} \delta^i \cdot \frac{dc_p(\cdot)}{dn_A(r)} - \eta(r) = 0 \tag{6.9}$$

$$\dot{\eta} = -\frac{\partial H(\cdot)}{\partial N_A(r)} = -\left[c_A + \frac{d \sum_{i \in N_A(r)} c_A^i}{dN_A(r)} - c_c(\cdot) - (N(r)-N_A(r))\cdot\frac{\partial c_c(\cdot)}{\partial N_A(r)} \right] \tag{6.10}$$

$$\dot{N}_A = \frac{\partial H(\cdot)}{\partial \eta(r)} = -n_A \tag{6.11}$$

$$N_A(0) = P = N(0) \tag{6.12}$$

$$N_A(r_f) = 0 = N(r_f) \tag{6.13}$$

As η gives the shadow price for the state variable N_A, it actually gives the marginal value of keeping a commuter an additional unit of distance in the alternative mode, measured outwards from the CBD. Therefore, this value has a close relationship to the spatial distribution of the optimal parking fees, which, through their impact on individual behaviour as stated in (6.3), should ideally induce individual commuters to behave so as to satisfy the above first-order conditions. From (6.3), it follows that individual commuters base their behaviour on the spatial pattern of the respective cost components of commuting. Taking the space-derivative of (6.9), and after substitution of (6.10) we obtain:

$$
\frac{d\left[(N(r)-N_A(r))\cdot\dfrac{\partial c_C(\cdot)}{\partial n_A(r)}\right]}{dr} + \frac{d\gamma(r)}{dr} + \frac{d\delta^i\cdot c_p(\cdot)}{dr} + \frac{d\displaystyle\sum_{i\in n_A(r)}\delta^i\cdot\dfrac{dc_p(\cdot)}{dn_A(r)}}{dr}
$$

$$
+\ c_A + \frac{d\displaystyle\sum_{i\in N_A(r)}c_A^i}{dN_A(r)} - c_C(\cdot) - (N(r)-N_A(r))\cdot\frac{\partial c_C(\cdot)}{\partial N_A(r)} = 0 \qquad (6.14)
$$

as a necessary condition for the optimal spatial allocation of parking. A comparison of (6.14) with individual optimizing behaviour as in equations (6.3)−(6.5) reveals that optimality requires the following pricing strategies:

$$
t_A = c_A \qquad (6.15)
$$

$$
\frac{df_p(r)}{dr} = \frac{dN_C(r)\cdot\dfrac{\partial c_C(\cdot)}{\partial n_A(r)}}{dr} + \frac{d\displaystyle\sum_{i\in n_A(r)}\delta^i\cdot\dfrac{dc_p(\cdot)}{dn_A(r)}}{dr} + N_C(r)\cdot\frac{\partial c_C(\cdot)}{\partial N_C(r)} + \frac{d\gamma(r)}{dr} \qquad (6.16)
$$

where $N_C(r)$ is substituted back for $N(r)-N_A(r)$. Equation (6.15) implies that the p.u.d. tariff for the alternative mode should equal its p.u.d. marginal cost. It is now *ex post* easy to see why it was permissible to speak so loosely of the 'general alternative mode'. As long as the (uncongested) alternatives are priced at their marginal cost, individual maximizing behaviour is efficient. That is, it does not matter that for some commuters r_A^i is the point at which they for instance start walking (and presumably $c_A=0$ and only c_A^i matters), whereas for others it may be the point where they take public transport, and presumably both c_A and c_A^i matter. It may also be the point where they start walking to the nearest public transport stop, when explicitly taking account of the fact that public transport usually cannot be used from every distance preferred. Marginal cost pricing ensures efficiency, and choices among the alternative modes can be left to the market as long as these alternatives are indeed uncongested.

Equation (6.16) defines the slope of what can be called the optimal parking fee gradient. Clearly, in the static setting with given patterns of land use, and given patterns of car ownership, there is no need to worry about the actual values of parking fees, but merely about their spatial distribution. From (6.16), it follows that the slope of the parking fee gradient should exactly reflect the p.u.d. increase in the external part of the three types of congestion considered (parking−road, parking−parking, and road−road, respectively), and the increase in the residual parking cost.

One of the most interesting aspects of (6.16) is that it is apparently possible to overcome the difficulty of regulatory parking policies not being capable of differentiation according to distance driven, by specifying the appropriate spatial pattern of parking fees, making individuals respond to spatial parking fee differentials. The model even allows a relaxation of the assumption of each commuter travelling all the way up to the CBD. As long as they travel in the same direction, optimal parking fee gradients as described by (6.16) may be derived. However, the scope for such policies will increasingly be eroded when the actual spatial patterns within the city move away from the monocentric, unidirectional (that is, linear or at least radial) city shape assumed above. Clearly, the same objection can be raised against many other concentric models applied in urban economics.

The fact that only spatial parking fee differentials matter, and not the absolute values of parking fees, critically hinges on the rigidities assumed. In particular, because commuters are assumed not to respond in terms of car-ownership, nor in terms of job, and because neither households nor employers are assumed to relocate, the constant term in the actual parking fee gradient chosen is nothing more than a lump-sum tax to which commuters cannot respond. Without explicit relaxation of these assumptions, it can be noted that a choice of:

$$f_p(r_f) = \gamma(r_f) \tag{6.17}$$

implies that commuters living at r_f, and owning a car, are exactly charged for their external costs, since the fee $p_f(r_A^i)$ they face then amounts to:

$$f_p(r_A^i) = N_C(r_A^i) \cdot \frac{\partial c_C(\cdot)}{\partial n_A(r_A^i)} + \sum_{i \in n_A(r)} \delta^i \cdot \frac{dc_p(\cdot)}{dn_A(r_A^i)} + \int_{r_A^i}^{r_f} N_C(x) \cdot \frac{\partial c_C(\cdot)}{\partial N_C(x)} dx + \gamma(r_A^i) \tag{6.18}$$

Additionally, spatially differentiated 'lump-sum' subsidies to car owners according to:

$$s(r) = \int_r^{r_f} N_C(x) \cdot \frac{\partial c_C(\cdot)}{\partial N_C(x)} dx \tag{6.19}$$

imply that all car-owning commuters face a budget effect equal to the external costs they cause, since then we find:

$$
\begin{aligned}
f_p(r_A^i) - s(r^i) = {} & N_C(r_A^i) \cdot \frac{\partial c_C(\cdot)}{\partial n_A(r_A^i)} + \sum_{i \in n_A(r)} \delta^i \cdot \frac{dc_p(\cdot)}{dn_A(r_A^i)} \\
& + \int_{r_A^i}^{r^i} N_C(x) \cdot \frac{\partial c_C(\cdot)}{\partial N_C(x)} dx + \gamma(r_A^i)
\end{aligned}
\tag{6.20}
$$

Clearly, as commuters without a car do not pay parking fees, nor need they receive the subsidies $s(r)$ given by (6.19).

Apart from satisfying some sense of equity, the additional policies of (6.17) and (6.19) may turn out to provide optimal incentives in terms of car-ownership and residential location, which were left aside in this model.

6.5   Conclusion

This chapter presented an economic analysis of regulatory parking policies. Although parking levies are the first-best payment vehicle for charging the use of scarce parking space, such levies can only be a second-best alternative for the regulation of other road transport externalities. The reason is that parking policies take place at the end of a trip, which generally rules out differentiation according to trip length, roads followed, or vehicle used. With this in mind, regulatory parking policies were considered that aim merely at optimizing congestion on an urban road network and optimizing the activity of parking itself.

In Section 6.3, a simple diagrammatic analysis was presented, which allowed for a comparison between two basic forms that regulatory parking policies might take: regulatory parking fees versus physical restrictions on parking space supply. Three reasons why the use of time-variable parking fees is superior to mere physical reductions in parking space supply emerged: an information argument, a temporal efficiency argument and an inter-temporal efficiency argument.

Section 6.4 contained a spatial parking model, indicating that under certain assumptions, it is possible to overcome the difficulty of regulatory parking policies not being capable of differentiation according to distance driven by specifying the appropriate spatial pattern of parking fees, making individuals respond to spatial parking fee differentials.

Although regulatory parking policies are merely a second-best alternative to road pricing, there may also be some specific advantages. Since parking policies already exist in many cities, the extension to regulatory parking policies as discussed in this chapter may be more acceptable to the public than the introduction of a completely new system such as ERP. The introduction may also be easier from a technical point of view. However, also a number of fundamental weaknesses of regulatory parking policies can be mentioned. In the first place, regulatory parking policies will always contain some distortive elements and will therefore remain a second-best option by nature. Secondly, there are two groups of car drivers that will be able to escape the parking policies: those who are parking on private parking space, and the so-called through-flow (see also Section 3.5). A third fundamental drawback is the risk of adverse spill-over effects to adjacent areas (see also Chapter 11).

Despite these fundamental objections, regulatory parking policies, preferably supported by supplementary instruments such as fuel taxes for the regulation of distance dependent externalities, are likely to offer an interesting alternative for urban traffic regulation, especially as long as road pricing is not yet introduced on a large scale. The potential power of regulatory parking policies has recently been underlined by several empirical studies (see Small, 1992a, pp. 126–128; and Willson and Shoup, 1990).

7   TRANSPORT, SPATIAL ECONOMY AND THE GLOBAL ENVIRONMENT[1]

7.1   Introduction

Although the notion of 'Sustainable Development' has become a key concept in environmental economics and in popular political jargon, rigorous analytical support and unambiguous interpretation of its features are lacking. This is especially so in fields closely related to, but not at the core of environmental economics; such as transport economics. The last decades have witnessed a stream of economic studies in the field of transport and environment, which typically rely on the neoclassical concept of external costs, and are performed in static, partial equilibrium settings (see the foregoing chapters and the references therein). While the results of such studies may underpin the need to develop a more stringent line of environmental transport policies, many important issues are left untouched. Apart from difficulties of coming to a satisfactory mapping between external cost approaches and the paradigm of sustainability, a partial approach to transport related phenomena can overlook the fact that most transport demand is derived, usually depending on spatial patterns of economic activity, and spatial and modal patterns of infrastructure supply. Therefore, 'optimal' levels of transport and 'optimal' Pigouvian transport taxes may actually suffer from second-best biases, since they are derived under the assumption of a first-best world.

This chapter focuses on interdependencies between transport, spatial economy and the environment in the context of policies designed to achieve a global environmental target, and hence investigates the consequences of the derived nature of the demand for transport for the regulation of its externalities. The spatial price equilibrium (SPE) approach is adapted to analyse the environmental sustainability of spatio-economic structure, and to evaluate first-best and second-best regulatory policies. A small scale version of this model is then used to perform a number of

---

[1]This chapter is partly based on an earlier contribution (Verhoef and Van den Bergh, 1996) to a book on spatial equilibrium modelling (Van den Bergh, Nijkamp and Rietveld, 1996), and partly on an article that will appear in *Environment and Planning A* (Verhoef, Van den Bergh and Button, 1996).

numerical simulations, investigating market based versus sustainable spatio-economic configurations with first-best and second-best policies.

Section 7.2 discusses some issues that become relevant when studying the environmental impacts of transport from a sustainability rather than an external cost perspective. In Section 7.3, these ideas are translated into a spatial price equilibrium model. Using a condensed simulation model based on this general model, Section 7.4 focuses on the optimal sustainable spatio-economic system, comparing it with the market based configuration. In Section 7.5, second-best transport policies are considered, namely the case where the transport regulator has no control over regulation in other sectors. In Section 7.6, endogenous environmental technologies are introduced, which allows for comparisons between emission taxation and activity taxation. Section 7.7 contains the conclusions.

7.2   Transport and environmental sustainability: a conceptual framework

'Sustainable Development' is usually interpreted in terms of the commitment of the present generation to act consistently with future as well as present needs. After the publication of the Brundtland Report (WCED, 1987), the concept has received much attention and some political support. However, it has challenged and still challenges economic environmental analysis in several ways.

Starting from the treatment of environmental degradation in the neoclassical context of externalities, it is clear that a consistent consideration of 'future needs' in terms of inter-temporal externalities and efficiency is bound to be hampered by practical and theoretical obstacles. Among these are issues concerning discount rates, consumer sovereignty, and uncertainty (Pezzey, 1993; Van den Bergh, 1996). Consequently, any satisfactory incorporation of the concept of sustainable development within a neoclassical framework, where the valuation of inter-temporal environmental spill-overs should be based on future willingness to pay for avoiding these effects, seems beyond reach. Rather, in addition to allocative efficiency, the concept of sustainability seems to call for a scale dimension when considering environmental regulation from the economic perspective (Daly, 1989). A possible approach to the operationalization of this scale dimension has been put forward by Siebert (1982) and Opschoor (1992), who suggest application of the 'Environmental Utilization Space' as a restriction on the extent to which a generation should be allowed to use natural resources (see also Opschoor and Weterings, 1994). The specification of a set of upper bounds to a generation's allowable environmental claims could be based on ecological phenomena such as carrying and regenerative capacities of ecosystems, and would be the domain of biology and ecology rather than economics.

Furthermore, through its focus on the long run and system-wide issues, the paradigm of sustainability embraces a much 'broader' connotation than does the notion of externalities. In terms of modelling characteristics, this points towards the application of dynamic general — rather than static partial — analyses. Whereas the consideration of dynamics in relation to sustainability is often cast in terms of aggregate macro-economic growth models (Toman, Pezzey and Krautkraemer, 1994), a more disaggregate systems analysis becomes particularly relevant when studying the sustainability of an open system such as a region or a sector (Van den Bergh and Nijkamp, 1994). Therefore, this chapter will focus on economy-wide and spatial interactions. Dynamics will not be treated explicitly. This reflects some steady state view of spatial sustainable development. It allows to concentrate on the consequences of the interactions between transport, the economy and the environment in a spatial context when comparing market-based and sustainable systems. Both sectoral and spatial disaggregation will thus be accounted for.

As the goal of sustainability reflects an orientation towards the long run behaviour of a well-defined, closed system, some complications arise in interpreting 'sustainable transport'. In particular, it is not straightforward how sustainability should or could be defined for a sub-system, because of interdependencies with other sub-systems. Clearly, the virtue and stability of regional or sectoral 'sustainability' are questionable when the overall system to which this region or sector belongs does not behave in a sustainable manner. Besides, environmental claims from different, economically related regions or sectors often infringe on the same global environmental goals, such as emissions of greenhouse gases. As a consequence, regulation on the level of a sub-system may often, indirectly, either benefit from synergetic side effects, or suffer from counterproductive compensatory effects in related sub-systems. It is important to investigate the potential impacts of such interdependencies upon the effectiveness of environmental regulation aiming at global targets.

In short, sustainability as such seems to be a concept much more applicable to closed, full systems than to open sub-systems. Hence, when considered on the level of a sub-system, sustainability calls for analyses allowing for consideration of all sorts of feedback effects with the 'macro' system. A necessary condition for a transport system to qualify as 'sustainable' can then be that its operation should not be inconsistent with overall sustainability. Overall sustainability refers to a sustainable level of overall activity, a sustainable spatial organization of these activities, and a supporting infrastructure network which is able to serve the transport flows resulting from this organization without conflicting with sustainability criteria. The crucial issue is, therefore, not a quest for 'sustainable transport' as some independently defined goal. Rather, the relevant ultimate target is overall sustainability, implying certain necessary

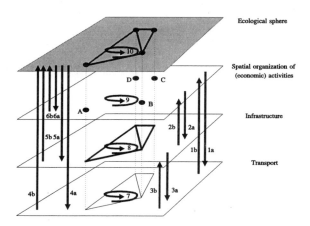

*Figure 7.1   Transport, spatial economy and the global environment
            in a multi-layer representation*

features of transport. The policy issue is the attainment of sustainability,
given the policy instruments available, and taking account of possibly
counteracting individual behaviour.

Figure 7.1 serves to illustrate such a comprehensive approach. Four
different, but closely related and interacting layers are distinguished. As a
start, consider the second layer, which represents the spatial organization
of (economic) activities. The parentheses indicate that a broad definition
of the term 'economic' is used, including all possible kinds of productive
and consumptive activities. It is assumed that these activities are
concentrated in various nodes, labelled A−D. At this level of abstraction,
one of the nodes may be taken to represent a more spacious 'node' such
as the agricultural sector. Due to specialization of these nodes, fed by
comparative advantages, scale economies or agglomeration economics, the
nodes are not self-sufficient: the bundle of goods and factors supplied
within a node is not the same as the bundle demanded at prevailing local
market prices, and, therefore, inter-nodal trade takes place. This trade is
made possible by means of the presence of infrastructure in the third layer,
and gives rise to all sorts of transport activities in the fourth layer. Finally,
the upper layer represents the ecological sphere.

The arrows indicate various interactions that may occur in the system.
The arrows on the right hand side describe issues which are traditionally
at the heart of regional and transport economics. From the right to the left:
1a indicates that the demand for transport is a derived demand, following
from the spatial organization of economic activities. Conversely, 1b
represents the effect of transport on the spatial distribution of activities.

Arrows 2a and 2b show that the construction of infrastructure depends on the spatial distribution of economic activities, but that the supply of infrastructure may in turn affect the development of the economic system. Next, 3a represents the restrictions that the existing infrastructure pose upon transport activities, whereas 3b indicates that an increasing demand for transport may eventually result in the construction of additional infrastructure.

The arrows on the left-hand side represent the additional interactions involved when considering the question of ecological sustainability. The three ascending arrows 4b−6b indicate the environmental degradation resulting from transport activities, the existence of infrastructure, and other economic activities. These effects will, to some extent, be localized. This is represented by the reprint of the spatial structure of the other layers in the ecological sphere. Other environmental externalities will be non-localized, and this is represented by the shading of the ecological layer. The three descending arrows 4a−6a indicate that the state of the environment may in turn affect the other three layers. In particular, environmental degradation may affect both the productivity and the utility in the second layer. Additionally, the productivity in the transport sector, and the quality of, and possibilities for, infrastructure supply may depend on environmental characteristics.

Finally, interactions may occur within each layer. The curved arrows may for instance represent: congestion effects in transport (7); inter- and intra-modal network dependencies in infrastructure (8); any form of economic interdependencies (9); and physical interactions within the ecosystem (10).

It is clear that a serious consideration of the issue of sustainable transport results in the adoption of a quite complex system of multilateral spatio-dynamic interactions. Traditional economic approaches regarding the relation between transport and environment, in contrast, usually concentrate exclusively on the outer left arrow 4b, and only on its static, non-localized component.

7.3 Transport and environmental sustainability in a spatial price equilibrium approach

In the following sections, the implications of the above issues are considered within the framework of a static spatial price equilibrium (SPE) approach. Both a general model and a small-scale simulation version have been developed. More detailed discussions of these models can be found in Verhoef and Van den Bergh (1996) and Verhoef, Van den Bergh and Button (1996). In the analysis, an exogenous global environmental restriction represents the environmental utilization space, and satisfaction of this restriction is taken as a necessary prerequisite for overall sustainability. It is important, however, to stress that the analysis could refer to any global environmental target, be it sustainability or any other less ambitious goal.

The SPE methodology, first presented by Samuelson (1952) and further developed by Takayama and others (Takayama and Judge, 1971; Takayama and Labys, 1986), has the property that equilibrating transport flows between two nodes come into existence as soon as the difference between nodal prices exceed transport costs. Both nodes benefit from such trade, and overall efficiency increases. Usually, SPE models are used to analyse spatial interactions in terms of commodity flows, with flexible prices clearing spatial excess demands and supplies for given transport cost structures and local demand and supply structures. A more general interpretation of SPE can embrace flows of production factors and intermediates, and even passenger transport. An advantage of the SPE approach is its close relation to traditional welfare economic modelling, thus lending itself to formulations in terms of welfare maximization, and derivations of associated optimal policies in a spatio-economic equilibrium setting.

In a general SPE setting with $J \cdot I$ spatially differentiated markets (for J goods and I nodes, $J \cdot I$ local demand relations and $J \cdot I$ local supply relations are assumed to exist) and M modes, the social optimization problem of maximizing net quasi welfare, subject to the constraint implied by the environmental utilization space, to individual maximizing behaviour, and to some relevant non-negativity constraints, can be represented by the following Kuhn–Tucker specification:

$$
\begin{aligned}
\Phi = &\sum_{i=1}^{I}\sum_{j=1}^{J}\int_0^{Y_i^j} b_i^{\,j}(\psi_i^j)\,d\psi_i^j - \sum_{i=1}^{I}\sum_{j=1}^{J}\int_0^{X_i^j} c_i^{\,j}\!\left(e_i^{\,h}(X_i^{\,h})\,\forall\,h,\chi_i^j\right)d\chi_i^j - \sum_{i=1}^{I}\sum_{j=1}^{J}\varepsilon_i^j\cdot e_i^{\,j}(X_i^{\,j}) \\[4pt]
&-\sum_{\substack{o=1}}^{I}\sum_{\substack{d=1\\d\neq o}}^{I}\sum_{j=1}^{J}\sum_{m=1}^{M} Z_{od}^{jm}\cdot t_{od}^{jm}(Z_{od}^{hm}\,\forall\,h,I_{od}^{\,m}) - \sum_{\substack{o=1}}^{I}\sum_{\substack{d=1\\d\neq o}}^{I}\sum_{m=1}^{M} C_{od}^{\,m}(I_{od}^{\,m}) \\[4pt]
&-\sum_{\substack{o=1}}^{I}\sum_{\substack{d=1\\d\neq o}}^{I}\sum_{m=1}^{M} \varepsilon_{od}^{Zm}\cdot e_{od}^{Zm}(Z_{od}^{jm}\,\forall\,j) - \sum_{\substack{o=1}}^{I}\sum_{\substack{d=1\\d\neq o}}^{I}\sum_{m=1}^{M} \varepsilon_{od}^{Im}\cdot e_{od}^{Im}(I_{od}^{\,m})
\end{aligned}
\qquad (7.1\text{a})
$$

$$
+\;\lambda_E\cdot\!\left[E^{\,*} - E\!\left(e_i^{\,j}(X_i^{\,j}),e_{od}^{Zm}(Z_{od}^{hm}\,\forall\,h),e_{od}^{Im}(I_{od}^{\,m})\right)\,\forall\,i\;\forall\,j\;\forall\,o\;\forall\,d\;\wedge o\neq d\;\forall\,m\right] \quad (7.1\text{b})
$$

$$
+\;\sum_{i=1}^{I}\sum_{j=1}^{J}\lambda_{M_i^j}\cdot\!\left[c_i^{\,j}\!\left(e_i^{\,h}(X_i^{\,h})\,\forall\,h,X_i^{\,j}\right) + \pi_i^j + \gamma_i^j - b_i^{\,j}(Y_i^{\,j})\right] \qquad (7.1\text{c})
$$

$$
+\;\sum_{\substack{o=1}}^{I}\sum_{\substack{d=1\\d\neq o}}^{I}\sum_{j=1}^{J}\sum_{m=1}^{M}\lambda_{N_{od}^{jm}}\cdot\!\left[c_o^{\,j}\!\left(e_o^{\,h}(X_o^{\,h})\,\forall\,h,X_o^{\,j}\right) + \pi_o^j + t_{od}^{jm}(Z_{od}^{hm}\,\forall\,h,I_{od}^{\,m}) + \tau_{od}^{jm} + \gamma_d^j - b_d^{\,j}(Y_d^{\,j})\right]
$$

$$
(7.1\text{d})
$$

s.t.: $\quad Z_{ii}^{j} \geq 0 \quad \forall i \; \forall j \quad$ (7.1e)

$\quad Z_{od}^{jm} \geq 0 \quad \forall o \; \forall d \wedge o \neq d \; \forall j \; \forall m \quad$ (7.1f)

$\quad I_{od}^{m} \geq 0 \quad \forall o \; \forall d \wedge o \neq d \; \forall m \quad$ (7.1g)

with: $\quad Y_{i}^{j} = \sum_{\substack{o=1 \\ o \neq i}}^{I} \sum_{m=1}^{M} Z_{oi}^{jm} + Z_{ii}^{j} \quad \forall i \; \forall j \quad$ (7.1h)

$\quad X_{i}^{j} = \sum_{\substack{d=1 \\ d \neq i}}^{I} \sum_{m=1}^{M} Z_{id}^{jm} + Z_{ii}^{j} \quad \forall i \; \forall j \quad$ (7.1i)

$\quad p_{i}^{j} = b_{i}^{j} - \gamma_{i}^{j} = c_{i}^{j} + \pi_{i}^{j} \quad \forall \; Z_{ii}^{j} > 0 \quad$ (7.1j)

$\quad p_{d}^{j} = b_{d}^{j} - \gamma_{d}^{j} = c_{o}^{j} + \pi_{o}^{j} + t_{od}^{jm} + \tau_{od}^{jm} = p_{o}^{j} + t_{od}^{jm} + \tau_{od}^{jm} \quad \forall \; Z_{od}^{jm} > 0 \quad$ (7.1k)

and: $\quad i,o,d \in \{1,2,...,I\} \wedge o \neq d; \quad j,h \in \{1,2,...,J\}; \quad m \in \{1,2,...,M\} \quad$ (7.1l)

Y_i^j is the consumption of good j (j=1,2,...,J) in node i (i=1,2,...,I), and X_i^j is the production of good j in node i. The functions b_i^j and c_i^j give the marginal benefits of consumption and the marginal production costs for good j in node i, respectively. Z_{ii}^j gives total intra-nodal deliveries of good j within node i, which are assumed not to require any transportation; that is, nodes are assumed to be spaceless points. Z_{od}^{jm} represents total deliveries of good j from node o (origin; o=1,2,...,I) to node d (destination; d=1,2,...,I), using transport mode m (m=1,2,...,M). The average transport costs of shipping good j from node o to node d with mode m are given by t_{od}^{jm}. I_{od}^m gives the capacity of infrastructure of type m between o and d in that particular direction, and C_{od}^m gives the associated total costs of infrastructure provisions, including depreciation and maintenance. Average transport costs t_{od}^{jm} are assumed to be negatively related to the relevant infrastructure capacity I_{od}^m available, and positively related to all deliveries on that particular link, Z_{od}^{hm} (for h=1,2,...,J), representing congestion effects.

The physical parameters e_i^j give the total local environmental emissions associated with the production of good j in node i. These may directly affect marginal production costs for local sectors c_i^j, which are non-decreasing in any local emissions e_i^h (where h=1,2,...,J), reflecting possible adverse effects of local environmental degradation on productive activities. Additionally, the extent to which overall nodal indirect money metric welfare in node i is directly adversely affected by local emissions is given by $\sum_j \varepsilon_i^j e_i^j$, where ε_i^j gives the nodal shadow price for sector j's emissions in node i associated with environmental values in addition to the direct effects on production costs. For instance, ε_i^j includes consumers' valuation of environmental goods. The total non-decreasing physical environmental effects of the usage and existence of infrastructure of type m between o and d are given by e_{od}^{Zm} and e_{od}^{Im}. As is the case for production, $\varepsilon_{od}^{Im} \cdot e_{od}^{Im}$ and $\varepsilon_{od}^{Zm} \cdot e_{od}^{Zm}$ give the associated extent to which instantaneous indirect money metric welfare is adversely affected by these effects along link o−d.

Apart from the instantaneous localized environmental effects, all physical parameters e have their respective non-decreasing effects on a global environmental parameter E. The global environmental utilization space is given by a maximum allowable level of E, denoted E^*. The model could of course be extended to multiple environmental effects (that is, various e's and E^*'s). This, however, would complicate the model considerably, without providing any major additional insights into the central research questions of the analysis. It may be noted that the emission factors e are source specific, thus already allowing for considerable heterogeneity in the environmental model.

Finally, considering the markets, p_i^j is the local price for good j in node i. The government is assumed to be able to regulate by means of specific producers' taxes π_i^j on the production of good j in node i; consumers' taxes γ_i^j on the consumption of good j in node i; and mode specific transport taxes τ_{od}^{jm} on deliveries of good j from o to d. The λ's are Lagrangian multipliers. In particular, the multiplier λ_E ($=\partial\Phi/\partial E^*$) can readily be interpreted as the shadow price for meeting the sustainability constraint.

Problem (7.1) can be summarized as maximizing instantaneous welfare, including instantaneous external costs, subject to the sustainability constraint – which is no part of instantaneous welfare, but is to be met for the sake of future generations – and subject to individual maximizing behaviour. It is shown in Verhoef and Van den Bergh (1996) that problem (7.1) may have an infinite number of internal solutions due to interdependencies between production, consumption and transport. This demonstrates that, in a more comprehensive setting, optimal regulatory taxes cannot be set in isolation, but requires consideration of both market failures and taxes applied elsewhere in the economic system. The most straightforward among the optimal tax schemes is to put consumption taxes γ_i^j equal to zero, and to impose the following regulatory taxes:

$$\pi_i^j = \left[\sum_{h=1}^{J} \frac{\partial C_i^h}{\partial e_i^j} + \varepsilon_i^j + \lambda_E \cdot \frac{\partial E}{\partial e_i^j}\right] \cdot \frac{\partial e_i^j}{\partial X_i^j} \quad \forall i \ \forall j \tag{7.2}$$

$$\tau_{od}^{jm} = \sum_{h=1}^{J} Z_{od}^{hm} \cdot \frac{\partial t_{od}^{hm}}{\partial Z_{od}^{jm}} + \left[\varepsilon_{od}^{Zm} + \lambda_E \cdot \frac{\partial E}{\partial e_{od}^{Zm}}\right] \cdot \frac{\partial e_{od}^{Zm}}{\partial Z_{od}^{jm}} \quad \forall o \ \forall d \wedge o \neq d \ \forall j \ \forall m \tag{7.3}$$

Equations (7.2) and (7.3) indicate a direct application of the *Polluter Pays Principle* by imposing environmental taxation on productive activities, and a composite congestion and environmental tax on transport activities. Optimal investment rules for infrastructure are finally given by:

$$-\sum_{j=1}^{J} Z_{od}^{jm} \cdot \frac{\partial t_{od}^{jm}}{\partial I_{od}^m} = \frac{\partial C_{od}^m}{\partial I_{od}^m} + \left[\varepsilon_{od}^{Im} + \lambda_E \cdot \frac{\partial E}{\partial e_{od}^{Im}}\right] \cdot \frac{\partial e_{od}^{Im}}{\partial I_{od}^m} \quad \forall I_{od}^m > 0 \tag{7.4}$$

It is evident that this model, because of its generality, will not easily yield any manageable solutions. In order to investigate its full comparative static properties, a small simulation version of this model was developed in Verhoef, Van den Bergh and Button (1996). The outcomes of this model are discussed in the following sections.

7.4 Optimal spatial sustainability versus market outcomes

For the simulations, a number of simplifying assumptions are made: only one good, two nodes, and one uncongested transport mode with a given level of infrastructural capacity are considered, and emissions only inflict upon one common global environmental target, namely the environmental utilization space. Some simulation results obtained with this condensed model are presented in this section, comparing market outcomes versus first-best sustainable spatio-economic configurations.

Before turning to these results, first the 'base case' will be discussed. The demand functions for the good are assumed to be linear and identical for both nodes (R=A,B), with intercepts $d_R=80$ and slopes $a_R=-0.5$. The supply functions of the two nodes are both linear but different, with intercepts $s_A=25$ and $s_B=5$; and slopes $b_A=1.5$ and $b_B=0.5$: production is more efficient in node B than it is in node A. Transport costs are equal to 5, which is smaller than the autarky price difference, and hence equilibrating transport flows will exist. As expected, in the trade equilibrium, B will be the net exporter with exports $F_B(=-F_A)=30$, which exactly compensates for the nodal imbalances implied by $Q_A^T=20$ and $Y_A^T=50$ at the after trade nodal price $P_A^T=55$; and $Q_B^T=90$ and $Y_B^T=60$ at the after trade nodal price $P_B^T=50$. In comparison with the autarky situation, total welfare in node A increases from 756.25 to 925, and in node B from 2812.5 to 2925.[2] Both nodes, therefore, benefit from trade; as they would with voluntary trade. By setting emission factors for production at $e_A=e_B=10$, and for transport at $e_T=15$, total emissions of 1550 result in the unregulated trade equilibrium: $E_A=200$; $E_B=900$ and $E_T=450$. Transport thus accounts for about 30% of the emissions. The environmental utilization space E^* is set at 1000.

To illustrate the SPE methodology in combination with the environmental model, in the first simulation the two production structures are gradually interchanged. On the right hand of Figure 7.2, the base case is found; on the left hand, $s_A=5$ and $b_A=0.5$, and $s_B=25$ and $b_B=1.5$. Moving right, s_A (s_B) is increased (decreased) by 1 each step; and b_A (b_B) is increased (decreased) by 0.05. The simultaneous variation of the four

---

[2]Welfare here is a narrowly defined concept, measured as the sum of consumer and producer surpluses, and does not include environmental values because environment is treated as a constraint rather than as a temporal externality. Therefore, in the simulations, it will be found that this narrowly defined welfare will *decrease* due to regulation.

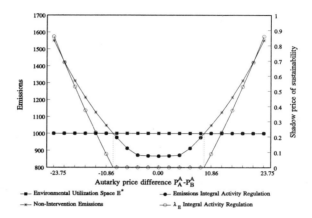

*Figure 7.2   Emissions in the market based and the optimal
              sustainable spatial equilibrium, and the shadow price
              of sustainability*

parameters is summarized along the horizontal axis by their impact on the
autarky price difference $P_A^A - P_B^A$, with the autarky prices being the nodal
prices that would arise in absence of trade. Given the identical demand
structures, this simulation yields symmetric results, with identical nodes,
as reflected by $P_A^A - P_B^A = 0$, in the centre.

NI	non intervention
NIE	non-intervention emissions
EUS (E*)	environmental utilization space
IAR	integral activity regulation
TVR	transport volume regulation
IER	integral emission regulation
TER	transport emission regulation

Table 7.1   Some abbreviations used in Chapter 7

Figure 7.2 focuses on environmental issues. From the curvature of the non-
intervention emissions NIE (see Table 7.1 for the various abbreviations
used), it is clear that the more the two nodes differ, the higher emissions
will be, due to the induced transport flows. Alternatively, when the two
nodes are identical, in the centre of the figure, NIE fall within the
environmental utilization space E* and the shadow price of sustainability
λ_E is zero. The basic relation between NIE, E*, and emissions and λ_E under
integral activity regulation (IAR) is obvious. As long as NIE<E*, no
regulation is needed, and emissions with IAR are equal to NIE. When

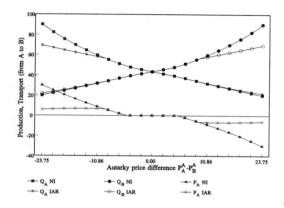

Figure 7.3   Production and transport in the market based and the optimal sustainable spatial equilibrium

NIE>E*, regulation is necessary. This is reflected in a positive shadow price of sustainability λ_E. The larger the difference between NIE and E*, the higher this value of λ_E.

The spatio-economic impacts of regulation, as well as some typical SPE characteristics, are shown in Figure 7.3. First, with identical nodes and autarky prices, no trade takes place; when the autarky price difference exceeds the transport costs, the node with the lower autarky price becomes the net exporter. When NIE exceed E*, free market activity levels are excessive. Figure 7.3 shows that the more different the nodes are, the larger the discrepancy between non-intervention and sustainable levels of trade and nodal specialization. For the optimal sustainable spatial configuration, production and transport have to be increasingly restricted. Given the identical demand structures, this implies a relatively stronger restriction in production in the exporting node than in the importing node, as can be seen on both ends of Figure 7.3.

7.5   Second-best transport volume regulation

The same modelling framework can be used to evaluate various second-best policies. Second-best regulation of road transport, particularly in the case of congestion, has received quite some attention over the last years (see the foregoing chapters and the references therein). However, except for studies on the dependencies between urban land use and congestion (see Section 6.4), such analyses typically consider transport in isolation from other economic activities. This partial equilibrium approach to transport ignores that transport demand is often a derived demand, depending on spatial patterns of economic activity, and spatial and modal patterns of infrastructure supply. Therefore, 'optimal' levels of transport and 'optimal' Pigouvian transport taxes derived in such analyses may suffer from second-best biases. Indeed, considering transport in isolation is equivalent to assuming that first-best conditions apply to the entire spatio-economic system. A main advantage of the above SPE model is that it offers an analytical framework for investigating these issues, and the associated complexities of different sectors infringing on the same global environmental targets.

The second-best case where the regulator is capable of regulating the transport sector only, and has no influence over regulation in the production sectors, is considered here. This could correspond to the situation of a relatively small transit region, concerned with the impact of its 'through-put' on some global environmental amenity, but unable to directly influence environmental policies in the nodes of origin and destination. The Netherlands are a good example. Although such a regulator cannot directly affect production and consumption, its transport policies will indirectly affect overall production and consumption. Ignoring all instantaneous externalities in the framework set out in equation (7.1), and considering only the impact of emissions on the sustainability constraint, it can be shown that for the general model discussed in Section 7.3 the following optimal second-best regulatory transportation taxes apply:

$$
\tau_{od}^{jm} = \sum_{h=1}^{J} Z_{od}^{hm} \cdot \frac{\partial t_{od}^{hm}}{\partial Z_{od}^{jm}} + \left[\varepsilon_{od}^{Zm} + \lambda_E \cdot \frac{\partial E}{\partial e_{od}^{Zm}} \right] \cdot \frac{\partial e_{od}^{Zm}}{\partial Z_{od}^{jm}}
$$

$$
+ \frac{\left[\varepsilon_o^j + \lambda_E \cdot \dfrac{\partial E}{\partial e_o^j} \right] \cdot \dfrac{\partial e_o^j}{\partial X_o^j} - \pi_o^j}{1 - \dfrac{\partial c_o^j}{\partial X_o^j} \bigg/ \dfrac{\partial b_o^j}{\partial Y_o^j}} + \frac{\gamma_o^j}{1 - \dfrac{\partial b_o^j}{\partial Y_o^j} \bigg/ \dfrac{\partial c_o^j}{\partial X_o^j}}
$$

$$
- \frac{\left[\varepsilon_d^j + \lambda_E \cdot \dfrac{\partial E}{\partial e_d^j} \right] \cdot \dfrac{\partial e_d^j}{\partial X_d^j} - \pi_d^j}{1 - \dfrac{\partial c_d^j}{\partial X_d^j} \bigg/ \dfrac{\partial b_d^j}{\partial Y_d^j}} - \frac{\gamma_d^j}{1 - \dfrac{\partial b_d^j}{\partial Y_d^j} \bigg/ \dfrac{\partial c_d^j}{\partial X_d^j}}
$$

(7.5)

(Verhoef and Van den Bergh, 1996). Equation (7.5) gives the second-best regulatory tax that trades off, in the most efficient way, the three impacts of (a) directly reducing emissions from transport; (b) indirectly reducing the emissions from production in the node of origin o; and (c) stimulating production and hence emissions in the node of destination d. For impacts (b) and (c), an important question is the extent to which producers' taxes π_i^j on the production of good j in node i(=o,d) differ from the optimal

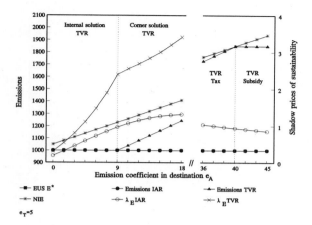

Figure 7.4   Emissions and shadow prices of sustainability under IAR and TVR

level; see the numerators of the associated terms. In the simulations with the condensed model, the focus is on how the underlying spatio-economic system might affect the efficiency and effectiveness of such second-best transport policies in comparison with first-best regulation where the regulator can set an optimal mix of transport and production taxes.

Figure 7.4 considers emissions and shadow prices of sustainability under both policies. Along the horizontal axis, the emission coefficient in the node of destination e_A is raised from 0 to 45; in comparison with the base case, e_T is set at 5 rather than 15. Furthermore, $\pi_A = \pi_B = 0$. The underlying spatio-economic structure has an important impact on the performance and potential of second-best regulation. On the left-hand side, this structure is relatively favourable for such policies. Not only does second-best transport volume regulation (TVR) have a favourable direct impact on emissions of transport itself, it also induces a shift from consumption of imported goods towards the purchase of locally produced goods in node A, which are produced in a relatively environmentally friendly way compared to node B. When moving right, however, this favourable indirect effect of transport policies is gradually eroded. Up to the point where $e_A=9$, this shows in an increasing discrepancy between the shadow prices of sustainability λ_E for both policies. This shadow price not only depends on the extent to which NIE exceed E^*, as illustrated by the gradual increase of λ_E for IAR. In addition, this shadow price also depends on the efficiency (and effectiveness; see below) of regulation itself.

When e_A exceeds the value of 9, TVR is no longer capable of meeting the sustainability constraint. In this regime, 'optimal' TVR consists of the

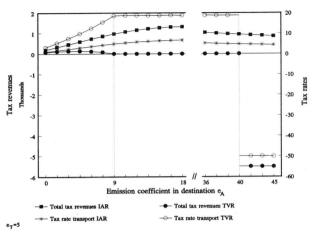

Figure 7.5   Regulatory tax rates and revenues under IAR and TVR

corner solution of prohibitive taxation with zero transport (Figure 7.5). Here, λ_E for TVR should no longer be seen as the 'shadow price of sustainability', but rather as the 'shadow price of reducing emissions as much as possible'. The effectiveness and efficiency of TVR increasingly falls short of those of IAR, as shown by the increasing difference of emissions and λ_E for both policies in Figure 7.4. With prohibitive transport taxation, total regulatory tax revenues will be zero. With IAR, internal solutions will generally result, implying positive tax revenues for the regulator (see Figure 7.5).

When e_A increases further, a point will be reached where TVR becomes completely ineffective and inefficient. In this simulation, e_A=40 creates that particular unfavourable combination of parameters where transport regulation has no effect whatsoever on total emissions. Here, the direct environmental impacts on emissions from transport are completely compensated for by additional emissions from increased local production in the node of destination; an increase induced by the transport policy itself. Here, λ_E for TVR approaches infinity.

When moving beyond this point, we end up in a third regime, where second-best TVR is in the form of transport subsidization rather than taxation. Transport taxation would be counter-productive, as it induces more emissions from production in the node of destination than it reduces transport emissions. As shown in Figure 7.5, the best thing the TVR regulator can do is to subsidize transport in a way that local production in node A is completely reduced to zero. In this case, TVR transport subsidies should be direction specific, which is never the case for transport taxes. Simulation results not depicted graphically here show that under this

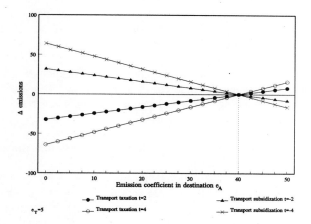

Figure 7.6   The effectiveness of TVR in a spatio-economic setting

regime, narrow welfare under TVR falls considerably, and goes below welfare under IAR, even though the sustainability constraint is not met with TVR. Such TVR subsidization obviously creates severe distortions in the spatio-economic system.

The curvature of λ_E under IAR deserves some attention. The fact that it is rising on the left-hand side of Figure 7.4 reflects that the economy as a whole becomes more polluting due to the increase of e_A. In that light, the flattening of curve's slope on the left-hand side, and its decline on the right-hand side may seem perverse. The explanation lies in the fact that the shadow price λ_E is attached to the factors e_i in the optimal tax rules. The increase in e_A, therefore, in itself has a deflating impact on λ_E. The observed pattern arises from the combination of both effects.

Although one might argue that this situation of TVR subsidization is quite extreme and unrealistic because one would not expect a transport regulator in the sort of transit region considered to actually subsidize transport for environmental reasons, the simulation has important implications also for a less ambitious transport regulator. The underlying spatio-economic equilibrium processes leading to the pattern seen in Figure 7.4 cannot be ignored, and will affect the effectiveness of any form of transport regulation. This is illustrated in Figure 7.6, where the impact of four different levels of transport taxes ($\tau=-4$, $\tau=-2$, $\tau=2$ and $\tau=4$) on total emissions is seen for various levels of e_A. On the left-hand side, taxes have a favourable impact on total emissions because of their direct effect on transport, as well as the indirect impact of stimulating a production shift from node B to A; the impact naturally being greater the higher the tax. With an increasing emission coefficient, however, these impacts decline, and beyond $e_A=40$, the transport regulator would find total emissions increasing more, the higher the transport tax charged. Transport subsidization is necessary if TVR is to reduce total emissions. If he is not inclined to subsidize transport, the best thing the regulator can do is to keep transport taxes at zero.

These simulations demonstrate the sometimes unexpected effects of transport regulation when considered in the context of a full spatio-economic setting, including the interdependencies between transport and the spatial pattern of economic activities.

7.6   Endogenous environmental technologies: emission charging versus activity regulation

This section discusses simulations in a model with endogenous environmental technology. Here, regulation by taxation based on production and transportation volumes is no longer first-best, since it fails to provide any incentives to reduce emissions through cleaner environmental technologies. The impacts of such integral activity regulation (IAR) will be compared with the first-best option of marginal external cost pricing or integral emission regulation (IER).

First, the modelling of environmental technologies will now be discussed in the context of the simulation model, although the principles equally hold for the more general model (7.1). It is assumed that application of improved environmental technologies in the production process shifts the cost curves for the good upwards, and that it increases the private cost of transport t. For modelling the costs of abatement technologies, therefore, the marginal cost of emission reductions per unit of production are assumed to be independent of the total level of production, and the marginal costs of emission reductions per unit of transport are assumed to be independent of the total level of transport activities. Consequently, such improvements affect marginal production and transport costs, and are, therefore, assumed to be embodied in products and transport activities. In an alternative formulation, abatement technologies could be assumed to be embodied in fixed capital, which would merely affect fixed costs, leaving marginal production and transport costs unaltered.

The private gains of environmental improvements are assumed to be solely in terms of reductions of the regulatory tax sum to be paid. This is in line with the assumption that the environmental utilization space is an external constraint, and not an argument in current actors' individual utility functions. Environmental degradation is not defined in terms of instantaneous external costs, and E^* is only to be met for the sake of future generations. Secondly, it reflects that the global natural environment is in many instances a public good, implying that 'free riding' is the rational strategy for individual actors. It is assumed here that in each of the three sources of emissions, namely the two production sectors and transport, actors can reduce the value of e_i below the initial non-intervention value e_i^0 at quadratically increasing cost $\frac{1}{2} \cdot k_i \cdot (e_i^0 - e_i)^2$, under the restriction that negative values of e_i are not possible. With optimal emission taxation, the actors will then set e_i to solve:

$$\underset{e_i}{\text{MIN}}\left(\frac{1}{2} \cdot k_i \cdot (e_i^0 - e_i)^2 + \lambda_E \cdot e_i\right) \tag{7.6a}$$

Price-taking behaviour is reflected here by actors not considering the impact of their behaviour on λ_E. From (7.6a), it can be shown that emission taxation provides the optimal incentives to undertake the socially optimal level of environmental investments: the first term gives the economic costs of such investments, whereas the second term gives the economic costs of not undertaking them. Minimizing (7.6a) is, thus, in line with overall efficiency, and leads to the following equilibrium levels of e_i:

$$e_i^* = \text{MAX}\left\{ 0, e_i^0 - \frac{\lambda_E}{k_i} \right\} \tag{7.6b}$$

When λ_E is sufficiently large or k_i is sufficiently small in equilibrium, e_i^* will be zero, whereas it will approach e_i^0 in the opposite cases. A comparison of the model without endogenous environmental technology with the present one in the first place enables an assessment of the potential impacts of endogenous environmental technological development. It can also be interpreted as comparing the features of 'emission taxation' to 'activity taxation' (that is: production and transport taxation). In many instances, regulatory tax schemes are not, or cannot, be based on actual emissions, but are based on related variables such as total production or total mobility instead, like fixed environmental taxes per product or per vehicle mile. Such taxes do not directly induce technological solutions to environmental problems, because actors do not receive a direct reward for their efforts since the tax does not depend on actual emissions (see also Chapter 3). In such cases, price-takers will not undertake environmental investments, and the model as discussed in Section 7.4 remains valid.

A final model is based on the second-best case in Section 7.5, with transport emission regulation (TER) rather than transport activity regulation. Here, (7.6a) and (7.6b) only hold for the transport sector (be it, that e_T^* will generally have a different value than in case of first-best policies and should for that reason actually be replaced by, for instance, e_T^{**}), while e_A^0 and e_B^0 remain valid.

Turning to the simulation results now, the most straightforward variables to consider are k_A, k_B and k_T, reflecting the marginal costs of abatement technologies for each of the three sources of emissions. In the first simulation, these three parameters were simultaneously raised by a factor 1.5 each step, from 0.003 up to a level of 12, the base values of 0.2 for each of these parameters being in the centre. The impacts are as

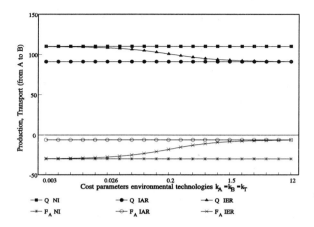

Figure 7.7   Overall production and transport under IAR and IER

expected. With low values of k_S, the discrepancy between IAR and IER is large, whereas at high values, the two forms of regulation practically converge. The higher the cost of implementing environmental abatement technologies, the more producers and suppliers of transport services will respond to regulation by reducing the size of their activities instead of adapting cleaner technologies. This follows directly from equation (7.6a), which states that under IER, suppliers minimize the sum of the regulatory tax rate and the per unit expenditures on abatement technologies.

The effect on the shadow price of sustainability, not shown graphically, is that λ_E for IER will increase from almost zero for very low values of k_S up to the level for IAR (0.86) at very high values. This is closely related to the fact that with IER, and at low values of k_S, the original non-intervention overall levels and patterns of production and transportation can be maintained under regulation by meeting the sustainability constraint through relatively cheap technological solutions, directly implying a low shadow price of sustainability. Alternatively, when abatement becomes more expensive, technological solutions becomes less attractive, and the sustainability constraint will have to be met by adaptations in production and transport levels, as is the case under IAR. Figure 7.7, showing total levels of production and transport under non-intervention (NI), IAR and IER, is illustrative.

Apart from k_S, other parameters will have their impact on the relative performance of IAR and IER. Figure 7.8 focuses on the impact of demand elasticity at the importing node on the levels of λ_E. Along the horizontal axis, the slope of the demand curve D_A (a_A), is gradually raised (by a factor 1.5 each step), while d_A is simultaneously increased in order to

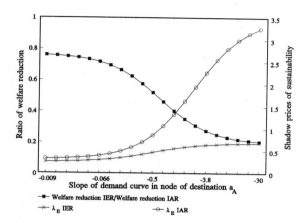

Figure 7.8   *Shadow prices of sustainability and ratio of welfare reduction for IAR and IER*

maintain the same non-intervention levels of consumption and production. In this way, both the demand for the good and for transport becomes more inelastic when moving right. As a result, it becomes increasingly difficult to restrict activity levels to meet the sustainability constraint.

This is reflected in the curvature of λ_E for IAR. Also λ_E for IER increases when moving towards more inelastic demand at the node of destination, but the increase is not as strong as for IAR. This increasing discrepancy shows that under IER, polluters have a greater incentive to invest in abatement technologies rather than to restrict production when demand is more inelastic. In this way, they keep the shadow price of sustainability relatively low. This implies that under first-best IER, the total 'offer' that a society has to make to keep emissions at E^* is smaller than under IAR. Figure 7.8 shows a direct link between the relative values of λ_E for both policies and the relative welfare reductions due to both policies. But also, from the private perspective, the producers of emissions can make considerable savings by trading off abatement against activity reductions. This is illustrated in Figure 7.9 for tax rates and the per unit of production expenditures on abatement in the local production sector in node A. The same patterns are found for total tax sums and total expenditures on abatement.

The simulations discussed show that the shadow price of sustainability not only depends on the extent to which non-intervention emissions exceed the environmental utilization space. In addition, the other key factor determining the value of this shadow price is the 'quality' of the environmental policies deployed to meet this restriction.

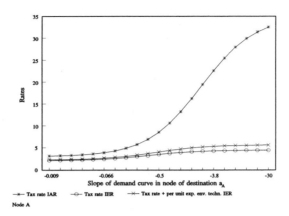

*Figure 7.9   Marginal taxes and per unit outlays on abatement
technology for IAR and IER*

Finally, the simulation from Section 7.4 can be used for an integral
comparison of TVR, IAR, IER, and the fourth possible form of regulation
mentioned above, namely transport emission regulation (TER). In Figure
7.10, the values of λ_E for the four policies are shown. As long as NIE$\leq$E*,
these shadow prices are all equal to zero; when NIE$>$E* however, they
diverge. As expected, λ_E for IER is lower than λ_E for IAR, and both fall
short of the λ_E's for transport regulation. This shows that, the more
'perfect' regulation is, the lower is the shadow price of sustainability.

More surprisingly, λ_E for TVR is, over a considerable range, lower than
λ_E for TER, whereas one would expect the opposite for the same reason
that TER seems closer to first-best standards than TVR. In fact, it is. The
reason that this is not reflected in λ_E is that λ_E is a marginal variable. At
the margin, the shadow price of sustainability for TER is higher than it is
for TVR where the larger restriction in transport volumes has a bigger
indirect impact on production and emissions by the production sectors.
This favourable side effect of transport regulation is less strongly present
when the suppliers of transport services are not confined to cutting down
the overall transport volume, but can also respond to regulation by
adopting abatement technologies. When looking at total welfare however
(not shown graphically), not merely evaluated at the margin, the impact of
TER and TVR on overall welfare is almost identical. A close inspection
of the numerical values of the welfare levels indeed shows that welfare
under TER is always above, or at least equal to welfare under TVR.
Again, welfare under IER is the closest to welfare under non-intervention,
with IAR between IER and both forms of transport regulation.

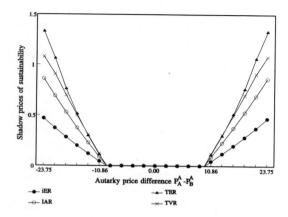

Figure 7.10 Shadow prices of sustainability for various types of regulation

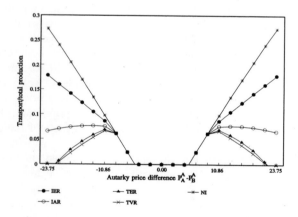

Figure 7.11 Ratio of transport to total production for various types of regulation

Figure 7.11 demonstrates that this ranking in welfare of the four types of regulation is closely connected to the extent to which the original spatio-economic structure is affected by regulation. The ratio of total transport to total production is taken for this purpose. With larger differences between the production structures of both nodes, non-intervention results in the greatest degree of specialization. Regulation in terms of IER, IAR, TER and TVR will, in that order, restrict such specialization, where for extreme differences between the nodes in terms of production structure, either form of second-best transport regulation may require a total prohibition of transport and trade.

7.7   Conclusion

In the foregoing analysis, interdependencies between transport, spatial economy and the environment were investigated in the context of regulatory environmental policies aimed at a global environmental target, defined in terms of the environmental utilization space as a prerequisite for global sustainability. A general SPE-model and a condensed small scale simulation version of it were discussed. The results from these models provide comparative static insights into issues that are important in the formulation of environmental and transport policies when considered from the viewpoint of global sustainability rather than from the more narrow perspective of a partial equilibrium externalities approach. The analysis thus focused on the system-wide connotation of the concept of sustainability.[3]

A binding environmental utilization space results in a positive, system-wide social 'shadow price of sustainability'. This can be interpreted as a counterpart to the concept of marginal external costs in more traditional economic approaches to environmental policy. The level of this shadow price not only depends on the extent to which non-intervention emissions exceed the global environmental target, but is, in addition, inversely related to the quality of the environmental policies pursued. In particular, when including the possibility of environmental abatement technologies in response to regulation, the lowest values for this shadow price, as well as the highest values of narrowly defined welfare after regulation, are found for the first-best policy mix of emission taxation in each of the polluting sectors.

Application of system-wide marginal tax rules based on this shadow price leads to the most cost-effective way of achieving global environmental targets. In a comprehensive setting in which interdependencies are allowed for, such optimal regulatory taxes cannot be set in isolation, but require consideration of both market failures and taxes applied elsewhere in the economic system.

---

[3]The dynamic aspects of sustainability were ignored. Clearly, however, the present approach could be made dynamic. In that case, the environmental utilization space E^*, as well as the shadow price of sustainability λ_E, would become endogenously determined. Such a model might for instance be used to study the issue of energy use by transport. However, whether this still results in manageable models, such as the one in equation (7.1), remains to be seen.

However, in many cases, such first-best policies cannot or will not be applied. In such instances, one needs to derive the optimal second-best policies within a model that takes account of the likely sectoral and spatial spill-overs that such policies may induce. In particular, environmental transport policies conducted in isolation have indirect side-effects. These side-effects may be advantageous, since a reduction in transport will generally lead to a reduction in overall trade and production. In some instances, however, notably if the local production sector in the importing node is relatively polluting, induced production shifts may partly or even completely offset the envisaged positive impacts of transport regulation. The analytical model used presents a framework for investigating such interdependencies.

For transport policies conducted in isolation, the difference between overall efficiency of transport volume regulation and that of transport emission regulation need not be large. Whereas the latter has an advantage of inducing the application of abatement technologies in the transport sector, the former is likely to result in a larger reduction of transport volumes, which often has a larger indirect impact on the spatio-economic structure by its limiting impact on production and emissions in the production sectors.

Consequently, for the realization of global environmental targets, the formulation of isolated transport policies is not as straightforward as is sometimes believed. One would prefer to apply a first-best policy mix in which all sectors can simultaneously be regulated. If this is not possible, the transport regulator should give close consideration to the environmental implications associated with the induced shifts in the spatio-economic structure due to the transport policies considered.

This chapter then, concludes the analysis of the efficiency aspects of the regulation of road transport externalities. Although the goal of allocative efficiency is an important one for the economic evaluation of such policies, the distributional impacts and social feasibility of regulation have proven to be at least as important in the practice of policy formulation. These issues will be dealt with in the next part of the book.

PART III

EQUITY ASPECTS AND SOCIAL FEASIBILITY OF REGULATION

8   EFFICIENCY AND EQUITY IN EXTERNALITIES[1]

8.1   Introduction

The concept of external effects has been in the interest of economists ever since the days of Marshall and Pigou. Along with the development of the field of environmental economics, the theory of externalities remained of great importance in economic science (see Cropper and Oates, 1992). An important drawback of the potential Pareto improvement criterion usually applied in analysing the economics of externalities, however, is that it is solely concerned with efficiency aspects (see also the analyses in the previous part of the book). It deliberately bypasses matters of equity, because problems associated with inter-personal utility comparison can thus be avoided. Still, in the practice of policy making, equity considerations are often at least as important as matters of efficiency. This part of the book is concerned with such equity aspects, and with related issues of social feasibility of externality regulation. After considering the welfare effects of an externality and its regulation for both its generators and its receptors in this chapter, Chapter 9 refocuses on road transport by discussing the trade-off between efficiency, effectiveness and social feasibility in the regulation of road transport externalities. Chapters 10 and 11 subsequently present some empirical analyses concerning these matters.

This chapter discusses the compatibility of optimization and compensation of an external cost. Therefore, without letting go of the relatively strong efficiency concept of potential Pareto improvements, it will be investigated whether satisfaction of a rather intuitive equity concept, namely compensation, is possible. Several forms of regulation and internalization will be considered, in different model settings. First, Section 8.2 gives some definitions of the concepts involved. Next, Section 8.3 contains a graphical presentation of the basic model. In Section 8.4, a more general external cost function is analysed, in which allowance is made for abatement and defensive activities. In Section 8.5, some dynamic aspects are discussed, concerning entry−exit behaviour of the receptor(s) and the supplier(s) of an externality. Finally, Section 8.6 contains the conclusions.

---

[1]This chapter is based on an earlier article in *Environment and Planning A* (Verhoef, 1994b).

It may be stressed at the outset that the analysis applies to the regulation of externalities in general. Therefore, the discussion, although often applicable to the regulation of (road) transport externalities, in particular environmental externalities, is phrased in general terms.

8.2   Some concepts involved with external effects

In Chapter 2, it was argued that externalities comprise both efficiency aspects and equity aspects, which do not necessarily have the same policy implications. The first have to do with the fact that, in presence of externalities, the competitive market outcome is not Pareto efficient. The second relate to the fact that the receptors of a negative (positive) externality are clearly worse (better) off at any non-zero level of the effect, unless compensations take place. This distinction between efficiency and equity aspects leads to a distinction between the optimization and the compensation of externalities. In this section, some definitions of these and other concepts to be used in the remainder of this chapter will be given in order to secure an unambiguous interpretation of the analysis.

The optimization of an external effect can be defined as follows: an externality is optimized when its level is consistent with optimal resource allocation according to the compensation criterion. Therefore, the commonly used concept of the 'Pareto optimal level' of an externality implies acceptation of the potential Pareto improvement criterion for the evaluation of social welfare. According to the strict Pareto criterion, an external cost generating activity is not allowed to be set up unless its victims are at least compensated. By the same criterion however, such an activity, once in existence, cannot be restricted or banned unless the generator is compensated. The potential Pareto criterion, on the other hand, is concerned solely with allocative efficiency, and allows such activities to expand as long as the victims can hypothetically be compensated, regardless of whether such compensations actually do take place.

The actual compensation of an external effect can be defined as follows: an externality is compensated when a (financial) transaction takes place between the supplier and the receptor of the effect, which compensates for the receptor's welfare effects due to the externality. Apart from such 'full' compensation, over- (under-) compensation occurs when more (less) than the full value of the effect is compensated.

Next, the internalization of an external effect involves the removal of its external character, making it 'internal to the economic process' (Mishan, 1971, p. 3): an externality is internalized if a market for the effect comes into being.[2] Internalization typically involves either the

---

[2]Pigouvian taxation is often referred to as 'internalization' of an externality. However, such market-conform regulation actually does not satisfy the definition of internalization.

creation of a market on which the externality is traded, or a gathering of interest, such as a merger in case of a producer–producer externality, the standard example being water pollution by an upstream firm damaging the product of a downstream firm. The former requires the assignment of property rights, after which 'Coasian negotiations' between the supplier and the receptor of the effect will lead to the social optimum – at least in theory (Coase, 1960).

Finally, the term regulation will be used for direct government intervention regarding the externality, by means of, for instance, price instruments, command and control measures, or any other means. Therefore, government intervention aiming at internalizing the externality, and thus having the market leading to the efficient outcome, is not headed under regulation here. Regulation in the above sense, in contrast, requires ongoing government intervention regarding the externality.

In the following sections, it will be investigated whether the satisfaction of a rather intuitive equity criterion, namely 'compensation', is possible without violating the efficiency criterion of optimization, for several forms of regulation and internalization, and in different model settings.

8.3   A basic model

Figure 8.1 provides the standard textbook presentation of a negative external effect. A certain actor, 'the producer', performs an activity Q, from which he enjoys net private benefits (private benefits minus private costs). However, he causes an external cost – say, pollution – to another actor: 'the victim'. The curves represent the marginal net private benefits (MNPB) and marginal external cost (MEC) of production. Without government intervention, a production level of Q^0 prevails, where net private benefits are maximized. The social optimum is Q^*, where the net social benefits (net private benefits minus external cost) are maximized, and the dead-weight welfare loss, triangle E, is avoided. In the optimum, a certain part of the external cost remains existent (C). Clearly, the optimization of an external effect does not mean its minimization or maximization.

In the literature, certain 'standard' schemes can be found which yield this social optimum. Three categories of such schemes are considered in the following analysis. First, two forms of regulation are distinguished: quantitative restrictions[3] and Pigouvian taxation. The second scheme is direct compensation from the producer to the victim. Finally, two forms of internalization are considered: a gathering of interest through a merger of the victim and the producer, which will often be impossible for very practical reasons; and the assignment of property rights concerning the

---

[3]Tradable permits are not considered because the model contains only one producer.

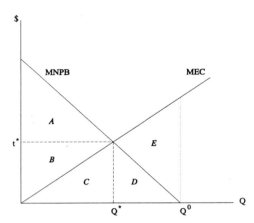

Figure 8.1   A basic model of external costs

externality, either to the producer or to the victim, which is assumed to result in Coasian negotiations.

Table 8.1 shows the distributional impacts of these schemes. Although in this simple setting each of them yields the efficient outcome, that is the maximum social welfare of $A+B$, they have different distributional implications. Most of the values in Table 8.1 can easily be verified with reference to Figure 8.1. However, Coasian negotiations deserve some closer attention. Here, the distributional implications depend on the distribution of property rights as well as on individual bargaining skills. The former determines the direction of the financial transfer; the latter determine its size. For both distributions of property rights, transfers between the extremes in Table 8.1 may occur. These boundary values follow from the fact that the MNPB gives the producer's minimum willingness to accept (maximum willingness to pay) for decreases (increases) in production, whereas MEC represents the victim's minimum willingness to accept (maximum willingness to pay) for increases (decreases) in the production level.[4] Note that, when the property right is assigned to the producer, the associated financial transfer has the direction opposite to compensation of the external cost. Full compensation takes place when the property right is assigned to the victim, while the producer is the extreme best bargainer. As a matter of fact, direct compensation can

---

[4]The maximum transfer from the victim to the producer $(D+E)$ mentioned assumes that the producer is truthful. If he pretends considering a production level above Q^0, the victim is willing to pay more than $D+E$ in order to secure Q^*. The victim does not have a comparable possibility of 'cheating'.

be seen as a restricted case of Coasian negotiations. The property right is implicitly assigned to the victim, but he is not allowed to bargain over the size of the compensation.

	Producer	Victim	Regulator	Social
NON-INTERVENTION	$A+B+C+D$	$-C-D-E$	0	$A+B-E$
REGULATION:				
Quantitative restriction (Q^*)	$A+B+C$	$-C$	0	$A+B$
Pigouvian tax (t^*)[1]	A	$-C$	$B+C$	$A+B$
DIRECT COMPENSATION	$A+B+C-(C)=A+B$	$-C+(C)=0$	0	$A+B$
INTERNALIZATION:				
Gathering of interest	$A+B$		0	$A+B$
Coasian negotiations[2a]	$A+B+C+(D+E)$	$-C-(D+E)$	0	$A+B$
Coasian negotiations[2b]	$A+B+C+(D)$	$-C-(D)$	0	$A+B$
Coasian negotiations[3a]	$A+B+C-(C)=A+B$	$-C+(C)=0$	0	$A+B$
Coasian negotiations[3b]	$A+B+C-(A+B+C)=0$	$-C+(A+B+C)=A+B$	0	$A+B$

Terms between brackets indicate financial transfers between the producer and the victim.

[1]	It is assumed that the producer and the victim do not consider the allocation of Pigouvian tax revenues.
[2a]	Property right lies with the producer; the producer is the extreme best bargainer.
[2b]	Property right lies with the producer; the victim is the extreme best bargainer.
[3a]	Property right lies with the victim; the producer is the extreme best bargainer.
[3b]	Property right lies with the victim; the victim is the extreme best bargainer.

*Table 8.1	The individual welfare positions associated with different schemes for optimizing externalities in a basic model*

Table 8.1 indicates that the actors have different rankings of the different schemes. The producer prefers Coasian negotiations with the property rights assigned to himself. He may then realize a welfare level above the level he enjoys with unrestricted production. Second favourite is non-intervention. Next comes a quantitative restriction, followed by direct compensation and finally either Coasian negotiations with the property right assigned to the victim, or Pigouvian taxation, depending on the distribution of bargaining skills (the ranking of these latter three depends on the assumption of rising marginal external cost). The victim prefers receiving the property rights and the associated Coasian negotiations. Next comes direct compensation, followed by any form of regulation. Then comes Coasian negotiations with the property rights assigned to the producer and finally non-intervention. The 'gathering of interest' possibility can for obvious reasons not be qualified along this criterion.

These rankings may to some extent explain why some policies are used more often than others. For example, considering regulation, the producer prefers a quantitative restriction to Pigouvian taxation, whereas the victim is indifferent, assuming he does not consider the possible allocation of the tax revenues. A vote-maximizing government may therefore prefer to use command-and-control measures rather than economic instruments, which seems to be confirmed by practical evidence[5] (see also Pearce and Turner, 1990, pp. 96–8).

A shortcoming of the foregoing analysis is that the MEC- and MNPB-curves are assumed to be stable, and do not shift in response to different distributions of wealth as considered in Table 8.1. For the producer, this assumption is not problematic as long as it is assumed that he is a profit maximizer. However, when the victim is a utility maximizer, such an approach is legitimate only when his marginal utility of income is constant. This is for instance the case when his utility function is quasi-linear. For such utility functions, Hicksian welfare measures (equivalent variation, compensating variation) coincide with the Marshallian consumer surplus, and the victim's valuation of the external cost, and therewith the position of the EC-curve, is independent of income and therefore of any compensations paid or received (see Varian, 1992, ch. 10).

The conclusions of the basic model presented in this section are fairly straightforward. Both direct compensation and internalization of the external cost, as well as (optimal) regulation, lead to its optimization. On the other hand, neither regulation nor internalization in general leads to full compensation. After optimization by means of regulation, the victim of the effect is still confronted with the optimal level of the externality. Coasian negotiations with the property rights assigned to the victim leads to an outcome where the externality is optimized and the victim is at least fully compensated. When the producer receives the property right, the associated transfers have the opposite direction. However, in this basic setting, the optimization and compensation of an external cost are certainly not necessarily incompatible.

8.4   Modelling abatement and defensive measures

In the above model, the actual level of external costs depends on the level of the activity only. In order to reduce the external cost, the producer of the effect can only reduce his activity. On the other hand, the victim can only passively suffer from the damage done to him. Often, however, the producer may also reduce the external cost by performing abatement activities, and the victim may protect himself against the negative effect by means of defensive measures. Such possibilities are often relevant for

---

[5]Other possible reasons for preferring either price or quantity measures have been put forward. Weitzman (1974), in his seminal paper, focuses on the relative efficiency of both types of regulation under uncertainty (see also Baumol and Oates, 1988). A bit closer to equity arguments as considered here, Buchanan and Tullock (1975) argue in another classic paper that quantity measures are preferred by producers since these can act as a barrier to entry and may therefore leave them with higher profits.

environmental externalities. For instance, polluting factories may be equipped with cleaner technologies, and victims of noise annoyance may decide to protect themselves by means of double glazing. In particular, defensive activities are relevant for the issues considered in this chapter, since the compensation of external costs is often said to remove the victim's optimal incentives to protect himself against the externality, thus inducing inefficiencies (see Baumol and Oates, 1988, p. 24) and ruling out the compatibility of optimization and compensation. The following general external cost function can be used to investigate this issue:

$$EC = EC(Q,D,A) \tag{8.1}$$

where EC is the external cost; Q is the level of the externality causing activity; D is the level of the victim's financial outlays on defensive measures; and A is the level of the producer's financial outlays on abatement activities. The following functional characteristics, representing the most plausible case, are assumed to apply:

$$EC_Q > 0 \text{ and } EC_{QQ} \geq 0 \tag{8.2a,b}$$
$$EC_D < 0 \text{ and } EC_{DD} > 0 \tag{8.2c,d}$$
$$EC_A < 0 \text{ and } EC_{AA} > 0 \tag{8.2e,f}$$

which indicate positive non-decreasing marginal external cost of the activity and positive diminishing marginal effectiveness of both kinds of measures (subscripts denote partial derivatives). In addition, it may be postulated that:

$$EC_{DQ} = EC_{QD} < 0 \tag{8.2g}$$
$$EC_{AQ} = EC_{QA} < 0 \tag{8.2h}$$
$$EC_{AD} = EC_{DA} > 0 \tag{8.2i}$$

The first two relationships (8.2g) and (8.2h) indicate that at higher levels of the activity, outlays on defensive and abatement actions will have more impact in terms of reducing the external cost; and, at higher levels of defensive or abatement outlays, a rise in the activity level causes smaller increases in the external cost. The third relationship (8.2i) states that at higher levels of defensive activities, the effect of increasing abatement will be smaller, and vice versa. Next, the producer's welfare function is given by his profit:

$$W^P = PB(Q) - PC(Q) - A - T = NPB(Q) - A - T \tag{8.3}$$

where PB(Q) is the private benefit and PC(Q) is the private (production) cost of the activity; NPB(Q) is the net private benefit. A positive T indicates a financial transfer from the producer to the victim. We assume diminishing marginal net private benefits:

$$NPB_{QQ} < 0 \tag{8.4}$$

The victim's money metric utility function is assumed to be functional separable in EC and D on the one hand, and the consumed bundle of goods other than defensive activities (represented by a vector **x**) on the other. This means that the preferences over the other goods are assumed to be independent of the preferences over EC and D, and that the vector demand $\mathbf{x}$ is only a function of the price vector $\mathbf{p}$ of these goods. The outlays on defensive measures D, as well as compensations T, influence the consumed bundle $\mathbf{x}$ only via the budget constraint. Taking the victim's income M and the price vector $\mathbf{p}$ as given, the victim's indirect money metric utility function, which will be called his welfare function, can then be written as:

$$W^V = e(\mathbf{p}, v(\mathbf{p}, M+T-D)) - EC(Q,A,D) \tag{8.5}$$

Here, v is the indirect utility function for the other goods, giving maximum utility available at given prices $\mathbf{p}$ and budget $M+T-D$ (that is, $v(\mathbf{p}, M+T-D) = \max_{\mathbf{x}} U(\mathbf{x})$ s.t. $\mathbf{px} = M+T-D$, where $U(\mathbf{x})$ is the direct utility function). The expenditure function e gives the minimum budget necessary for achieving a fixed level of utility and is therefore identical to the indirect money metric utility function. For given prices, the expenditure function is just the inverse of the indirect utility function. Furthermore, for given prices, the expenditure function is by definition equal to the budget: the minimum expenditure necessary to reach the maximum utility available at fixed prices and with a fixed budget is just equal to that budget. Therefore, the victim's welfare function (8.5) may be rewritten as:

$$W^V = M + T - D - EC(Q,A,D) \tag{8.6}$$

The simple postulation of EC as the external cost suffered by the victim hides one particular problem inherent to external effects, namely that they are unpriced by nature. Still, EC is defined as the monetary valuation of some physical external effect EF(Q,A,D) suffered, which is one of the arguments of the victim's direct utility function. For the fundamental relation between EF and EC, assume that defensive activities are not possible so that the D terms drop out of (8.6). It then follows from (8.6) that the victim is indifferent for simultaneous changes in T and EC, and therefore in M and EC, as long as:

$$dM - dEC = 0$$

In terms of direct utility U, this indifference translates into:

$$U_M dM + U_{EF} dEF = 0$$

Substituting the first equation into the second and rearranging, we find:

$$dEC/dEF = -U_{EF}/U_M \tag{8.7}$$

The relation between the physical effect and its monetary value (the external cost) not only depends on how seriously the effect harms the victim's utility ($-U_{EF}$), but is in addition inversely related to his marginal utility of income, or the value of money, U_M. This reflects the fact that the economic value of a negative external effect is defined as the victim's willingness to pay (WTP) for decreases, or willingness to accept (WTA) for increases in the physical effect. These values are lower, the higher the marginal utility for money (*ceteris paribus*, the lower the victim's income).

Intuitive objections against the implication that equal exposures to a physical effect imply, *ceteris paribus*, larger external costs for higher income groups than for lower income groups reflect either dissatisfaction with the existing income distribution, or the assignment of some demerit character of the effect for lower income groups. Therefore, straightforward application of the concept of external costs, even when explicitly taking account of equity aspects between its supplier(s) and its receptor(s), may ignore important equity aspects within the population of victims.

Returning to the model, the social money metric welfare function W can be defined as the sum of the individual welfare functions:

$$W = W^P + W^V = NPB(Q) - EC(Q,A,D) - A - D + M \qquad (8.8)$$

Social welfare maximization is realized according to the following first-order conditions:[6]

$$W_Q = 0 \Rightarrow EC_Q = NPB_Q \qquad (8.9a)$$
$$W_A = 0 \Rightarrow EC_A = -1 \qquad (8.9b)$$
$$W_D = 0 \Rightarrow EC_D = -1 \qquad (8.9c)$$

An intuitive interpretation of these results is that in the optimum, a reduction in the external cost is equally expensive for the three different ways of achieving it; that is, a reduction in the level of the activity, or increases in abatement or defensive outlays. For each option, the marginal value of reducing the external cost is equal to the marginal cost of doing so. It is assumed that an interior solution exists, where non-zero optimal values Q^*, A^* and D^* result in maximum social welfare W^*:

$$W^* = NPB(Q^*) - EC(Q^*,A^*,D^*) - A^* - D^* + M \qquad (8.10)$$

It will now be examined whether individual welfare maximization of the victim, maximization of (8.6), and the producer, maximization of (8.3), is consistent with social welfare maximization according to (8.9a−c).

Concerning the victim, as long as T is equal to zero, maximization of (8.6) is consistent with (8.9c). This indicates that the victim's behaviour is in general consistent with overall optimality: as long as the producer realizes Q^* and A^*, the victim has the optimal incentive to spend D^* on defensive activities. That is, (8.9c) gives the optimal condition for the victim's distribution of resources among the first and the second term on the right-hand side of (8.5). The outcome that the victim performs defensive activities up to the optimal level where $EC_D=-1$ is not very surprising once it is recalled that the marginal external cost is defined as the victim's willingness to pay for marginal reductions in the physical effect. Clearly, the possibility of defensive activities simply provides the victim with a means to express this willingness to pay in the market.

There are, however, three qualifications. In the first place, under free market conditions, the producer will generally set $Q>Q^*$ and $A<A^*$. Then, (8.2g) and (8.2i) together with (8.9c) imply $D>D^*$: the victim conducts

---

[6]The resulting extremum is of course a welfare maximum only if the associated Hessian satisfies the necessary criteria (when the principal minors duly alternate in sign, the first one being negative).

defensive actions up to a level optimal from his own point of view, but exceeding the overall optimal level D*.

Secondly, compensations may remove the victim's incentive to perform the optimal defensive activities. Two forms of compensation spring to mind: compensation of EC alone, which may be called the net external cost, and compensation of the sum of EC and D: the gross external cost. Direct compensation of the net external cost (T=EC) reduces (8.6) to:

$$W^V = M - D \qquad\qquad (8.6')$$

which is maximized for D=0. Alternatively, direct compensation of the gross external cost (T=EC+D) reduces (8.6) to:

$$W^V = M \qquad\qquad (8.6'')$$

which means that the victim is indifferent to the actual values of EC and D: his welfare is equal under all circumstances. The producer will in this case prefer the victim to undertake the optimal level of defensive outlays (see below). Clearly, under direct compensation there is no straightforward incentive for the victim to protect himself against the negative external effect. This is why Baumol and Oates (1988) claim that externalities should have an asymmetric price: "a non-zero price to the 'supplier' of the externality and a zero price for the consumption of the externality" (p. 29). However, any lump-sum compensation, whatever value it takes (net or gross external cost, or any other value), leaves the victim's incentive to conduct defensive measures intact. In that case, (8.6) can be written as:

$$W^V = M + \underline{T} - D - EC(Q,A,D) \qquad\qquad (8.6''')$$

Since $\underline{T}$ is constant, maximization is again realized according to (8.9c).

Thirdly, when the external cost is considered to have a demerit character, the social value of its 'consumption' is considered to be higher than the victim's valuation, and the level of defensive activities resulting from individual maximizing behaviour is consequently below the socially desirable level.

Turning to the producer now, maximization of (8.3) is generally not consistent with (8.9a) and (8.9b):

$$\max_Q(W^P) \Rightarrow NPB_Q = 0 \qquad\qquad (8.9a')$$
$$\max_A(W^P) \Rightarrow A = 0 \qquad\qquad (8.9b')$$

Production will be above, and abatement below the overall optimal levels. For optimal regulation, a quantitative measure regarding the level of the activity (Q^*) should now be accompanied by a quantitative duty, or standard, regarding the level of abatement activities (A^*). Likewise, Pigouvian regulation should provide the right incentive for the producer to choose both the optimal production level and the optimal level of abatement. This involves, apart from a tax on the activity, a subsidy on abatement; or a tax on the gap between the optimal and the actual level of abatement.[7] Of course, any combination of economic and non-economic incentives may be chosen here.[8]

Direct compensation of the net external cost (T=EC) will, according to (8.6'), result in D=0. The producer will then seek to maximize:

$$W^P = NPB(Q) - EC(Q,A,0) - A \qquad (8.3')$$

leading to second-best optimal levels of Q and A according to:

$$NPB_Q = EC_Q \qquad (8.9a'')$$
$$EC_A = -1 \qquad (8.9b'')$$

Unless the victim is somehow forced to perform defensive activities up to D^*, production will be below, and abatement above the optimal levels because of (8.2g) and (8.2i), implying deviations opposite to those in the non-intervention outcome. However, it is actually beneficial for the producer to propose direct compensation of the gross external cost (T=EC+D), simply because his maximization problem now in fact coincides with maximization of (8.8) according to (8.9a−c). Hence, he will try and persuade the victim to undertake defensive measures up to D^*. He may try to do so by means of mutually beneficial financial bids. Since D^* is the level of defensive activities where the potential benefits of bargaining are exhausted (see below), the optimal outcome may be expected. Again, direct compensations can be seen as a restricted form of Coasian negotiations. The property right is implicitly assigned to the victim, who is, however, not allowed to bargain so as to receive any transfers exceeding the gross external cost.

Lump-sum compensations, while preserving the right incentive for the victim, do not optimize the producer's behaviour, who will then maximize:

$$W^P = NPB(Q) - A - \underline{T} \qquad (8.3'')$$

which yields non-optimal values of A and Q according to (8.9a') and (8.9b'). Clearly, additional regulation of the producer is called for.

Finally, the internalization of the external cost is considered. First, a gathering of interest simply leads to the social optimum, since the common objective will be to maximize (8.8). Coasian negotiations are a bit more

---

[7]In order to derive the optimal subsidy on abatement activities, abatement can no longer be expressed as money expenditures, but some measure of 'units of abatement' should be introduced. Since this exercise does not yield important insights for the present purpose, it is left aside.

[8]It may be argued that the use of standards or taxation on the emitted physical effect EM, rather than concerning both the production level and abatement activities, would offer a much simpler device. The external cost will be a non-decreasing function of EM, so that a distinction can be made into EM(Q,A) and EC(EM,D) (and EF(EM,D)). However, the determination of optimal pollution standards or taxes is not possible without knowledge of relation (1). An optimal standard EM^*, consistent with $EC(Q^*,A^*,D^*)$ will dictate a least cost solution to the producer of Q^* and A^*. Likewise, the equivalent tax on pollution will amount to $EC_{EM}(EC^*)$, dictating the same values Q^* and A^*.

complex to deal with. However, assuming that the parties will bargain over Q, A, and D, the efficient outcome will be the sole equilibrium where no incentive for bargaining is left. This can be seen with reference to (8.9a−c). Consider the case where the victim receives the property right.

First, for any $Q < Q^*$: $EC_Q < NPB_Q \Rightarrow -W^V_Q < W^P_Q$. Consequently, there exists a marginal transfer (T_Q) from the producer to the victim for which $-W^V_Q < T_Q < W^P_Q$. Therefore, both parties can gain when Q is increased up to Q^*. For the same reason, $Q > Q^*$ will not occur. In that case, $EC_Q > NPB_Q$, and since the victim will at least require a marginal transfer equal to EC_Q ($> NPB_Q$), it is not optimal for the producer to choose any $Q > Q^*$. Similarly, for any $A < A^*$: $EC_A < -1 \Rightarrow W^V_A > 1$. Since $W^P_A = -1$, a marginal reduction in the transfer $(-T_A)$ exists for which: $W^V_A > -T_A > -W^P_A = 1$. Both parties can gain when A is increased up to A^*. $A > A^*$ will not occur, since in that case $W^V_A < 1$. The producer is better off compensating the victim than performing extra abatement activities. Finally, for every $D < D^*$: $EC_D < -1 \Rightarrow W^V_D > 0$. The victim will undertake the optimal defensive actions anyway, since his welfare will be maximized at the overall optimal D^*, where $EC_D = -1$ and $W^V_D = 0$. Moreover, the victim may try to bargain over this with the producer. If his bargaining position is strong enough, he may be able to make the producer compensate for the external cost resulting from below optimal defensive activities. The producer can gain reductions in the compensation equal to $-EC_D$ from increases in D, and there exists for every $D < D^*$ a marginal transfer (T_D) for which: $D_D = 1 < T_D < -EC_D$. Both parties can gain from increasing D up to D^*.[9] Again, $D > D^*$ will not occur; neither when the victim is to undertake the measures himself, nor when the producer is compensating for excessive external cost due to below optimal defensive actions. Along the same lines, it can be proven that also when the producer holds the property right, Q^*, A^*, and D^* result.

It may therefore be concluded that compensation and optimization are not necessarily at odds when defensive activities are possible; especially not as long as there are negotiations on these compensations.

8.5   Some dynamic aspects

8.5.1   *Optimal regulation of a localized undepletable external cost*
The conclusion in the previous section that a victim, certainly in absence of direct compensations, receives the optimal incentives for engaging in the optimal level of defensive activities rests on the critical assumption that he takes the values of Q and A as given. In fact, for every value of D other than D^*, there are suboptimal values $Q^x \neq Q^*$ and $A^x \neq A^*$ maximizing social

---

[9]It is now easy to verify that with direct compensations, the producer will try and persuade the victim to undertake D^*. If he does so by means of Coasian negotiations, D^* will indeed result.

welfare given the deviation $D^x \neq D^*$. Should the victim believe that, under a scheme of direct regulation of Q and A, these policies are adjusted in optimal response to the actual value of D chosen, his welfare function (8.6) can be written as:

$$W^v = M + T - D - EC(Q(D),A(D),D) \tag{8.11}$$

Maximization with respect to D now leads him to:

$$EC_Q \cdot Q_D + EC_A \cdot A_D + EC_D = -1 \tag{8.12}$$

Comparison with (8.9c) shows that behaviour described by (8.12) is inconsistent with overall optimality if $Q_D \neq 0$ and $A_D \neq 0$. That is, if the regulation of the producer is indeed adjusted in optimal response to deviations of D from D^*, so that $Q_D > 0$ and $A_D < 0$, we find $EC_D < -1$ and the first-order conditions for welfare optimization (8.9a−c) are violated. The victim performs defensive measures up to a certain level $D^x < D^*$. In (second-best optimal) response to this, the regulator will make the producer set $Q^x < Q^*$ and $A^x > A^*$. A welfare optimizing regulator with complete information can avoid this problem simply by not changing the incentives given to the producer in response to the victim's behaviour. Q_D and A_D in (8.12) are then equal to zero, and the victim is led to behave in line with overall optimality. However, the regulator may actually often wish to adjust the producer's regulation in response to the victim's activities. Particularly in dynamic contexts, where the victim(s) simply cannot be expected to react instantaneously to incentives given, the regulator may wish to do so in order to reach sequential social welfare maximization; that is, optimal social welfare in each period.

As an example, consider a localized, undepletable externality. One of the possible defensive measures a victim can take concerns moving out of, or not moving into, the area affected by the effect. However, the regulator may be uncertain about future developments in migration patterns, or may take the stance that it is undesirable to set the incentives to the producer according to their long-run optimal values since by doing so sequential welfare losses will occur as long as the long-run situation is not realized, let alone the question of how the long run should be defined. In such cases, the regulator may wish to make the producer act in optimal response to the number of victims, thus possibly inducing inefficient locational behaviour on behalf of these victims. The social welfare function can in this case be represented as follows:

$$W = NPB(Q) - A + N \cdot (M - EC(Q,A,D) - D) + LB(N) - LC(N) \tag{8.13}$$

where N gives the number of victims; M, EC and D are per capita variables. The undepletable character of the external effect, or the 'publicness of its consumption', is reflected by the fact that total net external costs are $N \cdot EC$. The victims are assumed to be identical, except for their valuation of living in the affected area. LB(N) gives the total location benefits enjoyed by the N residents due to the fact that they live in the area ($LB_N > 0$; $LB_{NN} < 0$). LC(N) gives the total private cost of location $(LC_N > 0)$; $LC_{NN} > 0$ can be postulated in order to indicate rising marginal cost of location. D reflects 'ordinary' defensive activities as considered in the previous section; the 'problematic' form of defensive behaviour here is locational behaviour.

Defining the short run as the period in which the number of victims N is constant, the short-run first-order conditions of (8.13) are found to be very much like $(8.9a-c)$:

$$W_Q = 0 \Rightarrow N \cdot EC_Q = NPB_Q \tag{8.14a}$$
$$W_A = 0 \Rightarrow N \cdot EC_A = -1 \tag{8.14b}$$
$$W_D = 0 \Rightarrow EC_D = -1 \tag{8.14c}$$

The policy implications are the same as those derived in Section 8.4, be it that the optimal Pigouvian taxes and subsidies, or physical measures, concerning Q and A now depend on the number of victims affected by the effect. Therefore, Q and A, and via these two also D, depend on the number of victims N when the government regulates so as to optimize social welfare in each period. Suppose N increases. From (8.2a,b) and (8.4), it follows that the optimal Q in (8.14a) decreases. From (8.2e,f), the optimal A in (8.14b) increases. From (8.2c,d) and (8.2g and i), the optimal D in (8.14c) therefore decreases, along with the decrease in the per capita optimal EC. By making the regulation on Q and A dependent on N, equation (8.13) can be rewritten as:

$$W^N = NPB(Q^N) - A^N + N \cdot [M - EC(Q^N, A^N, D(Q^N, A^N)) - D(Q^N, A^N)]$$
$$+ LB^N - LC^N \tag{8.13'}$$

Additional regulation of the (potential) victims is now necessary in order to reach overall optimality in terms of locational behaviour. This can be seen by comparing the actual incentives faced by the $N+1^{th}$ (potential) victim considering moving into, or out of the area with the total welfare effects of this move. The individual incentive partly depends on the question of whether compensation takes place; it is therefore useful to distinguish I^{EC}, giving the incentive when the victim receives no compensation and suffers the gross external cost, and I^{COM}, giving the incentive when the victim is compensated for the gross external effect:

$$I^{EC} = M - EC(Q^{N+1}, A^{N+1}, D(Q^{N+1}, A^{N+1})) - D(Q^{N+1}, A^{N+1})$$
$$+ (LB^{N+1} - LB^N) - (LC^{N+1} - LC^N) - W^0 \tag{8.15a}$$

and:

$$I^{COM} = M + (LB^{N+1} - LB^N) - (LC^{N+1} - LC^N) - W^0 \tag{8.15b}$$

where W^0 gives the money metric utility achievable in the best of the other possible locations, depending on the values of M, LB and LC on that location. Note that I^{EC} and I^{COM} are defined such that positive values indicate attraction to the affected area. The optimal incentive, taking account of all welfare effects due to the move of an additional victim into the area, amounts to:

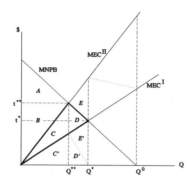

Figure 8.2   The welfare effects of an additional victim of a localized undepletable external cost

$$I^* = (NPB(Q^{N+1}) - NPB(Q^N)) - (A^{N+1} - A^N)$$
$$+ \{(N+1)\cdot[M - EC(Q^{N+1},A^{N+1},D(Q^{N+1},A^{N+1})) - D(Q^{N+1},A^{N+1})]$$
$$- N\cdot[M - EC(Q^N,A^N,D(Q^N,A^N)) - D(Q^N,A^N)]\}$$
$$+ (LB^{N+1} - LB^N) - (LC^{N+1} - LC^N) - W^0 \qquad (8.15c)$$

Therefore, I^{EC} and I^{COM} miss out on the following factors:

$$I^* - I^{EC} = (NPB(Q^{N+1}) - NPB(Q^N)) - (A^{N+1} - A^N)$$
$$+ N\cdot\{[M - EC(Q^{N+1},A^{N+1},D(Q^{N+1},A^{N+1})) - D(Q^{N+1},A^{N+1})]$$
$$- [M - EC(Q^N,A^N,D(Q^N,A^N)) - D(Q^N,A^N)]\} \qquad (8.16a)$$

and:

$$I^* - I^{COM} = I^* - I^{EC} - EC(Q^{N+1},A^{N+1},D(Q^{N+1},A^{N+1})) - D(Q^{N+1},A^{N+1}) \qquad (8.16b)$$

Equation (8.16a) gives the optimal attraction to the area minus the actual attraction in absence of compensations. The first two terms give the change in the producer's welfare due to changes in production and abatement levels. The overall sign of these two terms is negative since Q^* decreases and A^* increases when N increases. The last (large) term describes the change in the other N victims' welfare due to changes in the gross external effect; the overall sign is here positive because both EC and D^* decrease when N increases. The overall value of (8.16a), however, must be negative since it simply gives the change in common welfare of the producer and the N initial victims due to the entrance of the $N+1^{th}$ victim. Since their common welfare was initially optimized, it can only have decreased. Clearly, (8.16b) is also negative, and larger, in absolute terms, than (8.16a). Therefore, the actual attractions I^{EC} and I^{COM} are excessively large.

Figure 8.2 provides an illustration. A potential victim V considers moving to the affected area X; thus joining a first victim W that already lives there. Defensive and abatement measures are ignored, and the analysis relies on consumer surplus arguments. Prior to the contingent location of V, the socially optimal production level is given by Q^*. However, after V has decided to locate at X, the marginal external cost function becomes twice as steep: MEC^{II} rather than MEC^{I}, owing to the publicness of the external cost. As a consequence, areas between MEC^{I} and MEC^{II} have areas of equivalent size between the horizontal axis and MEC^{I}: $C=C'$, and so on. The optimal production level decreases from Q^* to Q^{**}, and the optimal tax increases from t^* to t^{**}.

With optimal adjustment of the production level, the decision of V to locate at X poses a welfare loss on the rest of the society of D. This is the algebraic sum of the decrease in the producer's benefit of $D'+E'+D = 2 \cdot D+E$, and the increase in W's welfare of $D'+E'$. Therefore, V's choice for locating at X is only efficient if it yields him extra welfare, compared to the second-best choice, of at least the optimal external cost he suffers from living there, plus the welfare loss he poses on the rest of the society: $C+D$. Consequently, the bold triangle represents the total (negative) incentive that V should receive for locating in the affected area in order to secure efficient location behaviour. This is equal to the decrease in optimal net social welfare, net of location benefits and costs, after V has located at X.[10] The victim should therefore not be compensated for C, and should be levied a 'location tax' D.

The absolute values of (8.16a) and (8.16b) give the general expressions for the optimal location taxes, to be levied on both potential and actual victims in order to sequentially optimize the number of victims. Also from (8.16a) and (8.16b), it follows that compensation is not in order here: the location tax implied by (8.16b) exceeds the one implied by (8.16a) exactly by the value of full compensation. Moreover, also lump-sum compensations as described in Section 8.4, which were lump-sum compensations of the gross external cost irrespective of the level of 'ordinary' defensive activities D undertaken, are ruled out. That is not surprising: 'true' lump-sum compensation in this setting would mean compensations independent of actual locational decisions. This underlines the small practical relevance of lump-sum compensations: in the case of a localized externality, lump-sum compensations involve payments to all potential victims, including everyone who might ever decide to move into the affected area. Such lump-sum compensations, of course, bare only very limited relation to the actual welfare effects of the externality and therefore make little sense from an equity point of view.

The optimal number of victims is illustrated in Figure 8.3. The horizontal axis gives the number of victims. MLB gives the marginal location benefits, defined here as $M+LB_N-W^0$. MOEC gives the marginal optimal gross external cost for additional victims as implied by (8.13') and (8.14).

---

[10] The optimal social welfare is $(A+B+C+D)$ before, and $(A+B)$ after V locates at X.

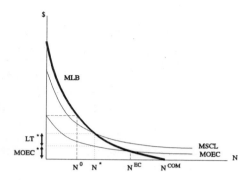

Figure 8.3   *The optimal number of victims of a localized undepletable external cost*

MSCL gives the marginal social cost of location including the welfare effects on the producer and the existing victims; it follows from adding the absolute value of (8.16a) to MOEC. The general shape of MOEC and MSCL follow from the notion that with an increasing number of victims, the marginal welfare effects of an additional victim will decrease. However, they will not become zero as long as the activity remains in existence. For convenience, zero land prices are assumed.

If the victims are compensated for the external cost, or if the external cost would not exist, N^{COM} victims choose the area as their location. However, without compensations, a certain number of potential victims will find that the external cost exceeds their marginal location benefit. Then, N^{EC} victims result. The socially optimal number of victims is given by N^*. Here, the marginal social cost of location is equal to the marginal location benefit.[11,12] This optimum can be reached by levying the optimal location tax LT^* and refraining from compensation of the optimal external cost $MOEC^*$. Finally, in absence of any regulation, N^0 victims result. The victims face the non-intervention level of the gross external

---

[11]Since MLB is zero at $N = N^{COM}$ whereas MSCL is never zero, there is a non-zero outcome N^* provided $MLB(0) > MSCL(0)$. Otherwise, the corner solution $N^* = 0$ prevails.

[12]The fact that N^0 is quite close to N^* indicates that non-intervention may lead to a total number of victims which might be somewhere near the optimal number, since the excess level of the external cost will to a certain extent serve as a substitute for the location tax. This, of course, does not mean that non-intervention may coincidentally lead to Pareto efficiency. Contrary to optimal regulation of the external cost and locational behaviour, non-intervention involves important welfare losses.

cost, which is equal to the optimal gross external cost for $N=0$. Figure 8.3 in fact describes situations where no land prices exist; in particular when the external effect affects a public area.[13] The allowance for flexible land prices does not really change the results. Only when the supply curve LC(N) is perfectly inelastic, all N's in Figure 8.3 coincide.[14] In that case, land price or rent adjustments would completely offset the effect of the external cost on the optimal and actual number of victims. Likewise, a location tax would immediately be absorbed by an equivalent drop in the land price, thus leaving the number of victims unaffected. Generally, the more elastic the supply of dwellings, the more relevant become the issues discussed above. Since the elasticity will increase with the time period considered, it is worth underlining that location taxes are more relevant in the longer run. Furthermore, it is perhaps important to stress here that the above model is relevant only for the small number case; when either the externality is not localized, or the number of victims goes to infinity, which will in reality of course occur jointly, the optimal location taxes can be shown to vanish.

Externalities thus have a reciprocal character. As soon as victims indeed value living in the affected area enough to be willing to accept the optimal incentive, this will be 'rewarded' with a decline in the optimal external effect. When a growing number of victims chooses to live in the area, the optimal production and hence the externality may be reduced to zero, reflecting that the existence of the activity at that location was apparently socially unwarranted.

8.5.2 Coasian negotiations on a localized undepletable external cost
The question rises whether Coasian negotiations would not offer a superior device in the case considered above. In fact, it is often asserted that Coasian negotiations are particularly relevant for small number cases, where high transaction costs are less likely to undermine their theoretical attractiveness. Since the concept of a localized externality implies some natural limit to the number of actors involved in the negotiations, it is worthwhile investigating the performance of this scheme under these circumstances. Section 8.4 demonstrated that Coasian negotiations provide

---

[13]For instance, Figure 8.3 may describe the optimal number of victims of external accident costs of road transport. Victims might be pedestrians, location now means walking along a road and MLB gives the benefits of walking. From an efficiency viewpoint, pedestrians should not be compensated for the expected accident costs posed upon them, and should actually be taxed for walking.

[14]Although the aggregate supply of land is usually perfectly inelastic, the supply curve for a sector (such as housing) is upwards sloping when the sector has to compete with others for the use of land.

short-run efficient outcomes as long as the negotiations simultaneously concern Q, A and D. Likewise, Coasian negotiations on a localized undepletable externality might preserve their efficient workings if, apart from negotiations on Q, A and D, additional negotiations on locational behaviour take place. Below, this is discussed in terms of equations (8.15) and (8.16), and [between square brackets] in terms of areas indicated in Figure 8.2. Three possible distributions of property rights are considered: (1) assigned to the producer, (2) assigned to the initially existing victim(s) only, and (3) assigned to all victims, including new entrants.

First, consider the case where the producer holds the property right. For the new optimum to settle after the location of the $N+1^{th}$ victim, the producer will require an additional transfer from all victims at least equal to the first two terms in (8.16a), abbreviated as ΔW^P [2·D+E]. The N existing victims are prepared to bargain over the location of the $N+1^{th}$ victim by offering (part of) their marginal benefit from his entrance. This benefit is given by the last large term in (8.16a), abbreviated as ΔW^{NV} [D'+E']. Clearly, up to the optimal number of victims, additional victims are willing to bare the sum of the 'new' optimal gross external cost represented by the last term in (8.16b), denoted GEC^{N+1} [C], and the additional transfer the producer requires in excess of what the N existing victims are willing to offer, given by $-(I^* - I^{EC})$ in (8.16a) [D]. Provided full negotiations take place on all relevant issues, including locational behaviour, the marginal potential victim faces exactly the optimal incentive I^* in (8.15c), and the overall optimal outcome might result. Only then are the possible mutual gains from negotiations exhausted.

Unfortunately, however, there is a particular problem associated with the assignment of the property right to the producer of an undepletable externality, which is closely related to the problem of voluntary private provision of public goods (see for instance Bergstrom, Blume and Varian, 1986). Suppose that N identical victims suffer from the externality, the size of which they can reduce either by offering the producer Coasian compensations for reductions in the emission (EM) of the externality, or by means of (private) defensive activities D. Without cooperation among the victims, each victim v can be assumed to exhibit 'Nash behaviour': when deciding on his bid b to be made to the producer, he takes the sum of the other victims' bids, B^{-v}, as given. Hence, a victim v acts so as to maximize:

$$W^v = M - EC(D, EM(B^{-v}+b)) - D - b \tag{8.17}$$

leading to:

$$EC_D = -1 \tag{8.18a}$$
$$EC_{EM} \cdot EM_b = -1 \tag{8.18b}$$

This behaviour is easily seen to imply underprovision of the 'public good' of reducing the emission. The optimal conditions for the victims' behaviour follow from maximization of their common welfare, being N times the representative victim's welfare W^V:

$$N \cdot W^V = N \cdot [M - EC(D, EM(N \cdot \beta)) - D - \beta] \qquad (8.17')$$

where β gives the average (per victim) Coasian bid. The first-order conditions are:

$$EC_D = -1 \qquad\qquad\qquad (8.18a')$$
$$EC_{EM} \cdot EM_\beta = -1/N \qquad\qquad (8.18b')$$

Equations (8.18b) and (8.18b') show that, due to the 'free-rider problem' associated with the voluntary provision of public goods, Nash behaviour implies individual 'undervaluation' of reductions in the emission with a factor which is proportional to the number of victims. Therefore, with the property right assigned to the producer of an undepletable externality, a below optimal reduction in the emission of the externality may result, and therefore an above optimal level of private defensive activities. Unless the victims gather their interests in some sort of victims' union, such Coasian negotiations do not lead to overall efficiency. However, individual victims will have an incentive to quit such unions and go free-riding, which makes the voluntary emergence of these unions unlikely.

In the second case, the initially existing victims possess the property right. The new short-run optimum is reached through some sort of two-stage bargaining between the new victim and the producer, where the existing victims act as an intermediate. For the optimal outcome to settle, the new victim should make a transfer to the existing victims which (at least) enables them to make a mutually profitable bid to the producer for reducing the externality. Such a bid in fact takes place in terms of a reduction in the producer's payment to them in exchange for further reductions in the emission. Since the existing victims have a certain interest in such reductions as well, the minimum transfer required from the new one amounts to $\Delta W^P - \Delta W^{NV}$ [D]. Furthermore, the new victim will receive no compensation for the gross external cost GEC^{N+1} [C]. Again, entrance is likely to take place up to the optimal number of victims. Note, however, that with more than one additional victim entered, the same free-rider problem as discussed above will emerge.

In the third case, the new victim receives a property right after having located in the affected area. Therefore, the free-rider problem will not occur. The minimum transfer a victim will then demand from the producer amounts to the optimal gross external cost GEC^{N+1} [C]. Potential victims initially face a below optimal, namely a zero, incentive for staying out of the affected area. Only if additional bargaining on locational decisions takes place will the optimal number of victims be reached. In the first place, the producer is prepared to offer payments up to the minimum transfer just mentioned (GEC^{N+1} [C]) in order to keep the new victim out. In addition, he is prepared to offer a payment up to the value of ΔW^P [$2 \cdot D + E$]. The existing victims, however, are prepared to pay the new one up to ΔW^{NV} [D+E] if he enters the area. At the margin therefore, the potential victim faces exactly the optimal incentive for entering the affected area, be it that in this case he foregoes a payment $GEC^{N+1} + \Delta W^P - \Delta W^{NV}$ [C+D] if he actually does enter. Clearly, this type of bargaining creates perverse incentives for 'potential' victims. Simply by threatening to enter the area, they are able to receive the payment just mentioned. If the producer and the existing victims decide not to make any such transfers in order to prevent this behaviour, potential victims clearly face a below optimal incentive for staying out of the affected area. Note that, under the second scheme, the existing victims do not have the same possibility for strategic behaviour. The incentive of the existing N+1th victim to move out is the sum $GEC^{N+1} + \Delta W^P - \Delta W^{NV}$ [C+D] he foregoes by not doing so. Obviously, he is only able to collect this money from the producer and the N other existing victims if he really does move out.[15]

In Section 8.4, direct compensations were found not to lead to inefficient behaviour of the victims in terms of undertaking below optimal defensive measures, provided negotiations on the level of defensive activities would take place. It is noteworthy that with localized undepletable externalities, direct compensation to new victims induce them to exhibit the strategic behaviour just discussed. That is, they are able to receive a payment $GEC^{N+1} + \Delta W^P - \Delta W^{NV}$ when threatening to enter the area. Hence, the negotiations which may follow from direct compensations in this case, although preserving the optimal marginal incentive, may actually provoke adverse strategic behaviour of potential victims.

It may therefore be concluded that, provided additional negotiations on locational decisions do take place, Coasian negotiations are only in principle capable of providing efficient outcomes in case of a localized undepletable externality. However, although Coasian negotiations are often thought to be especially attractive in small number cases, such as in the case of localized externalities, because of relatively low transaction costs, the envisaged efficient outcomes may be seriously endangered by induced strategic or free-rider behaviour.

8.5.3 Entry—exit decisions of producers

Entry—exit behaviour of producers plays an important role in the issue of Pigouvian taxation versus subsidization (see Pearce and Turner, 1990, pp.

---

[15]For the payments $GEC^{N+1} + \Delta W^P - \Delta W^{NV}$ mentioned in this paragraph actually to materialize, we have to assume some sort of trilateral bargaining over locational discussions. For instance, although the producer is prepared to pay $GEC^{N+1} + \Delta W^P$ to keep victims away, his actual offer in direct negotiations with them is $GEC^{N+1} + \Delta W^P - \Delta W^{NV}$ provided the other N victims let the producer know that they are willing to accept (demand) reductions (increases) in transfers received up to ΔW^{NV} when entrance (exiting) does take place.

107−109). Although the short-run responses to both measures will be the same, a subsidy will in the long run attract additional firms to the industry, whereas a tax will drive a number of firms out of the industry. This implies that the former will eventually result in higher production and pollution levels at the industry level than the latter. Cropper and Oates (1992) observe in this respect that only "...if firms bear the total cost of their emissions will the prospective profitability of the enterprise reflect the true social net benefit of entry and exit into the industry" (p. 682).

For the model considered in Section 8.3, only those schemes that charge the producer according to the full compensation criterion yield long-run efficient entry−exit behaviour of producers. These are compensation, Coasian negotiations with the property right assigned to victim, and Pigouvian taxation in case of constant marginal external cost.

For the case discussed in Section 8.4, the optimal charge for accomplishing long-run efficient producer entry−exit behaviour simply amounts to the gross external cost, provided that both production and abatement are optimal. As far as Coasian negotiations are concerned, the property rights should clearly be assigned to the victims from this point of view. In a competitive market equilibrium, entrance of new producers will take place until excess profits have disappeared. As a consequence, the maximum transfer victims are able to receive in such negotiations is then exactly equal to full compensation of the gross external cost.

Finally, in the case of localized external costs, such as discussed in the foregoing sub-sections, the producer's entry−exit behaviour is optimized when he faces the optimal gross external cost on a certain location. Whenever external costs differ between locations, for instance owing to differences in optimal numbers of victims, the producer will then receive the correct incentives for his locational decisions. Therefore, it may be concluded in general that the long-run efficiency condition for producers coincides with the equity condition of full compensation.

8.6   Conclusion
Externalities comprise both efficiency and equity aspects. The potential Pareto improvement criterion usually applied in analysing the economics of externalities is solely concerned with the former, because it bypasses the question of inter-personal utility comparison. However, in the practice of policy making, equity issues are often at least as important. This chapter investigated the puzzling relations between equity and efficiency issues in the economics of externalities. The main conclusions are as follows.

First of all, external costs, being the monetary value of some external effect, are defined in terms of the victims' willingness to pay for reductions in this effect. Since the individual willingness to pay for such reductions was seen to be inversely related to the marginal utility of money, an implication is that equal exposures to a physical effect imply, *ceteris paribus*, larger external costs for higher income groups than for lower income groups. Intuitive objections against this implication reflect either dissatisfaction with the existing income distribution, or the assignment of some demerit character of the effect for lower income groups. Straightforward application of the concept of external costs may therefore ignore important equity aspects within the population of victims. However, this chapter focused on equity aspects between the supplier(s) and the receptor(s) of the effect only.

In the most simple static model, allocative efficiency can be achieved by means of optimal regulation, internalization or direct compensation, although each of them has different distributional consequences. Compensation and optimization are therefore in principle perfectly compatible in such settings. When allowing for the possibility of defensive activities on behalf of the victim of an external cost, direct compensations may remove the optimal incentive to engage in the efficient level of defensive activities. This will not occur when the gross external cost rather than the net external cost is to be compensated, and negotiations between the producer and the victim on the level of defensive activities take place. Therefore, in a static setting, direct compensations are not necessarily incompatible with efficiency. Since direct compensation can be seen as a restricted form of assigning property rights to the victim, this is not too surprising; Coasian negotiations were seen to lead to efficiency in this setting. With the property right assigned to the victim, Coasian negotiations will in addition at least lead to full compensation of the gross external cost. Furthermore, Pigouvian tax revenues resulting from producer's regulation may be transferred in a lump-sum fashion to the victims without endangering the optimal outcome.

In a dynamic context, a regulator faces a particular difficulty when following a policy of 'sequential welfare optimization', which may be pursued because of uncertainty, or to avoid sequential short-run welfare losses. When direct regulation of the producer of the externality is adjusted in sub-optimal response to the victims' behaviour, below-optimal incentives for defensive behaviour result. It thus creates a need for regulation of victims, either in terms of subsidization of defensive activities, or in terms of taxation of a lack of defensive activities. The latter is particularly relevant in case of a localized externality, where a location tax was seen to be necessary in order to sequentially realize the optimal number of victims. Any form of compensation then acts against efficient location behaviour.

Interestingly, the performance of Coasian negotiations in such a localized-dynamic context was seen to be quite problematic. First, Coasian negotiations in this setting lead to optimization of the effect only if additional negotiations on locational decisions take place. However, although Coasian negotiations are often thought to be especially attractive in small number cases, such as localized externalities, the envisaged efficient outcomes may be seriously endangered by induced strategic or free-rider behaviour. Assigning property rights to the producer may result in free-riding of the victims in the process of Coasian negotiations, ruling out efficient outcomes. Comparable free-riding among 'new' victims may emerge when only the initially existing victims receive a property right. On the other hand, assigning property rights to all victims, including new ones, may provoke adverse strategic behaviour on behalf of 'potential' victims, since in this case the optimal locational incentive received is in terms of foregoing a payment. Secondly, the assignment of the property rights is not a matter as innocent as it is in static settings. In order to secure long-run entry – exit behaviour of producers, they should face incentives according to the equity criterion of full compensation. Since, in a competitive market equilibrium, entrance of new producers will take place until excess profits have disappeared and victims are not able to receive any Coasian transfers exceeding the gross external cost, the assignment of property rights to the victims is preferable from both an equity and a dynamic efficiency point of view. All in all, in a dynamic context, Coasian negotiations are certainly not as attractive as they may seem from a static perspective.

It can be concluded that, in a static context, the compensation and optimization of an external cost are more likely to be compatible as long as the victim(s) of the externality are actively engaged in direct negotiations over this compensation. In a localized-dynamic context, however, compensation is incompatible with optimization. Moreover, victims of an external cost should then even be charged for being a victim.

As already mentioned in the introduction to this chapter, the discussion was cast in rather broad terms, as it applies to the regulation of externalities in general. Many of the principles therefore hold for (road) transport, or airports, as well as for any other externality generating activity. Nevertheless, it may be mentioned that the possibly interesting case of intra-sectoral externalities, where the generators and victims of externalities are the same actors, was not considered here. It may prove worthwhile to investigate this issue explicitly in future work.

In the next chapter, the focus will be narrowed again to the regulation of road transport externalities.

9 THE TRADE-OFF BETWEEN EFFICIENCY, EFFECTIVENESS AND SOCIAL FEASIBILITY OF REGULATING ROAD TRANSPORT EXTERNALITIES [1]

1. Introduction

Returning more specifically to the regulation of road transport externalities, this chapter discusses the discrepancy that exists between the economic theory of the regulation of road transport externalities and observed practice. Although the principles of Pigouvian regulation and its attractive efficient properties have been known for over 70 years now, practical applications, in road transport as well as in other sectors, remain scarce. Lave (1995) summarizes this problem as follows: "It has been a commonplace event for transportation economists to put the conventional diagram on the board, note the self-evident optimality of pricing solutions, and then sit down waiting for the world to adopt this obviously correct solution. Well, we have been waiting for seventy years now, and it's worth asking what are the facets of the problem that we have been missing. Why is the world reluctant to do the obvious?" (p. 465). This important question has recently been addressed in a number of papers on the social and political feasibility of the regulation of road transport externalities, in particular related to congestion and road pricing (see Chapter 10 for a literature review).

In this chapter, the tension between the theory and practice of road transport regulation will be approached from the viewpoint of the trade-off between efficiency, effectiveness and social feasibility of regulation. Besides congestion, which is usually the central topic in such analyses, also other external costs of road transport (see Figure 2.2) are considered. Furthermore, besides direct demand management, also other regulatory instruments will be considered, namely indirect demand management and supply-side oriented policies. The chapter's structure is as follows. Section 9.2 addresses the fundamental trade-off between efficiency and feasibility of regulation in a simple model. In Section 9.3, the efficiency,

---

[1]This chapter is based on an article that will appear in *Transportation Planning and Technology* (Verhoef, Nijkamp and Rietveld, 1996b).

effectiveness and feasibility of various instruments for containing road transport externalities are discussed. Next, Section 9.4 focuses on the trade-off between efficiency, effectiveness and social feasibility of what will be called 'direct demand management'. Finally, Section 9.5 conludes.

9.2   Efficiency and social feasibility of regulation: a basic analysis

As discussed in Chapter 2, road transport causes intra-sectoral and environmental external costs, due to which the free market outcome exceeds the Pareto optimal level of road mobility. Figure 9.1 summarizes the problem. The market equilibrium N^0 is at the intersection of the demand curve, which is equal to the marginal private and social benefits $(D = MPB = MSB)^2$, and the marginal private cost curve (MPC). With identical road users, MPC may be equated to average social cost (ASC); it is positively sloped because of intra-sectoral externalities such as congestion. Taking account of intra-sectoral externalities, MSC represents marginal social costs; when accounting for the marginal environmental external costs MEC, TMSC gives the 'total marginal social costs'. Optimal road usage is therefore at N^*, where net social benefits, given by the area between the curves MPB and TMSC, is maximized, and the shaded welfare loss *hel* is avoided. Although diagrams such as Figure 9.1 are usually taken to represent the situation on a certain road on a certain time of day, the figure can also be seen as an abstraction for the more general road transport issue.

The identification of N^* as 'optimal' is of course contingent on the application of the − among economists − more or less commonly accepted potential Pareto criterion. However, this criterion to a considerable extent bypasses issues of equity (see Chapter 8), and therewith also the narrowly related issue of 'social feasibility' of regulation. This social feasibility is not so much dependent on the question of whether society at large benefits from regulation, but rather on the distribution of such a net welfare improvement − expressed, for instance, in the numbers of winners and losers, combined with the intensities of individual welfare changes. For example, in a very simple democracy where all decisions are taken by referendum, a rule of thumb might be that at least half of the voting population should benefit from a certain policy (change); otherwise it would not be accepted. Of course, most democracies do not operate in such a simple manner. Nevertheless, comparable decision and policy mechanisms will apply. In general, there will be some limit to the freedom of a democratically elected government, aiming at being re-elected, in the choice of their regulatory policies.

---

[2]Significant external benefits of road transport are not likely to exist; the benefits are usually either purely internal or pecuniary in nature (see Chapter 2). Hence, MPB and MSB are assumed to be identical in Figure 9.1.

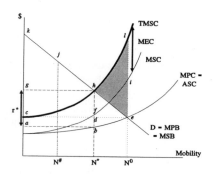

Figure 9.1   Welfare implications of regulating road transport externalities

To illustrate this, consider two 'textbook' instruments for achieving N^* in Figure 9.1: optimal physical regulation (a prohibition on mobility between N^* and N^0), and the optimal effluent fee r^*. Analogous to the analysis in Section 8.3, the distributional impacts of these policies are given in Table 9.1. It is assumed for the moment that both policies succeed in achieving the Pareto optimum.

	Road users: $0 - N^*$	Road users: $N^* - N^0$	Victims of the environmental externality	Regulator	Social (total)
Optimal physical regulation	*abdc*	*−beh* *+beif−abdc*	*filh*	0	*hel*
Optimal regulatory fees	*abdc−abhg=* *−cdhg*	*−beh* *+beif−abdc*	*filh*	*abhg*	*hel*

Table 9.1   The welfare effects of optimal physical regulation and optimal fees

With optimal physical regulation, the road users generating the optimal mobility N^* enjoy a welfare gain due to decreased congestion costs, which is represented by the rectangular *abdc*. Indeed, it is because of the existence of intra-sectoral externalities that in this case, in contrast to the analysis in Section 8.3, generators of external costs may actually benefit from regulation. Next, the mobility foregone, between N^* and N^0, incurs a loss of benefits equal to area N^*N^0eh and a reduction of internal private costs of N^*N^0eb, yielding a negative subtotal of *beh*. In addition, external congestion costs within this group will disappear, equal to the total reduction in external congestion costs *beif* minus the fraction *abdc* enjoyed by the remaining road users. Thus the total welfare effect given in the second column in Table 9.1 results. Finally, the reduction in the environmental externality implies a welfare gain to its victims equal to *filh*. Summing over the three groups, a social welfare gain equal to *hel* can then be derived.

Optimal regulatory taxation yields identical welfare effects for the mobility foregone, for the victims of the environmental externality, and for society at large. However, the remaining road users are now worse off, as total tax revenues *abhg* necessarily exceed the reduction in congestion costs *abdc*. These tax revenues of course accrue to the regulator, or more general, to the government.

Therefore, in this stylized setting, where the two instruments are equally efficient in terms of accomplishing N^*, they are certainly not equivalent in terms of social feasibility. The road users generating optimal mobility enjoy a welfare gain with physical regulation, whereas they are worse off with regulatory fees. Since the other groups are likely to be indifferent between both policies, physical regulation will be more socially feasible than regulatory taxation. If, in the case sketched above, the ratio of mobility and the number of road users is assumed to be constant along the horizontal axis, a majority of road users would even be in favour of physical measures, while all road users would be opposed to the fee. An important assumption here is that internal (time) costs do not differ among road users (see Chapter 10).

It is important to stress that the tax revenues are implicitly assumed to remain with the regulator, and that the various groups in society do not consider the possibility of benefitting from possible allocations of these financial means. Given the usual response to regulatory taxation ('the car as a cash-cow' or 'yet another tax', instead of: 'more money for beneficial public projects'...), governments should formulate convincing policy packages if such scepticism of tax payers is to be overcome (see also Chapter 10). In theory, it is by definition always possible to construct a lump-sum redistribution of means, including the tax revenues, such that everyone is better off after optimal regulation. This might, however, involve taxation of those benefiting from the reduced environmental externality.[3] In Section 9.4, the possible allocations of regulatory tax revenues will be considered in some more depth.

However, apart from differing in terms of social feasibility, different regulatory instruments will usually also differ in terms of efficiency. In fact, the above assumption of both instruments achieving optimality is

---

[3]Insofar as the environmental benefits are to be enjoyed by future generations, there will of course be a practical problem. To a limited extent however, this may justify the existence of public debts in the interpretation of postponed taxation.

quite unrealistic. This particularly holds for physical regulation: it is hard to envisage a regulator applying 'optimal' physical regulation by identifying and prohibiting the socially excessive mobility between N^* and N^0. In reality, with physical regulation, the regulator runs the risk of also affecting mobility with relatively high economic benefits (see Chapter 6). In contrast to fees, which will naturally make the road users give up mobility between N^* and N^0, where benefits fall short of the sum of the internal costs and the fee, a 'quasi-optimal' physical measure might in the worst case affect mobility between 0 and $N^\#$ (with $N^\# = N^0 - N^*$). Regulation may then even be inferior to non-intervention, like in the sketched case where the benefits foregone $0N^\#jk$ exceed the savings in social costs N^*N^0lh.[4] Such adverse effects may for instance occur with a physical measure such as the 'car-free Sunday'; temporarily applied in The Netherlands during the first oil crisis in 1973, and now again frequently mentioned in the public debate on transport and environment. It is very likely that road users would much rather give up part of the mobility generated on week days rather than on Sundays. If the benefits associated with some mobility on Sundays exceed those associated with some mobility on other days, such a measure is clearly not optimal from an efficiency perspective. In conclusion, with physical regulation, there is no guarantee that the remaining mobility represents the highest benefits.

This may in turn negatively affect the policy's social feasibility. Although the majority of the initial road users may still benefit from some physical measure, the benefits foregone are higher than in the optimal case. While a referendum among road users may therefore still result in acceptance, the higher these benefits foregone, the more likely the measure is to provoke resistance and protest.

The main conclusion to this basic analysis therefore is perhaps a bit discouraging: there appears to be some inverse relation between the efficiency and the social feasibility of regulatory instruments for containing road transport externalities.

9.3 The efficiency, effectiveness and social feasibility of regulatory instruments for containing road transport externalities

Although the model discussed in the previous section clearly demonstrates the tension between the efficiency and the feasibility of regulation in road transport, it is too simple to allow for a broad evaluation of the various possible instruments.

This is in the first place related to the fact that the road transport sector is a complex one, also from the viewpoint of regulation. In the previous

---

[4]Furthermore, with physical regulation it is conceivable that, owing to its favourable effect on user costs, latent demand to the right of N^0, insofar as it is not affected by the prohibition, will be provoked.

section, some complications resulting from the market's atomistic structure were mentioned: there are many, in comparison to the market's size relatively small sources of externalities. Other complexities have been dealt with in previous chapters, such as problems of heterogeneity among externality generators (Chapter 3), network complications (Chapter 4), and the derived character of transport demand (Chapter 7).

Secondly, rather than just the two archetypical instruments discussed in the previous section, there is a whole range of regulatory instruments for containing road transport externalities. In this section, the effectiveness and efficiency (Section 9.3.2) and social feasibility (Section 9.3.3) of these instruments will be discussed. First of all however, these concepts of effectiveness, efficiency and feasibility as such are discussed in some more depth in Section 9.3.1.

9.3.1   Effectiveness, efficiency and feasibility of regulation

From this chapter's perspective, one may distinguish three main criteria for the evaluation of regulatory instruments. First, effectiveness refers to the extent to which an instrument is capable of accomplishing a certain goal at all, be it optimal external costs, or any other, perhaps less ambitious target. Secondly, efficiency refers to the extent to which the accomplishment of such a goal yields the highest possible net social benefits, defined as the difference between social benefits and social costs. Hence, in the sequel, 'efficiency' does not merely refer to the binary question of 'to be or not to be Pareto efficient', but is instead used as a more continuous criterion (this is the very reason for distinguishing between the effectiveness and the efficiency of regulation). If excessive benefit losses due to a certain policy are interpreted as social costs, efficiency in the above sense represents the 'social cost-effectiveness' of regulation.

Clearly, effectiveness and efficiency are closely related: when a certain goal can be reached against relatively low social costs (efficiency), the realization of that goal (effectiveness) may generally be easier. Still, the distinction can be useful in practice. For instance, high effectiveness does not necessarily imply high efficiency; consider, for instance, the complete prohibition of road transport. Also the reverse needs not necessarily hold (see the discussion on attitude policies in Section 9.3.2).

Thirdly, feasibility refers to all factors influencing the possibility and probability of the introduction and application of a certain policy instrument. Table 9.2 provides an overview of factors underlying these three main criteria. It would take too long to discuss each of these factors separately here; in the remainder of this chapter, most of them, when relevant, will be addressed. A couple of points, though, are worth noting before proceeding.

Effectiveness	Efficiency			Feasibility		
	Narrow efficiency	*Broad efficiency (additional factors)*	*Narrow social feasibility*	*Broad social feasibility (additional factors)*	*Other feasibility concepts*
* Avoidability *Controll- ability * Counter- productive side effects * Reliability * Adaptation possibilities (to remain effective with expected growth of road mobility)	* Differentiation according to individual benefits * Differentiation according to individual external costs: vehicle, time of driving, route, trip length, driving style * Avoidability * Controllability * Unwarranted or counter-productive side effects * Reliability	* Implemen- tation costs * Application costs * Maintenance costs	* Numbers of winners and losers * Intensity of welfare changes, accounting for contingent direct or indirect compensation of welfare losses (including regulatory taxes)	* User- friendliness * Transparency * Allocation of contingent tax revenues * Effect on income distribution * Justice * Anonymity and privacy * Way of introduction * Adjustment possibilities for road users * Familiarity * Economic feasibility * Technical feasibility * Institutional feasibility	*Economic feasibility* * Broad efficiency and effectiveness *Technical feasibility* * Availability of technologies * Reliability *Institutional feasibility* * Level of organization (lobbies) of winners and losers * Relative strength of interest groups *Legislative feasibility* * Compatibility with legal framework *Political feasibility* * All other feasibility concepts * Personal perceptions of politicians * Party political factors * International political constraints

Table 9.2   Possible (sub-)criteria for the evaluation of regulatory instruments for containing road transport externalities

First, space and time are important exogenous elements to Table 9.2. The spatial scale of a policy may to a large extent determine its effectiveness and efficiency, for instance for reasons of avoidability (consider fuel taxes or parking policies); as well as its feasibility (feelings of fairness).

As far as the time element is concerned, the effectiveness, efficiency, and feasibility of certain instruments may in the long run often be different from their short-run counterparts. In general, one would expect the former to exceed the latter, because in the long run people will have more opportunity to adapt to the regulation. Apart from that, attitudes and preferences themselves may change over time, implying that what seems unpopular beforehand, may gain public acceptance after implementation. An example could be the policy of speed limits: after a system of strict speed limit enforcement had been operated on the Dutch A2 highway between Utrecht and Amsterdam for a number of months in 1995, most users were pleased because of the positive impact on congestion.

In other words, the performance of a certain instrument in terms of the criteria mentioned in Table 9.2 often depends on the questions of (1) on which spatial scale the instrument is to be used, and (2) the time period considered.

Next, the distinction made for efficiency into a narrowly and a broadly defined concept deserves some attention. The narrowly defined concept is in line with the discussion in the previous section; for the broadly defined concept, additional factors also play a role. These factors are related to the 'cost of regulation', which may make it worthwhile not to opt for generally rather costly 'first-best' instruments, but to rely on less perfect, but considerably cheaper alternatives instead. A topical example here is the question of whether to use an electronic road pricing system for the regulation of congestion, and if so, whether to implement the system for the entire road network (see also Chapters 3 and 4).

As far as the 'feasibility' of regulation is concerned, different perspectives may be taken. Apart from the social feasibility considered in the remainder of this chapter, one could distinguish various other factors influencing the possibility and probability of a certain policy to be introduced. The economic feasibility refers to the extent to which net social benefits can be expected from a policy, and is therefore directly related to the broadly defined efficiency and effectiveness. The technical feasibility is a straightforward concept, and needs no further comments.

The institutional feasibility is closely connected to the level of organization of winners and losers of a policy, and the relative strength of these interest groups. When considering the regulation of environmental externalities of road usage, one could here for instance think of the extent to which interest groups such as the road lobby, the automobile industry, industrial interest groups, and environmental pressure groups succeed in affecting both the public opinion and the political process. Also, the extent to which these groups compete or collaborate is an important matter here.

The legislative feasibility refers to the extent to which a certain policy is compatible with the existing legal framework. An example underlining the importance of such factors is given by the fact that in 1994, an experiment with a separate carpool lane on the Dutch A1 highway, near Amsterdam, was eventually terminated by court for the reason that the concept of 'carpool lanes' had no legal interpretation.

The political feasibility includes all factors that might influence the political decision making process. Apart from the other feasibility concepts, all of which may be expected to play a role at some stage in the political process, personal perceptions of politicians may be crucial for the political feasibility of regulation. Also, party political factors (for instance, related to the interests of a party's traditional adherence, to a party's general ideology, and to voting deals in parliament), and even parliamentary presence during votes may eventually tip the balance when it comes to actual policy formulation and decision making. Finally, especially for relatively open countries like The Netherlands, international constraints such as imposed by the EU or other international institutions (the GATT) may pose restrictions on the options open for the regulation of transport.

For the social feasibility, which refers to the extent to which resistance from the public at large against an instrument is (or can be) avoided, again a distinction is made into a narrowly and a broadly defined concept. The narrowly defined concept is in line with the discussion in Section 9.2 and captures the numbers of winners and losers and the intensities of welfare changes. For the broadly defined concept, additional factors also become relevant. These are for instance factors of a psychological, sociological, or cultural nature. In addition, the economic, technical and institutional feasibility may also have a major impact on the question of whether a certain policy will eventually be acceptable to the public at large.

It is clear from Table 9.2 that the different feasibility concepts are certainly not independent; they merely reflect the primary perspective taken when considering issues of feasibility. In the sequel, we confine ourselves to the welfare economic perspective, and therefore to issues of effectiveness, efficiency and social feasibility. We now turn to a qualitative evaluation of the various possible forms of regulation of road transport externalities according to these three criteria.

9.3.2   The efficiency and effectiveness of various regulatory instruments

Table 9.3 gives an overview of the main possible regulatory instruments for containing road transport externalities. A rough distinction is made into three main policy fields: direct demand management, indirect demand management and supply-side oriented policies. Below, it will be argued that these three main fields should be seen as complementary rather than as purely substitutable. Therefore, a meaningful comparison between instruments from different main fields in terms of efficiency and effectiveness is not really possible, since the overall performance of regulation will, to a considerable extent, depend on the coordination of instruments originating from these three different main fields (see, for instance, the analysis in Chapter 7). Furthermore, it should be noted that many instruments may have impacts in more than one main field, both because of substituting behaviour of road users (for instance, theoretically speaking, first-best policies in the first column will lead to optimal behaviourial responses in each of the three main fields), and because of the nature of the instruments as such (note the occurrence of speed and fuel policies in the first and the third main field).

The first two columns of Table 9.3 contain pricing instruments, comparable to the 'fee' in the previous section. Still, these instruments certainly do differ in terms of efficiency. From an efficiency point of view, perfect marginal external cost pricing is optimal, by providing the efficient incentives to simultaneously change behaviour in each of the three main fields.[5] The narrow efficiency therefore is optimal. Such first-best policies, however, will be difficult or even impossible to conduct in practice for both theoretical and practical reasons. It is, for instance, difficult to assess the impact of driving style on marginal external costs; it is perhaps even more difficult to apply perfectly differentiated fees according to driving style. Therefore, 'first-best' is used more as a theoretical bench-mark, than as a practical policy alternative here.

First-best policies	Direct demand management			Indirect demand management	Supply-side oriented policies
	Second-best demand management	*Third-best demand management*	*Other direct demand policies*		
* Marginal external cost pricing, e.g. by means of: - Perfectly fluctuating electronic road pricing with perfect information provision - Perfect emission charges - Optimal combination of second-best instruments	* Imperfect electronic road pricing * Parking fees * Toll booths * Fuel taxes (effect on road transport demand) * Peak hour permits * Cordon charges * Area licenses * 'Feebates'	* Restriction of parking space * Car-free (sun)days * Minimal vehicle occupancy * Odd/even number plates on odd/even days only * Speed limits (effect on demand) * Traffic calming by means of physical characteristics of road infrastructure	* Attitude and persuasion policies, for instance, by means of public campaigns	* Stimulation of alternative transport modes, such as public transport * Physical planning and spatio-economic policies * Spreading of working and shopping hours * Stimulation tele-activities	* Technology policies (vehicles) * Fuel policies: fuel quality, and effect on fuel efficiency of vehicles * Speed policies (effect on safety and emissions) * Infrastructural policies (effect on congestion and safety) * Telematics policies (efficiency of road usage)
* Differentiated or simple system of tradable permits					

Table 9.3   Various regulatory instruments for containing road transport externalities

The pricing instruments in the second column are therefore classified as 'second-best', since perfect fee differentiation, and hence perfect incentive provision, is not possible. Welfare losses in comparison with first-best regulation are practically unavoidable (see Part II). For instance, parking

---

[5]The reason then for listing first-best policies under 'direct demand management' is that, with an elastic demand for road transport, the first behavioural adaptations may be expected to be in terms of reductions in mobility. Still, my reluctance to classify first-best policies merely as 'direct demand management' is reflected by the physical lay-out of Table 9.3; in particular by printing 'First-best policies' bold-faced and by shifting it a bit upwards in comparison to the headings of the other sub-categories of 'direct demand management'.

fees can hardly differentiate according to trip length or vehicle used, which renders such a policy a quite inefficient tool for containing environmental externalities. On the other hand, parking fees may be quite efficient for the regulation of urban congestion (see Chapter 6). In contrast, fuel taxes may be quite efficient for the regulation of environmental externalities, as long as not strongly time and place dependent, whereas they will perform poorly for the regulation of congestion. The extent to which the instruments in the second column approach the 'first-best' ideal thus strongly depends on the extent to which the fee provides optimal incentives by differentiating according to marginal external costs (see Chapter 3).

Although second-best policies may have a smaller than optimal narrow efficiency, the costs of regulation are likely to be lower than those for instruments more closely approaching first-best standards such as electronic road pricing with perfect information provision, or ingenious pollution pricing mechanisms. This will positively affect the broad efficiency. Finally, when well combined, these instruments may approach the optimal fee differentiation when considering all externalities of road usage. This is the reason for mentioning this possibility in the first column.

In addition, also the effectiveness of the pricing instruments in the second column will usually fall short of first-best standards. Avoidance may be a problem, such as private parking or through-traffic with parking fees (see Section 3.5), 'rat-running' (see Chapter 4), or trans-border fuel purchases − often implying increased mobility − in case of fuel taxes.

The last second-best instrument mentioned concerns 'feebates'. The aim of such policies is to design a budget-neutral set of Pigouvian taxes for high externality generators, such as dirty cars, and subsidies for low externality generators in order to accomplish a favourable shift towards, for instance, cleaner technologies (see Button and Rothengatter, 1996). Such pricing policies are not first-best, in which case all external costs are taxed, not subsidized. In particular, they will generally result in an above optimal overall level of the externality (see also Section 8.5.3). Still, they may provide strong incentives for favourable substitution.

Divided over the first two columns, there is a somewhat different group of pricing instruments: tradable permits. Such systems can be envisaged in various forms, such as vehicle permits, vehicle-kilometre permits, fuel permits, or tradable peak-hour smart cards for ERP systems. The narrow efficiency will, to a considerable extent, depend on the degree of differentiation (area, time of driving, etc.) within the system. For the broad efficiency, it will in particular be important to keep transaction costs down. In the next sub-section, some possible applications of tradable permits for road transport regulation will be mentioned.

The instruments in the third column are classified as 'third-best', because the price mechanism is not used. These instruments are therefore instances of what was called 'physical regulation' in Section 9.2. Apart from a lower narrow efficiency, these instruments can also be expected to be less effective than second-best demand management policies; due to, for instance, easier avoidability (for instance, rescheduling with car-free Sundays), and unwarranted or even counterproductive side effects (such as increased driving around in search of a parking spot after a restriction in parking space supply). However, the broad efficiency of these instruments will usually be positively affected by the absence of tolling mechanisms, making the costs of regulation generally lower. Speed policies and infrastructural measures, insofar as directed to demand reduction, are somewhat out of place in this column. With these instruments, road users pay a 'fee' in terms of time rather than money. However, since these time costs are bygone, and do not generate redistributable financial means, these instruments are listed under 'third-best' rather than 'second-best' demand management.

The fourth and fifth column of Table 9.3 contain a number of regulatory instruments which are not directly comparable to those discussed in Section 9.2. These policies aim at accomplishing favourable, inward shifts of the demand curve, rather than movements along this curve.

This may, for instance, be aimed at by means of direct instruments, such as attitude and persuasion policies. Without the support of other forms of direct demand management, these instruments − mentioned in the fourth column − are not likely to be very effective, as their impact is completely contingent on voluntary response (Tertoolen (1994) provides a psychological analysis of voluntary car mobility reduction). Still, insofar as these instruments do succeed in reducing road transport demand, this can be expected to take place in a quite efficient way, as road users themselves can decide whether to be influenced, implying that mobility with relatively high benefits will generally remain unaffected. One has to be careful in this respect, however, since it is not clear whether the preferences before or after the persuasion should be taken as a frame of reference. A very convenient assumption to make would be that the ordering of the vehicle-kilometres along the horizontal axis of Figure 9.1 remains unaffected due to persuasion. Then, such policies can be classified as efficient in the narrow definition.

A rather different group of policies aiming at inward shifts of the demand curve for road transport is given by 'indirect demand management' in the fifth column, such as the stimulation of alternative, less distortive modes of transport (Rienstra, Vleugel and Nijkamp, 1996), spatio-economic policies (see Chapter 7), peak flattening through adaptation of working or shopping hours, or trip suppression by stimulation of tele-activities [see, however, Jones and Salomon (1993), and Mokhtarian, Handy and Salomon (1994) for some critical remarks]. Such instruments may be quite effective in the reduction, or spreading of the demand for road transport, particularly because they affect factors behind this derived demand. Moreover, without using these instruments, the regulator may very well be confronted with a highly inelastic demand for road transport, which may frustrate efforts in direct demand management.

Finally, the last column contains a number of 'supply-side oriented' policies, aiming at shifting the external cost function downwards. Both financial and command-and-control regulations are possible, for instance, directed to vehicle technology (the catalytic converter) or fuel quality (lead-free petrol). Geerlings (1996) discusses the adoption processes and the associated difficulties of such technology based strategies. Insofar as speed policies have a favourable effect on emissions, safety, or congestion, they also belong to this category. Infrastructural policies may be used to relieve congestion, be it at the risk of provoking latent demand, adversely affecting environmental externalities. Such policies may also be directed to issues of road safety, or could be used to give priority to certain types of road usage, like bus lanes, carpool lanes, or carpool parking facilities. Finally, new telematic technologies can be used to relieve non-recurrent congestion effects (see Chapter 5). These supply-side oriented policies may be rather effective in reducing the externalities per vehicle-kilometre. However, such gains often evaporate − at least to a certain extent − because of volume effects (see Table 2.1), which gives rise to the necessity of combining these instruments with demand management policies.

This brings us to the existence of interdependencies and interactions between the various instruments mentioned. First of all, optimal first-best marginal external cost pricing, in the first column, will in theory provide road users with the optimal incentives to adjust their behaviour in terms of, for instance, modal choice (fifth column), carpooling (fourth column), cleaner fuel and/or vehicles (sixth column), trip timing (fifth column), and adjustments in the locations of their various activities (fifth column). However, even when applying first-best demand-management policies, it is likely that the government should still have to play an important role in these fields. This is particularly due to the likely existence of various types of market failures and rigidities; for instance, in the supply of infrastructure, in the supply of alternative, often public, transport services, in the organization of carpool schemes, in research and development in fuel and vehicle technologies, or in spatio-economic development and physical planning. In general, the less efficient and effective the instruments in the first main field are used, the more important stringent policies in the other two main fields will be. Reversely, policies in these latter two main fields will be more effective, the more road users − through direct demand management − receive incentives to adjust their behaviour in the preferred direction.

Ideally, one would aim at a balanced development of the three main fields distinguished in Table 9.3: direct demand characteristics, factors behind that demand, and factors on the supply side. This implies that in policy formulation, one should give serious consideration to the interactions between these fields, both via market processes and because of interdependencies between the instruments as such. The overall efficiency and effectiveness of the policy package will first and foremost depend on the consistency of policies from these three main fields (see the discussion on λ_E in Sections 7.5 and 7.6). It is worth stressing again that instruments from different main fields can generally not be seen as pure substitutes. Only in very extreme cases, where externalities completely vanish because of a certain policy would the necessity of such coordination disappear. This would, for instance, be the case if an entirely environmentally friendly, silent, safe and 'congestion free' car were developed.

9.3.3   The social feasibility of various regulatory instruments
Having considered issues of efficiency and effectiveness, now the social feasibility of the various instruments listed in Table 9.3 will be discussed.

Considering the first main field of direct demand management first, one of the conclusions in Chapter 3 can be used to compare first-best and second-best pricing instruments. The fact that the optimal second-best fee is a weighted average of the optimally differentiated first-best fees implies that, for road users generating relatively low externalities (for instance, driving relatively clean vehicles), the narrowly defined feasibility (see Section 9.3.1) of first-best effluent taxation will exceed that of second-best regulation. The opposite of course holds for road users generating relatively high externalities. This may have a positive effect on the broad social feasibility of first-best taxation in comparison with second-best taxation, as it is less likely to provoke feelings of injustice. On the other hand, the broad social feasibility of an instrument such as electronic road pricing may be negatively affected for reasons of unfamiliarity and privacy. This argument, however, becomes less relevant now that smart-card technologies are available. In addition, its introduction may very well be interpreted as an additional form of taxation, inducing stronger resistance than does an increase of existing fees such as fuel taxes or parking charges (see also Chapter 10). Hence, neither for the narrowly nor the broadly defined feasibility concept can a straightforward ranking of first-best and second-best effluent taxation be given.

Both of them, however, are likely to be outperformed by third-best measures when it comes to the narrow social feasibility. Each of the three types of regulation aims at a reduction in road usage; with pricing instruments however, this goal is pursued by making the road users pay charges (see Section 9.2). In this respect, a noteworthy position is taken by 'tradable permits'. The narrow feasibility of such schemes may considerably exceed that of other pricing instruments, because the regulator can in principle distribute the permits for free. When subsequent trading of these permits takes place, there is a zero-sum game, in terms of financial flows, for the traders involved (note, however, that not all of these traders necessarily have to be initial externality generators). This is obviously not the case for effluent taxation, unless accompanied with a non-distortive compensation scheme. As the regulator can decide about the initial distribution of the permits, he is equipped with a potentially strong means of affecting the narrow social feasibility of regulation. The broad social feasibility of such schemes, however, will generally be negatively affected for reasons of unfamiliarity, and does also strongly depend on the costs and efforts of trading.

A practical application of tradable permits in road transport regulation was the vehicle quota system in Singapore in its first year (Koh and Lee, 1994).[6] Another tradable permit scheme related to transport is the successful USA's lead trading programme, designed to reduce lead from 1.1 grams/gallon for large refineries in 1982 to 0.1 grams/gallon for all refineries after five years (Hahn, 1989). Button (1993b) mentions the USA's Corporate Average Fuel Economy Standards (CAFE) programme, introduced in 1975, as another example of the application of tradable permits in the transport sector.[7] Also other schemes have been proposed. Rothengatter (1989), for instance, suggests car ownership permits differentiated according to emission classes. Goddard (1996) discusses the applicability of a tradable permit scheme for regulating road transport externalities in the Mexico City area. Clearly, there appears to be room for using such schemes in the regulation of road transport externalities.

Feebates, like tradable permits when distributed for free, also imply a zero-sum game, in this case for the population of regulatees. For the same reason then, also feebates are likely to outperform effluent taxation when it comes to the social feasibility of regulation.

Finally, the group of attitude and persuasion instruments may generally be expected to have a relatively high social feasibility, since the road users' contingent response to such instruments will have to be voluntary.

---

[6]Although the 'certificates of entitlement' (COEs) in this scheme were initially indeed transferable, stories about huge profits earned by speculators made the Singapore government decide to terminate tradability in most categories after October 1991, restricting the programme to a monthly sealed-bid tender auction. However, this did not reduce COE prices (Koh and Lee, 1994).

[7]This programme was designed to make car manufacturers' fleets conform certain standards: the harmonic average fuel consumption had to be 18 miles/gallon in 1978 and 27.5 miles/gallon in 1985. By leaving the exact strategies to conform these standards to the manufacturers, they could improve the fuel efficiency of those types of vehicle where this was most economical. However, although such a scheme allows for what can be seen as firm-internal trading, external trading is not possible.

For the second main field, 'indirect demand management', the social feasibility of regulation will first and foremost depend on the nature of the measures taken. Policies such as prohibitions and taxation, for example, in physical planning, are less popular and socially feasible than policies conducted in terms of stimulation and subsidization, such as the supply of additional public transport or telematics networks.

Thirdly, in a qualitative sense, instruments from the third main field of supply-side oriented policies often seem to provoke relatively limited resistance, especially when comparing them to direct demand management. This may partly be explained by the fact that the former do not directly threaten the 'freedom of mobility'. On the contrary, road users may very well realize that, for instance, technology based solutions can provide some guarantee for retaining road mobility. Furthermore, insofar as technology based instruments do affect the price of mobility, road users may feel that they get some 'value for money' in terms of, for example, a cleaner car or higher quality fuel, whereas effluent taxes are usually considered as losses from the individual point of view. Finally, instruments related to the supply, maintenance and quality of infrastructure, as well as the legislation on traffic rules, are traditionally seen as the government's responsibility, and may therefore have a relatively high broad social feasibility.

To conclude, it can be noted that, as is the case for efficiency and effectiveness of regulation, a comparison of the social feasibility of instruments from different main policy fields cannot easily be made. This requires further research, not in the last place on the interdependencies between these instruments. However, for direct demand management, the trade-off between efficiency, effectiveness and social feasibility of regulation can be discussed in some more depth on a theoretical basis — especially when focusing on the narrowly defined concepts. This is the topic of the next section.

9.4   Towards a trade-off between efficiency, effectiveness and social feasibility of regulation in road transport

This section focuses on the apparent necessity to come to some trade-off between the efficiency, effectiveness and feasibility of regulation in road transport. The discussion is confined to instruments from the first main field of direct demand management. Furthermore, the discussion is restricted to the trade-off between the narrow social feasibility on the one hand, and a combined narrow efficiency/effectiveness measure on the other; a combination which makes sense because of the close relationship between the two.

In Figure 9.2, the four categories of direct demand management distinguished in Table 9.3 are ordinally classified according to these two criteria. Their relative positions are based on the discussion in Section 9.3. The most favourable area in Figure 9.2 is of course the upper-right corner, where both the narrow social feasibility, and the narrow efficiency and effectiveness are relatively high.

On the left-hand side of Figure 9.2, the regulatory fees can be found, with a relatively low narrow social feasibility. The bench-mark of first-best fees is by definition more narrowly efficient than second-best fees, and is in addition likely to be more effective. As indicated by the arrows however, the efficiency of second-best policies approaches first-best standards when the fees are more differentiated according to individual marginal external costs. The same holds when the policy has only limited unwarranted side-effects, and when it is relatively difficult to avoid.

The narrow feasibility of effluent taxation, be it first-best or second-best, can be increased by 'ear-marking' of the tax revenues, and reserving them for certain goals. These goals should, for this purpose of social feasibility, of course be as much as possible in the interest of road users.[8] In terms of Figure 9.1 and Table 9.1, this means that road users consider a certain proportion of *abhg* no longer as a pure loss. Three types of such ear-marking will briefly be discussed below.

The most straightforward possibility is more or less direct compensation of the fees charged. The problem then of course is how to do this without eroding the regulatory impact of the fees. In the most extreme case of direct and complete restitution, the fee would have no impact at all, and the market would return to the non-intervention outcome N^0 in Figure 9.1. In Figure 9.2, this illustrated by the south-eastly directing arrow. This problem can only be avoided if 'lump-sum' compensation were possible. Unfortunately, the concept of pure lump-sum payments is mainly a theoretical bench-mark construction, with only limited practical relevance.

The second type of ear-marking however, being the variabilization of road taxes, can be considered as a (not inexhaustible) form of lump-sum compensations. Such a simultaneous introduction of effluent taxes and lowering of fixed taxes can offer an important possibility of avoiding resistance against regulatory taxation (see also Chapter 10).

The third form of ear-marking is often the theoretically most elegant one: the usage of regulatory tax revenues for covering the costs of measures from the third main field of supply oriented policies. For instance, for congestion, it can be shown that under certain assumptions the revenues of optimal congestion tolls are just sufficient to cover the cost of the optimal supply of road infrastructure (Mohring and Harwitz, 1962). The proverbial knife then cuts from three sides: the regulatory impact of

---

[8]If the allocation of these revenues is not directly in the interest of road users, the feasibility may even be negatively affected. This recently happened in the Dutch province of Drenthe, where the road lobby accused the regional authorities of 'legal theft' after the news had spread that the extra revenues of increased road taxes would be used for a subsidization scheme for thatched roofs.

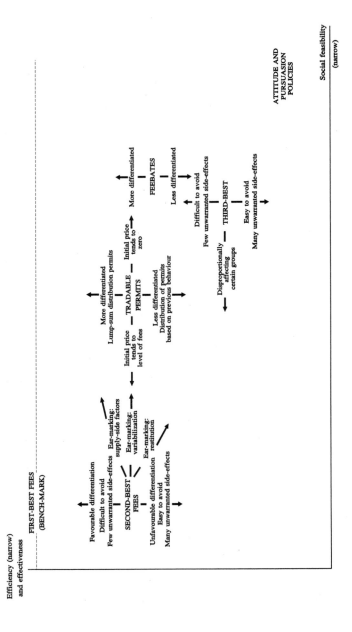

Figure 9.2   *The trade-off between efficiency, effectiveness and social feasibility of direct demand management for the regulation of road transport*

the fee, the increased feasibility of regulation, and the positive impacts of supply-side oriented policies. In Figure 9.2, this is depicted by the arrow pointing north-eastly.

The narrow feasibility of tradable permits strongly depends on the question of how these permits are to be issued. If they are sold, the narrow feasibility will decline as the initial price approaches more closely the level of corresponding regulatory fees. When these two become equal, no trade will take place, since only those road users that were prepared to pay a fee would purchase a permit. The two instruments are then equivalent: the narrow feasibility will strongly depend on the allocation of the revenues, whereas the efficiency and effectiveness will depend on the degree of differentiation within the system. In the other extreme, where the permits' initial price tends to zero, the narrow feasibility will of course increase. However, the efficiency will then more and more depend on the question of how the permits are to be distributed. If the initial distribution depends on revealed mobility behaviour, for instance, in some previous period, then a situation comparable to direct restitution of tax revenues might arise. If road users know that a large share of the money spent on permits will be refunded in a next period in the form of free permits, strategic behaviour can arise, which, although it cannot affect the effectiveness, may have a negative impact on efficiency.[9] A lump-sum distribution of permits is therefore preferable from an efficiency point of view.

Tradable permits, when distributed for free, may have a narrow feasibility comparable to that of third-best regulation. Moreover, this latter may even be exceeded if certain groups are disproportionally affected by such third-best regulation, as outlined in Section 9.2 and indicated by the leftwards pointing arrow. Tradable permits then have the advantage of allowing such groups to retain their mobility by purchasing permits from those who derive less benefits from mobility. Since such trade takes place voluntarily, it can only positively affect the social feasibility in comparison to third-best regulation, where such trade is not possible. As depicted by the vertical arrows, the efficiency and effectiveness of third-best policies will particularly depend on the avoidability, and the extent to which unwarranted side effects occur.

Feebates may also be more socially feasible in the narrow sense than third-best policies, because some generators of externalities are made better off with feebates. On the other hand, of course, high externality generators will prefer physical restrictions to feebates, so that an unambiguous conclusion cannot be drawn. The efficiency of feebates will usually be lower than that of second-best fees. This is easy to see after realizing that

---

[9]Only if capital markets operate perfectly, and everybody has the same perception of the expected price in the next period, this need not be a problem.

a system of feebates would, in second-best maximization problems such as discussed in Chapter 3, add a restriction to the Lagrangian, namely that the total sum of tax revenues be zero. Comparing feebates with freely distributed tradable permits, it can first be hypothesized that the narrow social feasibility will be comparable, because both result in zero-sum games. Tradable permits however, are likely to be more efficient and effective, since 'winners' in terms of cash money win because they decide not to use the car, whereas with feebates they win because they do decide to use the car. Moreover, tradable permits may generally be more effective because a clear target for the overall level of the externality can be set.

The position of attitude and persuasion policies follows directly from the discussion in the previous section. Although quite feasible, and not particularly inefficient, such instruments will most likely turn out not to be very effective.

It is important to stress that the above discussion is confined to the narrowly defined efficiency and feasibility concepts. For the broad concepts, the relative positions of the instruments in Figure 9.2 may be different. The broad efficiency of first-best charging will often be negatively affected by the costs of differentiated toll collection. The same can be said for tradable permits when considering transaction costs. Also the broad feasibility of these instruments may be negatively affected for reasons of unfamiliarity; whereas second-best instruments will often benefit from already being used to some extent. However, in the qualitative framework presented above, it is not possible to discuss these broader concepts without speculation, which is the reason for restricting the analysis to the narrowly defined concepts. The following two chapters will provide some empirical evidence on these matters.

Finally, the discussion was restricted to a partial setting. This means that potential benefits of effluent fees in terms of reaping 'double dividend' by offering possibilities to lower distortive taxes elsewhere in the economy, typically on labour, are not accounted for. In principle, common neo-classical economic wisdom teaches that a shift from taxation of consumption, production or labour towards taxation of externalities should increase social welfare (Sandmo, 1975; Atkinson and Stiglitz, 1980, pp. 451–454). Recently, however, this appealing idea of 'double dividend' has been challenged by authors like Bovenberg (1995), who put forward 'excess burden' arguments against environmental taxation. The claim is that such taxes, which will eventually be borne by labour, may lead to unemployment. In response, it can be argued that starting from a second-best world where labour taxes are set too high, a fiscal reform may still have a positive effect on employment (Carraro and Soubeyran, 1995). However interesting this discussion may be, this does not seem the right place to repeat the arguments. The interested reader may consult the above references.

9.5   Conclusion

This chapter discussed the tension between theory and practice of regulation of road transport externalities by linking this to the trade-off between efficiency, effectiveness and social feasibility of regulation. Since there is a certain limit to the freedom of a democratic government in formulating their regulatory policies, this is a highly important, but yet hardly explored, research area. Unfortunately, there appears to be some inverse relation between the efficiency and effectiveness of regulation on the one hand, and its social feasibility on the other. However, the regulator is not merely restricted to making a negative trade-off between efficiency, effectiveness and social feasibility of regulation. From a more positive perspective, there appears to be room for strategies aiming at increasing the efficiency and effectiveness of regulation, given a certain social feasibility, and *vice versa*.

Four important trajectories in this respect may be (1) the usage of tradable permits; (2) the usage of feebates; (3) the formulation of well balanced mixes of second-best and third-best policies, approaching first-best standards as much as possible; and (4) 'ear-marking' of regulatory tax revenues. In the latter case, the aim is to turn potential Pareto improvements as much as possible into strict Pareto improvements, without eroding the efficiency and effectiveness of regulation. As long as regulation leads to net social welfare gains, a strict Pareto improvement is theoretically possible. In practice however, this requires quite some creativity in finding ways of redistribution that are as much as possible lump-sum in nature. Usage of tax revenues for financing supply-side oriented policies, and variabilization of road taxes can play an important role in this respect. From a broader perspective, the social feasibility of regulation may be increased by compensations in other taxes, as well as by making the public aware of the benefits, and perhaps necessity of environmental improvements (see also Chapters 10 and 11).

Furthermore, the coordination of policies is an important strategic weapon. This holds both for the combination of second-best policies, and for the coordination between direct demand management, indirect demand management and supply-side oriented policies. This latter issue is of particular importance for the overall efficiency and effectiveness of the whole policy package, and hence also for its social feasibility via the extent to which instruments will have to be used disproportionally stringently because of lacking policies in the other fields.

Finally, from a long run perspective, it is important that the choice of a policy package is such that it remains capable of meeting the criteria of efficiency, effectiveness and social feasibility, also in the light of the expected continuing growth in the demand for transport. Furthermore, more stringent policies are preferably to be introduced as soon as possible; not only because of the current size of road transport externalities, but also because current mobility patterns provoke and facilitate shifts in the factors behind the demand of transport, for instance in terms of spatial organization, that will undoubtedly negatively affect the effectiveness and social feasibility of future regulation.

Clearly, the theoretical approach in the foregoing chapter, besides having the advantage of allowing for a rather broad view, has the specific disadvantage that empirical questions remain unanswered. The following two chapters study such questions, beginning with the social feasibility of congestion pricing in Chapter 10.

10 THE SOCIAL FEASIBILITY OF ROAD PRICING: A CASE STUDY FOR THE RANDSTAD AREA

10.1 Introduction

Road pricing[1] is a highly controversial topic, and debates about its desirability tend to be heated. Economists often seem surprised by the difficulties they face in communicating this 'obviously good idea', and apparently have done a bad job so far in convincing politicians and the public at large of the beneficial efficient properties of road charging (Arnott, De Palma and Lindsey, 1994). Moreover, even academics themselves appear to have rather strong and passionate, but diverging opinions on the issues of road congestion and congestion charging, witness the relatively large number of comments and replies that papers on these topics seem to trigger (Foster, 1974, 1975 versus Richardson, 1974, 1975; Else, 1981, 1982 versus Nash, 1982; Andrew Evans, 1992, 1993 versus Hills, 1993; and Lave, 1994, 1995 versus Verhoef, 1995).

The apparently limited social and political feasibility of road pricing has led various authors to study this problem from different perspectives. However, empirical research into this important issue is scarce. Nevertheless, it is evident that, no matter how important theoretical reasoning may be for understanding the pro's and con's of road pricing, its feasibility will in the end be an empirical matter. This chapter discusses the outcomes of a survey among morning peak road users in the Dutch Randstad area. The main aim of the survey was to provide an exploratory analysis of road users' opinions on road pricing. The data set allows to identify a number of key factors that determine these opinions. Both personal characteristics are considered, such as income, and trip related variables, such as trip purpose, trip length, and the severity of congestion. Apart from that, various important related matters are analysed, such as the reasons why peak hour travellers dislike congestion, the willingness to pay for time gains, considered alternatives for road usage in the morning peak,

---

[1]The term 'road pricing' usually refers to congestion pricing in the literature. Also this chapter concentrates on congestion pricing; road charges for environmental externalities are not considered.

and last but not least various possible allocations of revenues. In addition to the efficiency of various forms of congestion pricing as studied in Part II, this chapter therewith provides insight into the social feasibility.

The chapter starts with a brief literature review in the next section. The study design and some general results are presented in Section 10.3. The exploratory analysis of the opinions on road pricing in Section 10.4 is ordered according to the structure of the recursive model that was designed for this purpose. Section 10.5 considers the allocation of revenues, and its impact on the feasibility of road pricing. Finally, Section 10.6 contains the conclusions.

10.2   The feasibility of road pricing: a brief literature review

This section provides a brief review of the literature on the feasibility of road pricing. A more extensive overview can be found in Emmerink, Nijkamp and Rietveld (1995).

The most simple economic analysis of the social feasibility of road pricing is presented in Figure 10.1. Here, road users are identical in all respects, apart from their marginal willingness to pay for a trip, represented by the demand curve $D = MPB = MSB$ (marginal private and social benefits, respectively). Due to congestion, marginal social cost (MSC) exceed marginal private cost (MPC), which are equal to average social cost (ASC). The free market outcome is at N^0, and socially optimal road mobility at N^*. The road price that accomplishes this optimum is the Pigouvian tax r^*, which is equal to the marginal external congestion costs $(MSC - MPC)$ in the optimum. Although this tax yields the social welfare benefit given by the shaded area, it is easy to see that, without redistribution of the optimal tax revenues $N^* \cdot r^*$, everybody is worse off due to road pricing, except the regulator. Those who remain using the road incur a net welfare loss of a, which consists of a time gain b on the one hand, and the necessarily higher road price r^* they have to pay for this on the other. Those who are taxed off the road incur welfare losses varying from 0, for the initial marginal user, to a, for the marginal 'non-user' after road pricing. Therefore, those who are taxed off the road generally incur smaller welfare losses than those who remain using it. Otherwise, the former would of course remain using the road.

It has been observed that these redistributional effects of road pricing may dominate the efficiency gains (Segal and Steinmeier, 1980; Andrew Evans, 1992). Andrew Evans (1992) questions the desirability of road pricing for this reason; among other reasons, such as the possibility of monopolistic pricing. The latter seems less of a serious concern in reality, given the reluctance of most governments to use price instruments to any significant extent anyway. Borins (1988) goes a step further, and draws the pessimistic conclusion that road pricing will "inevitably fail because it is an intrinsically unpopular policy in any democratic urban policy" (p. 43).

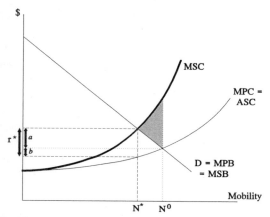

Figure 10.1 The social feasibility of road pricing in a basic model

A well established result from the literature, however, is that some road users may benefit from road pricing when heterogeneity of road users is allowed for. The typical case considered concerns income differences. Starting with Richardson (1974), most authors conclude that road pricing is likely to be regressive (Layard, 1977; Glazer, 1981; Niskanen, 1987; Arnott, De Palma and Lindsey, 1994[2])[3]. Clearly, stated this way, the non-intervention outcome is taken as a reference. Another way of looking at it is that higher income drivers suffer disproportionately from unregulated (excessive) congestion. From that perspective, it is of course questionable whether the progressive incidence of welfare losses due to unregulated congestion provides a sound basis for leaving this inefficiency in existence.

The regressive impact of road pricing can be illustrated as follows. Assume very simple individual utility functions $U^i(\mathbf{x},t)$, where $\mathbf{x}$ is the vector of consumption goods and t is the time spent travelling during the peak. Assuming utility maximizing agents who spend income M among goods $\mathbf{x}$ for given prices $\mathbf{p}$ such as to maximize utility, and utility to be functionally separable in time and consumption, so that a road price only affects utility from consumption of $\mathbf{x}$ owing to its effect on the budget, individual i's money metric welfare is given by:

$$W^i = (M^i - r) - VTT^i(t(r)) \tag{10.1}$$

---

[2]In addition, Arnott, De Palma and Lindsey (1994) conclude that a toll is likely to benefit drivers with relatively high scheduling costs.

[3]Foster (1974, 1975), in contrast, stresses that road pricing can be progressive, in particular when society is divided into 'rich' car owners and a 'poor' rest group.

where M^i is the individual's (exogenous) money income, r is the road price, and VTT^i is the individual's valuation of total travel time t. An individual who remains using the road after imposition of a toll[4] is indifferent to marginal changes in this toll if:

$dr = - dVTT^i$ (10.2a)

With an increase in r, the right-hand side becomes positive for an individual who remains using the road, because others will be priced off the road. Likewise, an individual is indifferent if:

$dM^i = dVTT^i$ (10.2b)

In terms of the direct utility function U^i, this indifference translates into (dropping superscripts i):

$U_M dM + U_t dt = 0$ (10.3)

where subscripts denote partial derivatives.[5] Substitution of (10.2b) into (10.3) yields:

$U_M dVTT + U_t dt = 0$ (10.4a)

which can finally be rewritten as:

$$\frac{dVTT}{dt} = \frac{-U_t}{U_M} \qquad\qquad\qquad (10.4b)$$

The left-hand side gives the individual's marginal value of time, or the willingness to pay for time savings, on the road. As is clear from (10.4b), this willingness to pay is positively related to the marginal utility of time $-U_t$, and inversely related to the marginal utility of income U_M. On the micro level then, one would expect the congestion toll to be beneficial, if for anybody, for those with a relatively high marginal utility of time and a relatively low marginal utility of income. The latter effect is directly responsible for the regressiveness of road pricing.

Giuliano (1992) notes that such equity considerations may merely "present an apparently legitimate basis for opposition that is actually motivated by other reasons" (p. 349), and Small (1983, 1992b) stresses at several places that road pricing may actually be progressive given certain redistributions of revenues. Nevertheless, the income transfers as such due to road pricing have played an important role in the discussion of its feasibility (Andrew Evans, 1992). Various authors have proposed schemes of spending the funds raised by road pricing in such a way that as many actors as possible eventually benefit, so that the opposition be minimized

---

[4] Those who are taxed off the road certainly will not benefit, since these people will have to choose an inferior alternative (otherwise, they would not have been on the road in the initial situation).

[5] U_M is therefore identical to the Lagrangian multiplier associated with the optimization problem $MAX_x U(x,t)$ s.t. $M - px - r = 0$, and hence represents the marginal utility of income (or money).

(Goodwin, 1989; Jones, 1991; Small, 1992b). Still, May (1992) asserts that "it has to be expected that any form of road pricing will introduce some inequities. The key is to keep these to a minimum" (p. 328). Daganzo (1995) approaches the issue from the other side, by proposing a combination of rationing and pricing that reduces the size of money transfers. Else (1986) mentions the possibility of leaving road users a choice between paying a toll or queuing (see also Chapter 4). Others (Starkie, 1986; Poole, 1992; May, 1992; Lave, 1995) concentrate on various other aspects of road pricing, especially related to its introduction, that may help improve the public acceptability.

Notwithstanding the importance of the topic, and in spite of the impressive list of theoretical contributions, empirical research on the social feasibility of road pricing is scarce. Segal and Steinmeier (1980) and Small (1983, 1992b) use empirical bases for their simulation studies towards the distributive impacts of road pricing. Seale (1993) investigates London politicians' attitudes towards road pricing, and finds for instance that there is a positive correlation between knowledge of the concept, and the support for road pricing. Also for London, Sheldon, Scott and Jones (1993) report the results of an interview study among London residents. Some main conclusions are that road pricing is more likely to be accepted if the system is simple, enforcement is guaranteed, and when the revenues are used in a transparent manner; in particular, efforts should be made to neutralise any potential equity concerns. It is evident that, now that the introduction of road pricing is seriously considered at various places (see Table 3.1; and Small and Gomez-Ibañez, 1996), the importance of empirical investigation into this issue can hardly be overestimated. This was the reason for undertaking the present research.

10.3 Study design and some general results

Over the last decades, road charging, in various forms, has frequently been proposed as a means of reducing road mobility in The Netherlands, especially in the 'Randstad area'. This is the dense, central area in The Netherlands, including the relatively close cities of Amsterdam, Den Haag (The Hague), Rotterdam and Utrecht. At the time that the survey was held (June 1995, before summer holidays), the Dutch Parliament had just requested the Minister of Transport to make a new proposal on the introduction of road charging policies, where the planned year of implementation was to be shifted from 2001 to 1998, and a detailed policy design to be developed. A large share of road users in the Randstad can therefore be expected to be to some extent familiar with the concept of road charging, and with the possibility of its future introduction. This may partly explain the relatively high response rate (40%) to the questionnaire.

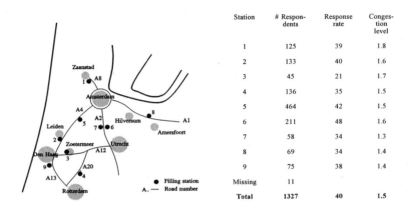

Station	# Respondents	Response rate	Congestion level
1	125	39	1.8
2	133	40	1.6
3	45	21	1.7
4	136	35	1.5
5	464	42	1.5
6	211	48	1.6
7	58	34	1.3
8	69	34	1.4
9	75	38	1.4
Missing	11		
Total	1327	40	1.5

Figure 10.2 The study area, response and congestion levels

The questionnaires were distributed among morning peak road users at filling stations between 7 and 10 a.m. Nine such stations were selected; contingent, of course, on their approval. Figure 10.2 shows the locations of these stations, with the numbers of respondents, the response rates, and the congestion levels expressed as the average reported ratio between travel time with congestion and free-flow travel time.

Like any feasible alternative, the distribution of questionnaires at filling stations has some potential drawbacks. The most important of these is probably the problem of biased sampling. First, people with a relatively high value of time in morning peak travel may be under-represented in the sample, because they may generally try to have their cars filled outside the morning peak. Secondly, people (more precisely, cars) driving a relatively large number of kilometres are probably over-represented, because they have to go to a filling station more often.

Whether these are truly problems of any significant size in this data set is uncertain. The potential problem of hurried ('high value of time') respondents, unwilling to cooperate in the survey for that reason, was minimized by having the respondents returning the forms by mail (postal free), so that they could complete it whenever it would suit them best. The potential impact of the second possible source of bias could be checked by weighting the response with the inverse of the yearly kilometres driven. It turned out that this did not strongly affect overall results such as given in Figures 10.3, 10.5 and 10.6. Moreover, for the regression analyses carried out in this chapter, this potential non-proportionality in the sample is not a point of concern, since it relates to an exogenous variable, namely the yearly kilometres driven.

It would take too long to discuss the questionnaire itself in great detail here. In short, it has the following structure. The first questions were related to the respondent's morning peak travelling behaviour; for instance, trip purpose, number of persons in the car, trip length, and trip time with and without congestion. Those who had indicated to have 'stable' morning peak travelling behaviour, often commuters, were asked for averages; those who often make different trips, like business travellers, were asked to report for the specific trip they had made when receiving the form.

Then followed some questions related to the 'disutility of congestion'. First, respondents could indicate to what extent they dislike travelling in congestion, then they were asked to report how important they find particular aspects of congestion, and finally, they were asked to indicate the extent to which they see congestion as a general social problem. Next, the respondents were asked for their opinion on road pricing, where the following answers were possible: 'no opinion'; 'bad idea'; 'moderate idea'; 'of course I do not feel like paying road charges, but nevertheless I think it is a good idea'; and 'good idea'. After explaining that the government could use the revenues for certain purposes, respondents could subsequently indicate their opinions on various possibilities. Finally, it was asked whether the respondent's opinion on road pricing is dependent on the allocation of revenues.

Then followed a set of questions with the aim of assessing the respondents' willingness to pay for time gains. For various road prices, varying from DFl 1 to DFl 10,[6] they could indicate either the minimum time gain they require to be satisfied with road pricing, or that they found the fee mentioned prohibitively high. In order to minimize 'protest bidding', being a maximum financial bid of 0 to express general protest against the instrument of road pricing as such, this question was not phrased in terms of maximum bids for given time gains. The equivalent protest bid of infinite time gains for a given road price indeed was not given by any respondent. Although the respondents were asked to imagine that they would not be compensated for the road price, they were subsequently asked whether they expect to be, for instance by their employer. Next, they could indicate which alternatives for their current behaviour they consider, should a road price become prohibitively high.

The final set of questions concerned personal characteristics, such as age, gender, education, occupation, income, and household size. In addition, the number of years one has a car at his or her disposal and the yearly number of car kilometres were asked.

The key variable to be analysed in the following sections concerns the morning peak road users' opinions on road pricing. These are summarized

---

[6]The exchange rate of the Dutch guilder (DFl) is DFl 2.06 = 1 ECU.

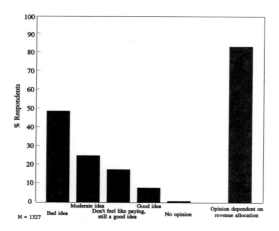

Figure 10.3 The morning peak road users' opinions on road pricing

in Figure 10.3. Almost 50% of the sample find road pricing a bad idea; increasingly positive judgements are given by descending numbers of respondents. About 25% think that road pricing is a good idea, even though most of them admit that they are of course not keen on paying for morning peak road usage. Although the general picture of the social feasibility of road pricing emerging from Figure 10.3 is not overly optimistic, it should be noted that, at least, this picture is more optimistic than the conclusion implied by the most basic model in Figure 10.1.

Presumably, there are certain factors that make road users' opinions on road pricing differ across individuals. These are investigated in the next section. One important factor for the overall feasibility of road pricing, however, is already depicted on the right-hand side of Figure 10.3: an overwhelming majority (83%) state that his or her opinion on road pricing depends on the allocation of revenues (see also Section 10.5).

10.4   An exploratory recursive analysis of morning peak road users' opinions on road pricing

10.4.1 The recursive model

One of the main aims of the survey was, apart from the sheer assessment of road users' opinions on road pricing (see Figure 10.3), to explore the factors that determine these opinions. The analysis thus gives an idea of which groups will be stronger opposed to road pricing, should it be implemented. The outcomes may therefore help the government in formulating supplementary policies that could help improve the social feasibility of road pricing. In particular, should the analysis reveal that certain groups of morning peak road users have disproportionately strong

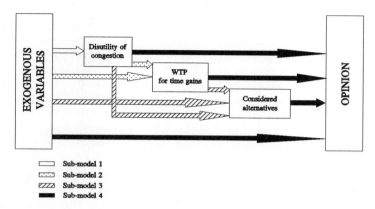

Figure 10.4 The full recursive model of peak hour road users' opinions on road pricing

negative opinions on road pricing, then specific side measures aiming at such a target group may help take away some of the resistance. The analysis also allows for an empirical validation of the hypothesis that road pricing is (perceived as) a regressive policy.

Section 10.4.5 discusses an ordered probit estimation of the opinions represented in Figure 10.3. Such an analysis has the disadvantage that only direct impacts of various individual characteristics on the opinion can be assessed. However, it is important to see whether some variables may also, or perhaps only, have an indirect impact, via other parameters. The recursive model as shown in Figure 10.4 was constructed in order to check for such indirect effects, and to assess the most important dependencies between the explanatory variables for the respondents' opinions on road pricing. In addition, the various sub-models of course may yield interesting results as such, and therefore deserve separate treatment.

Working backwards through Figure 10.4, the following general model structure is assumed. First of all, apart from a number of exogenous variables (income, education, etc.), the opinion on road pricing may depend on the considered alternatives for current behaviour should a road price become prohibitively high for the individual. Respondents who have relatively close alternatives (trip rescheduling, carpooling, or relatively attractive public transport) may be less opposed to road pricing than for instance those who have reported that they have no alternative for their current behaviour in the morning peak. Next, the 'classical' variable of willingness to pay (WTP) for time gains is of course included. Finally, various measures for the disutility of congestion are considered. Apart from the (marginal) disutility of time losses, which should in theory be captured in the WTP for time gains according to equation (10.4b) in Section 10.2, the disutility due to uncertainty, unpleasant driving conditions, and also the extent to which the respondent finds congestion a general social problem, may directly affect the opinion on road pricing, apart from any contingent impacts via the WTP for time gains.

Sub-model 3 investigates whether the reported alternatives to road usage depend on a number of exogenous variables, on the WTP for time savings (people with a higher WTP may choose other alternatives), and on the weights attached to the various inconveniences of congestion (because individuals can be expected to choose an alternative that does not have the inconveniences of congestion they find important).

Sub-model 2 is estimated to see whether the WTP for time gains indeed depends on income and disutility of time losses as implied by equation (10.4b), and if it additionally varies across individuals according to other characteristics. Apart from the disutility of time losses, also the disutility of congestion because of increased uncertainty and worsened driving conditions will be included. Hence, U_t in equation (10.4b) is broadened from time losses only, to include other inconveniences of congestion as well. Clearly, the marginal disutility of congestion as such cannot be measured directly. The answers to the various 'disutility of congestion questions' may actually be more related to the utility structure in general than to the marginal disutility of congestion. Nevertheless, in combination with the measures for the congestion actually experienced, the marginal disutility of congestion may be approximated sufficiently accurately.

Finally, sub-model 1 is estimated to see whether particular groups attach different weights to various inconveniences due to traffic congestion.

Before turning to the results, it is mentioned here that Appendix 10.A contains a list of variables, with their definitions, the abbreviations to be used below, and, for dummy variables, the reference groups considered.

10.4.2 The disutility of congestion

The logical start for the analysis of the social feasibility of road pricing is to assess the extent to which, and the reasons, road users dislike congestion. A number of questions were related to these matters, and the answers can be used as first proxies for the marginal disutility of congestion, like $-U_t$ in (10.4b). As mentioned above, however, the response to these question actually says more about the structure of the respondent's utility function than about the marginal disutility of congestion, which will also depend on the actual congestion experienced.

As far as driving in congested situations is concerned, represented by the variable DC, only 2.6% of the respondents do not dislike driving in congestion, or have 'no opinion'. The others have a moderate (25.0%), clear (41.2%) or strong (31.1%) dispreference for driving in congestion.

	Time losses DCT	Uncertainty DCU	Driving conditions DCD	Behaviour fellow road users DCF	Out-of-pocket costs DCM
Average	4.14	3.61	3.52	2.78	2.14
Std. dev.	0.98	1.24	1.19	1.31	1.13

N = 1327

Table 10.1   *The importance of various reasons for disliking congestion (scores on 5 point scales)*

The importance of various possible reasons why respondents dislike congestion is shown in Table 10.1. The average scores indicate that time losses (DCT) weigh most heavily, followed by uncertainty (DCU), unpleasant driving conditions (DCD) and the related behaviour of fellow road users (DCF), and finally the impact on the 'out-of-pocket' costs of road usage (DCM).

Finally, 1.5% of the respondents did not find congestion a general social problem, for instance, for environmental reasons or because of the impact on the economy; 2.6% have no opinion, and the rest find it an acceptable (16.4%), unacceptable (63.3%) or highly unacceptable (16.3%) problem. Clearly then, morning peak road users do consider congestion as a problem, both for private reasons, in particular time losses, uncertainty, and driving conditions; and for general reasons.

Sub-model 1 (see Figure 10.4) aims at investigating whether these judgements vary systematically across different groups of road users. Before turning to the results, it should be noted that for the other sub-models, the above variables were rescaled to dummies (DC34, DCT45, DCU45, DCD45, DCM45, DCF45, and CGP34) which take on the value of 1 if the respondent indicates an answer in one of the two highest categories. In order to maintain the compatibility of sub-model 1 with the other sub-models, therefore, binary probit analyses of these dummy variables, instead of multinomial ordered probit estimates, were used for sub-model 1. Table 10.2 gives the most important outcomes. A +sign (−sign) indicates a significant positive (negative) parameter estimate at the 0.1 level of significance; two and three +'s and −'s represent 0.05 and 0.01 levels of significance, respectively. Insignificance is reflected by no sign at all. DCF and DCM are not considered here; DCF due to its close connection with DCD, and DCM because it was not considered very important by most road users.

	DC34	DCT45	DCU45	DCD45	CGP34
Inc3					++
HHS2		−			
HHS1		− − −	− −		
Purpb			+++		+
Purpm	+				
Morn23		− −			
Mornle1		−			
Educ3		+			
Educ4		++			
Occuent			+		
Age2		− −			
Age3		− − −			
Sametrip			−		
lnCO/FR	+++	++	+++		+++
lnLength	+++	+++	+++		
YKM3					++
lik. rat. χ^2	73	67	91	30	52
sign.	0.000	0.000	0.000	0.272	0.002
pseudo R^2	0.07	0.06	0.07	0.02	0.06

N = 965

+/++/+++ (−/− −/− − −) denotes positive (negative) significant parameter estimate at the 0.1/0.05/0.01 level of significance (two-sided t-test)

The following variables were included in the regressions but had no significant impact in any of the estimates: Inc2, Compdk, Compy, Purpo, Educ2, Occuo, Gender, YC2, YC3, YKM2

Table 10.2   Summary of probit estimates for sub-model 1: the disutility of congestion[7]

The extent to which respondents dislike driving in congestion (DC34) strongly depends on the severity of congestion experienced (lnCO/FR: the natural logarithm of the ratio between travel time under congestion and free-flow travel time) and on the length of the trip (lnLength: the natural logarithm of trip length), is a bit higher for multi-purpose trips (Purpm), and does otherwise not vary systematically over different user groups. The

---

[7]Due to missing values, the sample size for the various regressions is N = 965. The detailed regression results from this and some of the following sub-models are not given for reasons of space. They are available from the author upon request.

element of time losses (DCT45) becomes less important for smaller households (HSS-dummies), which may reflect that a smaller household demands less of one's time budget. Furthermore, the importance of time losses decreases if one faces congestion on a less regular basis (Morn-dummies), and with age (Age-dummies). On the other hand, higher levels of education (Educ-dummies), more severe congestion and longer trips increase the importance of time losses. The latter two also determine the importance of uncertainty (DCU45), which is in addition positively affected for business trips (Purpb-dummy) and for entrepreneurs (Occuent-dummy), and negatively for one-person households and for those who usually make the same trip (Sametrip-dummy). The fourth column in Table 10.2 shows that the element of driving conditions (DCD45) does not at all vary systematically across user groups. However, as it is not clear beforehand why it should, this is not disappointing.

Finally, the extent to which one sees congestion as a general social problem (CGP34) increases with income, is higher for business travellers, increases with the severity of congestion witnessed personally, and is positively affected by the yearly number of kilometres (YKM3).

The measures for overall statistical fit are of course not impressive, but at least indicate that the models, except the one for DCD45, do make sense. Also in the following sections, and in Chapter 11, generally low measures for overall statistical fit will be reported. It is therefore good to stress at this point that the aim of the models is to identify the impact of certain parameters on the dependent variables studied. For that purpose, individual parameter estimates and t-statistics are relevant, and these are therefore the statistics that will be discussed. Obviously, due to the heterogeneity among respondents, and in light of the sort of questions studied in this and the following chapter, a high overall fit of the models simply cannot be expected.

The results of sub-model 1 then, are in most cases conform expectations; although it is noteworthy that income only plays a modest role as a discriminant.

10.4.3 The willingness to pay for time gains
One of the key variables in theoretical work on the social feasibility of road pricing is the value of time (see also Section 10.2). In the present survey, apart from asking for proxies for the theoretical determinants of this value of time according to equation (10.4b), respondents were asked to indicate minimum time gains they require for certain road prices, the answers to which imply a willingness to pay (WTP) for time gains. An individual's WTP for time gains was subsequently calculated as the average of the implied WTP's for time gains for each WTP question.

Since respondents are put in a hypothetical situation, all sorts of biases and distortions can be expected, comparable to those arising with contingent valuation studies (see Mitchell and Carson, 1989). Not in the last place, respondents may exhibit some sort of protest behaviour, in which case their disapproval of paying for time gains through the mechanism of road pricing as such would be reflected in lower WTP responses. Apart from that, the questions relate to time savings only, as opposed to time losses. For these reasons, the terminology of 'WTP for time gains', rather than the 'value of time', will be used below: the figures refer to the value of time savings that are non-voluntarily 'bought' through road pricing.

The problem of protest bidding was minimized by asking for minimum time gains instead of maximum money bids. Still, this is no guarantee for avoiding downwards biased WTP estimates. For instance, comparing the average WTP for time gains of DFl 10.46 per hour for commuters in this study to the value of time of DFl 18 for the same group in HCG (1990a) (see Table 2.4), this indeed seems to be the case. However, the HCG estimate is an average of valuations of time losses and time gains, the latter of which is about 50% below the former (HCG, 1990a). This implies that the present estimate of travel time gain valuations is actually quite close to the HCG estimation; especially when accounting for the uncertainty in estimates. For business trips, the difference is much larger: DFl 11.39 versus DFl 52. Here, however, it should be noted that the HCG estimate adds the employer's valuation of time to the traveller's own valuation (again weighted over gains and losses) of DFl 20. It can thus be concluded that the present WTP estimates for travel time gains are rather close to the HCG outcomes for the Netherlands. Finally, the confidence in the WTP values is further strengthened by the fact that the implied valuation of time gains of about 40% of net wages is well in line with other empirical work (see Small, 1992a, pp. 43−44).

For sub-model 2, the natural logarithm of the WTP for travel time gains (lnWTP) was regressed on a number of variables. A complication for this regression is the likely endogeneity of two particular variables, namely the length of the trip (lnLength) and the severity of congestion experienced (lnCO/FR). On the one hand, one would expect both variables to have a positive impact on the WTP for time gains, as both will have a positive impact on the marginal disutility of congestion. On the other hand, people with a high value of time, and therewith a high WTP for time gains, may try to avoid long trips in severe congestion, for instance by choosing their work and/or residential location accordingly. This would lead to a negative correlation between these variables and the WTP for time gains. This was indeed found with an ordinary least squares (OLS) estimate of the WTP for time gains: both parameters were negative, with high significance.

An appropriate technique for handling such endogeneity problems is the so-called 'two-stage-least-squares' (2SLS) procedure. In the first stage, the endogenous explanatory variables are regressed on a number of instruments, and the predicted values of these endogenous variables are subsequently used in the second stage. The resulting regression results are shown in Table 10.3.

Variables	ß	t-value	sign. t[#]	Variables	ß	t-value	sign. t[#]
DC34	−0.00	−0.02	0.982	Educ2	0.06	0.52	0.603
DCT45	0.02	0.27	0.787	Educ3	0.15	1.37	0.173
DCU45	−0.02	−0.29	0.775	Educ4	0.22	1.26	0.208
DCD45	0.03	0.66	0.507				
CGP34[*]	0.13	1.90	0.058	Occuent	0.13	1.46	0.144
				Occuo	0.18	1.38	0.169
Inc2	0.16	0.97	0.332				
Inc3[**]	0.32	2.36	0.018	Age2	0.10	1.36	0.176
				Age3	0.05	0.75	0.453
Carpool	−0.04	−0.57	0.567				
				Gender[**]	−0.15	−2.12	0.034
Compdk	0.09	1.22	0.225				
Compy[***]	0.21	3.31	0.001	lnCO/FR[a]	0.03	0.02	0.982
				lnLength[a]	−0.12	−0.19	0.846
Purpb	−0.00	−0.00	0.997				
Purpm	0.03	0.35	0.725	YC2	−0.08	−0.94	0.347
Purpo	−0.10	−0.49	0.623	YC3[**]	−0.19	−2.40	0.017
Morn23	0.18	1.23	0.219	YKM2	−0.06	−0.49	0.624
Mornle1	0.26	0.83	0.405	YKM3	0.00	0.01	0.993
				Constant	2.00	0.72	0.471
$R^2 = 0.10$							

N = 965

HHS2, HHS1 and Sametrip were not included in the second stage estimation for technical reasons: they had to be used as additional instrumental variables in the first stage. They were found to be insignificant in OLS estimations of lnWTP, both with and without lnCO/FR and lnLength.

[a]   Endogenous variable (predicted values were used in the second stage of the estimation)
[#]   Two-sided test for significance of t
[*]   Significant at the 0.1 level
[**]   Significant at the 0.05 level
[***]   Significant at the 0.01 level

Table 10.3   Second stage results of 2SLS regression for sub-model 2: the natural logarithm of the WTP for time gains

It is interesting to see that the parameter estimates for both lnCO/FR and lnLength then become insignificant. This means in the first place that the significantly negative effect on the WTP for time gains found with the OLS estimation was indeed due to the endogeneity of both variables.

However, after correcting for this, the expected positive impact on WTP is not found. Also the other variables capturing the respondents' disutility of congestion, as discussed in the previous section, remain insignificant. This is the case for the general personal disutility of congestion (DC34), as well as for the three dummies representing the most important reasons for disliking congestion (compared with equation (10.4b) also DCU45 and DCD45 were included as explanatory variables in the regression, because a positive impact of road pricing on travel times as well as on uncertainty and driving conditions can be expected). In contrast, the dummy capturing the extent to which the respondent sees congestion as a general problem (CGP34) is significant, showing that such respondents desire less time gains for road prices; presumably because they find that the policy serves a good general goal, apart from their own private interests.

The results therefore only partly validate equation (10.4b). The effect of income on the WTP for time gains in the denominator of (10.4b) is found, but the effect of the numerator, the marginal disutility of congestion, cannot be reproduced with the data set. A straightforward explanation is not easy to give. The insignificance of the DC-dummies might be due to the fact that the response to the various DC-questions is of course a subjective, rather than an objective, variable. Hence, the variation in this response may actually more strongly reflect other differences in personality than the 'objective' disutilities attached to congestion. For instance, it may reflect negative or positive mindedness in general, or perhaps the 'propensity to complain'. A more general explanation is that the income effect simply is by far the most dominant factor for the determination of the WTP for time gains according to (10.4b). To mention a related example, it is not unlikely that the revealed WTP for travelling first class by train or airplane may be much stronger related to income than to the marginal utility of luxurious travelling. If the reduction in congestion during the morning peak is regarded as a move towards 'first class' travelling, the analogy is complete.

Turning to the other variables now, the carpool-dummy is insignificant. Although the questions were phrased in terms of road prices per vehicle, these respondents apparently did not realize, or did not find it important, that this means that they can split the fee among all passengers in the car. Next, the dummy representing whether one expects to be able to be compensated for the road price (Compy) is highly significant. This is not surprising: it is more attractive to spend someone else's rather than one's own money on time gains. This issue of compensation of road prices will be discussed in some more detail in Section 10.4.5. In contrast to the expectation, the WTP for time gains does not vary systematically according to trip purpose. The generally higher values of time for business trips found in the literature is to a large extent related to the employer's valuation (HCG, 1990a), which is not considered here. The higher WTP that was found for business trips — as opposed to the reference group of commuters — is, in the present survey, in the estimation apparently fully explained by other factors, such as income, and the possibility of having the road price compensated. After a number of statistically insignificant variables,[8] a further significant result is that female respondents, for some reason, have a slightly lower WTP. Finally, respondents who have had a car at their disposal for more years (YC3) have a lower WTP, perhaps because they are more used to the 'right' to use roads for free.

In conclusion, comparing the results with the prediction of equation (10.4b), it appears that the WTP for time gains strongly depends on characteristics that are closely related to the financial sides to road pricing: income, and the question of whether one will be compensated for the road price are strongly significant explanatory variables. The variables related to the personal disutility of congestion do not significantly affect the WTP.

10.4.4 Considered alternatives for current behaviour

The primary goal of road pricing, being the reduction or even optimization of congestion, requires that some people be priced off the road at certain times and certain places. For the social and political feasibility of road pricing, it is important to see which alternatives such people consider after being priced off the road. The availability of relatively close alternatives, like trip rescheduling, or attractive alternatives, such as good public transport, may positively affect the individual's opinion on road pricing. Besides, it is important for governments to have an idea of the indirect impacts of road pricing before deciding whether to implement it. Therefore, respondents were asked to indicate the alternatives they consider, should prohibitively high road prices make them change behaviour. Multiple answers were allowed here, and Figure 10.5 shows that people indeed often consider various alternatives. The more drastic alternatives, such as searching for a new job or residence, or abandoning the trip, are seldom mentioned as the only alternative.

It is striking that the most often mentioned 'alternative' actually is no alternative at all. These are people that indicated that, in spite of a (from their point of view) prohibitively high road price, they will still stick to their current behaviour. To some extent, these may be respondents who misunderstand the term 'prohibitive': the road price apparently is not

---

[8]It might be argued that the 'Morn' dummies ought to be endogenized for the same reason as lnCO/FR and lnLength. There were two reasons for not doing so. First, positive parameter estimates for Morn1e1 and Morn23 could indicate an exogenous budget effect as well as an endogeneity problem. Secondly, and very practically, the fit of 2SLS estimates tends to decrease with the number of endogenized variables. Therefore, only those variables for which the endogeneity problem is evident and which are considered important variables in the estimation were endogenized.

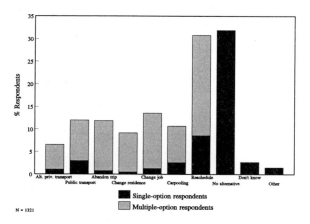

Figure 10.5 Considered alternatives for current behaviour in the morning peak after prohibitive road pricing

prohibitive at all since it does not make them change their behaviour. Apart from that, however, these may be respondents with a highly inelastic demand for morning peak automobile travel, who find a certain road price prohibitively high for its unacceptable budget effect, but indeed see no alternative for their current behaviour.

By far the most often mentioned 'true' alternative is trip rescheduling, which is encouraging for the likeliness of congestion reduction through 'peak spreading', but slightly discouraging as far as possible beneficial environmental side effects of congestion charging through modal split effects is concerned.

It is important to bear in mind that Figure 10.5 relates to the entire sample of respondents. In other words, it includes the considered alternatives for those respondents who are likely to remain using the road also with congestion pricing. It is therefore noteworthy that the shares of the various alternatives for the first 20% of road users, when ordered according to increasing WTP for time gains so that those with the lowest WTP are selected, are quite close to the shares implied by Figure 10.5. Therefore, the considered alternatives for these respondents, who are more likely to leave the road system after road pricing than the other 80%, are sufficiently well represented by Figure 10.5. For yet smaller groups of respondents, like the first 5%, the 'no-alternative' option and 'change job' option are over-represented in comparison with Figure 10.5. For the first group, a certain element of protest bidding could be present, where respondents give a relatively low WTP without seriously considering any alternatives. Those considering to change job may be respondents who are not very pleased with their present jobs anyway, and therefore only need a relatively small incentive actually to start looking for a new one; indeed, they may already be doing so.

Sub-model 3 questions whether the reported alternatives vary systematically across different groups of road users. For that purpose, various probit estimates were performed, assessing the impact of a number of potential explanatory variables on the probability of mentioning the most important alternatives in Figure 10.5. Because multiple alternatives could be indicated, a multinomial analysis is not possible here. Table 10.4 summarizes the results in the same format as Table 10.2 did for sub-model 1. A number of results stand out.

A high WTP for time gains makes people more likely to mention public transport as an alternative. This perhaps unexpected result may be due to the fact that these people anticipate being able to use their time well when travelling by public transport. The same may hold for carpooling when respondents foresee that they will not have to drive themselves each time. Furthermore, a high WTP makes people more likely to look for a new residence, and less likely to look for a new job due to road pricing. Whereas the first impact could reflect a relatively strong desire of high WTP respondents to cut on travel times by decreasing travel distances, the second effect is less easy to explain. It is not unlikely, however, that it reflects some link between the value of time and the sort of job, where jobs that are associated with higher values of time, holding income constant, are the sort of job one would rather not give up.

Next, the positive impact of CGP34 (congestion as a general problem) on the probability of trip abandonment is plausible. The highly significant impact of DCU45 (disutility of congestion because of uncertainty) on the propensity to change job (negative) probably indicates that, as is the case for higher values of time, jobs that are associated with a stronger desire for certainty in travel times, for instance because one has to meet an appointment, are also the sort of job one would rather not give up. The positive impact of DCU45 on the no-alternative option may simply reflect that these respondents find the other alternatives even more uncertain.

Persons from smaller households (HHS2, and almost significant for HHS1) are more inclined to change job, and, almost significant for HHS1 only, to change residence. Two-person households find it slightly less attractive to reschedule their activities. Carpoolers are inclined to carpool more often due to road pricing, and therefore less often see 'no alternative': they already have one.

Respondents who expect to be compensated do significantly less strongly consider alternatives other than the no-alternative option. This implies that this possibility of compensation may indeed to some extent undermine the effectiveness of road pricing. This issue will be discussed further in Section 10.4.5.

	Alt. priv. transport ALTOT	Public transport ALTPT	Abandon trip ALTAT	Change resid. ALTCR	Change job ALTCJ	Car-pooling ALTCP	Resche-duling ALTR	No alt. NO-ALT
lnWTP		+++		++	− −	++		
DCU45					− − −			+++
CGP34			++					
HHS2					+		−	
Carpool						+++		− − −
Compdk								++
Compy		− −		− −	−			++
Purpb					− −	−		
Purpm		−	+++				+++	
Mornle1		++					++	− −
Educ2	−							
Educ3	−		++			++		
Educ4	− −		++			+++	+++	−
Occuent		−			−			++
Occuo	+++	− −				− −		
Age2					− − −			
Age3	− −		+	−	− − −			
Gender	− −	−			+++			
Sametrip						++		− −
lnPT/CO		− − −	++					
lnLength	− − −	−		+++	+++			
YKM2		− −			+			
YKM3	−	− − −			+++		− − −	
lik.rat. χ²	69	165	87	41	137	194	56	105
sign.	0.000	0.000	0.000	0.163	0.000	0.000	0.007	0.000
ps. R²	0.17	0.22	0.09	0.06	0.17	0.29	0.05	0.09

N = 936 (due to inclusion of lnPT/CO, 29 cases had to be removed because of missing values)

+/++/+++ (−/− −/− − −) denotes positive (negative) significant parameter estimate at the 0.1/0.05/0.01 level of significance (two-sided t-test)

The following variables were included in the regressions but had no significant impact in any of the estimates: DC34, DCT45, DCD45, Inc2, Inc3, HHS1, Purpo, Morn23, YC3. YC2 had a negative impact on the probability of changing job and residence, but is not included in the table owing to a lack of interpretation.

Table 10.4   Summary of probit estimates for sub-model 3: considered alternatives for current behaviour

Business travellers (Purpb) are less inclined than the reference group of commuters to change job, or to go carpooling. Multi-purpose trips (Purpm) are less likely to be shifted towards public transport, but will either be abandoned or rescheduled. Infrequent morning peak road users (Mornle1) are relatively likely to choose public transport or to reschedule the trip.

The probability of other private transport declines with the level of education; the opposite holds for trip abandonment, carpooling and rescheduling. Entrepreneurs are less likely to use public transport or to change job, and more often see no alternative to current behaviour in comparison with the reference group of full time employees. Respondents with yet other occupations (Occuo) are more likely to opt for alternative private transport, and less likely to use public transport or to go carpooling.

Higher aged respondents are less likely to choose alternative private transport (presumably, often cycling), to change residence, or to change job. They are more likely to abandon the trip altogether. Also women are less likely to use alternative private transport, or public transport; they will relatively often look for a new job. Respondents often making the same trip, naturally, are more inclined to go carpooling.

The travel time ratio between public transport and (congested) road transport has, apart from the expected impact on the probability of choosing public transport, a positive impact on trip abandonment. Apparently, a low quality public transport connection often makes people give up the trip under road pricing. Trip length has the expected negative impacts on alternative private transport (cycling!), and on residence or job changes (positive). The reason for the negative impact on the public transport alternative is not clear. Perhaps respondents see public transport and job or residence changes as more or less competing alternatives.

Finally, the number of car-kilometres per year negatively affects the probability of choosing alternative private or public transport, which is presumably due to the respondent's 'car-mindedness'. It also negatively affects the propensity for carpooling but, for some reason, has a positive impact on the chance of looking for a new job. If these respondents have to drive many kilometres for their jobs, this latter effect may reflect dissatisfaction with too much driving in general.

10.4.5 Opinions on road pricing

This section discusses the outcomes of the final sub-model 4, which aims at providing an exploratory analysis of road users' opinions on road pricing (see Figure 10.3). A suitable statistical tool for analysing such data is the multinomial ordered probit model. This model does, first, justice to the fact that the response can only take on discrete values; and secondly, to the fact that the response is an ordinal variable. The analytical details of this model are given in Maddala (1983). In short, it aims at identifying the impact and significance of a number of explanatory variables on a discrete, ordered dependent variable, here the opinion on road pricing, and yields parameter estimates (β) like any other multiple regression. A specific characteristic is that, instead of one single constant, the model uses a number of constants (α), which define the various categories to which the underlying response variable is assigned in the estimation procedure.

Table 10.5 gives the estimation results. By far the most significant factor is the WTP for time gains, which has the expected positive impact on the opinion on road pricing. Also some of the variables that were seen positively to affect the WTP in Table 10.3 (Section 10.4.3) remain significant in the present estimation: Inc3 (the highest income group), CGP34 (congestion as a general problem), and Compy (the expectation to be compensated); all with expected signs. Other variables strongly influencing the opinion on road pricing are lnCO/FR (the severity of congestion experienced) and lnLength (trip length); also both with expected signs.

The opinion on road pricing is only to some extent dependent on the considered alternatives (see Section 10.4.4); in particular respondents who consider using public transport or going carpooling are significantly less opposed to road pricing than the reference group that indicated seeing no alternative. Finally, HHS1 (denoting single person households) and Purpm and Purpo (denoting multi-purpose trips and other purposes, respectively) have a direct positive impact on the opinion on road pricing.

Again, as in sub-model 2, the various personal disutilities of congestion have no direct significant impact on the opinion on road pricing. However, the severity of congestion (lnCO/FR) and trip length (lnLength), which will also influence the marginal disutility of congestion, and additionally have a great impact on the various 'inconvenience of congestion dummies' (see Table 10.2), are highly significant. This suggests that these variables may actually capture the disutility of congestion much better than the various DC-dummies; at least in the present estimation.

The direct and indirect impacts on the respondents' opinions on road pricing can now be traced in light of the full recursive model as given in Tables 10.2 – 10.5. Only the most outstanding results are mentioned here.

The severity of congestion (lnCO/FR), apart from its direct effect on opinions, also has an indirect impact via the extent to which the respondent sees congestion as a general problem (CGP34). The direct impact of trip length (lnLength), in contrast, is a bit dampened via its negative effect on the propensity to use public transport as an alternative. Nevertheless, these two variables, apparently, capture the personal disutility of congestion in the explanation of the opinion on road pricing.

Income, in particular the highest level Inc3, has a direct impact, and indirect impact via CGP34, as well as via the WTP for time gains (lnWTP). The latter also holds for the expectation to be compensated (Compy). Here, however, the positive direct and indirect effects are slightly dampened because of the negative effect on the propensity to use public transport. These results strongly underline the importance that road users attach to the financial aspects of road pricing.

Segmentation by trip purpose, in particular when focusing on the two main groups of business (Purpb) and the reference group of commuters, yields hardly any significant results, except from slightly diverging preferences for alternatives.

Variables	ß	t-value	sign. t#	Variables	ß	t-value	sign. t#
lnWTP***	0.55	9.49	0.000	Occuent	−0.11	−0.84	0.400
				Occuo	−0.00	−0.02	0.983
DC34	−0.04	−0.41	0.682				
DCT45	−0.14	−1.40	0.162	Age2	−0.05	−0.47	0.641
DCU45	0.02	0.23	0.818	Age3	0.11	0.90	0.369
DCD45	0.06	0.82	0.411				
CGP34***	0.32	3.00	0.003	Gender	0.02	0.20	0.838
Inc2	0.18	1.02	0.309	Sametrip	−0.13	−1.07	0.285
Inc3**	0.39	2.11	0.035				
				lnCO/FR***	0.56	2.93	0.003
HHS2	−0.13	−1.43	0.152	lnLength**	0.15	2.01	0.044
HHS1**	0.29	2.40	0.016				
				ALTOT	−0.11	−0.66	0.512
Carpool	−0.10	−0.82	0.414	ALTPT***	0.31	2.63	0.009
				ALTAT	0.03	0.27	0.786
Compdk	0.11	1.09	0.276	ALTCR	0.02	0.19	0.852
Compy**	0.22	2.37	0.018	ALTCJ	−0.03	−0.30	0.763
				ALTCP**	0.23	1.83	0.067
Purpb	0.10	0.71	0.480	ALTR	0.08	0.99	0.320
Purpm*	0.19	1.79	0.074	ALTO	−0.17	−0.81	0.417
Purpo*	0.50	1.70	0.089				
				YC2	−0.18	−1.41	0.158
Morn23	0.10	1.06	0.290	YC3	−0.17	−1.30	0.193
Mornle1	−0.07	−0.56	0.577				
				YKM2	−0.10	−0.74	0.459
Educ2	−0.02	−0.11	0.914	YKM3	−0.04	−0.27	0.786
Educ3	0.18	1.16	0.246				
Educ4	0.24	1.45	0.149				
Measures of fit:				**Constants:**			
likelihood ratio χ² (sign.)			224 (0.0000)	α_1***	2.19	4.84	0.000
−2 log lik. full model			2255	α_2***	3.05	6.71	0.000
−2 log lik. restr. model			2479	α_3***	4.00	8.66	0.000
pseudo R²			0.09				

N = 965

#	Two-sided test for significance of t
*	Significant at the 0.1 level
**	Significant at the 0.05 level
***	Significant at the 0.01 level

Table 10.5   Ordered probit regression results for sub-model 4: road users' opinions on road pricing

The impact of frequency of morning peak road usage (Morn-dummies) on the opinion on road pricing is only via a decreased probability of choosing the public transport alternative (ALTPT). Also the educational level (Educ-dummies) has no direct impact on the opinion, but a positive indirect impact via the increased probability of choosing carpooling as an alternative (ALTCP). Entrepreneurs (Occuent), as opposed to the reference group of full-time employees, have no significantly different opinions on road pricing, but indirectly have a more negative opinion via the lower propensity to choose public transport. Morning peak road users with 'stable' travel behaviour (Sametrip) only indirectly have a more positive opinion on road pricing due to their larger propensity to go carpooling.

Age has no significant effect at all; and female respondents are indirectly more opposed to road pricing because of their lower WTP and lower propensity to choose the public transport alternative.

The fact that one drives more kilometres per year by car (especially YKM3) makes people more likely to have a positive opinion on road pricing due to its effect on the extent to which congestion is seen as a general problem. However, a compensating negative effect is that these respondents are less likely to use public transport or to go carpooling with road pricing. No direct impact on the opinion was found. Respondents who have had a car at their disposal for a longer period (YC3) are only indirectly more opposed to road pricing via a lower WTP.

Finally, the extent to which respondents see congestion as a general problem (CGP34) has a positive impact on their opinion on road pricing; both directly, and indirectly via a higher WTP for time gains. This, in turn, has a direct positive impact, as well as an indirect positive impact via increased propensities to go carpooling and to use public transport with prohibitively high road prices.

This concludes the analysis of the morning peak road users' opinions on road pricing. Before turning to the next issue, namely the allocation of tax revenues, first a few words should be said about the effect of compensation of road prices. It has become clear that respondents who expect to be compensated have a higher WTP for time gains and a more positive opinion on road pricing − which is not surprising. However, the estimations in Section 10.4.4 demonstrated that these people, equally naturally, are not inclined to change their behaviour. On the one hand, it could be argued that this may frustrate the effectiveness of road pricing. To some extent, this is true. However, it should not be forgotten that, from the efficiency point of view, this need not be a problem. The employers' apparent benefits of having these employees travelling by car, in addition to their own personal benefits, may often put these employees on the left-hand side of the demand curve (see Figure 10.1). In that case, they indeed 'should' remain using the road after road pricing, as they are drivers with a relatively high social benefit of road usage. Insofar as this is not the case, employers may be expected to change their travel cost compensation programmes after implementation of road pricing. This then, may eventually lead to some of these people being priced off the road. Therefore, compensation of road prices *per se* causes no fundamental problem to the efficiency of road pricing. Nevertheless, this issue, as well as comparable matters of, for instance, tax deductibility of road prices, should be carefully investigated before implementing road pricing. These topics, however, are not of primary concern in the present study.

10.5   The allocation of revenues

The allocation of revenues raised with road pricing can be an important means of increasing its social feasibility. Consequently, various schemes of revenue allocation aiming at the minimization of social resistance against road pricing have been proposed in the literature (Goodwin, 1989; Jones, 1991; Small, 1992b). Also the results in the previous section indicate that road users are mainly concerned with the redistributional impacts of road pricing; this is in sharp contrast with the academics' main focus on the efficiency of road usage. From this perspective, the overwhelming majority of respondents who state that their opinion on road pricing is dependent on the allocation of revenues (83%; see Figure 10.3) is not surprising. Moreover, this fact should be taken very seriously in the formulation of road pricing schemes, as it may turn out to be one of the most crucial success factors for the social acceptance of road pricing.

One of the questions was directly related to this issue of revenue allocation. Respondents were asked to indicate their opinion on a number of possible allocations on a five point scale, varying from a 'very bad allocation of revenues' (1) to a 'very good allocation of revenues' (5). Figure 10.6 summarizes the results, by showing both the average and median scores for each alternative mentioned. The latter is included because, although being a bit less precise than the average scores, it reflects the opinion of the 'median voter', which is the decisive opinion in simple models of democratic decision making (see Atkinson and Stiglitz, 1980, ch. 10).

After having ordered the various alternatives according to decreasing popularity in Figure 10.6, a clear message arises. As expected, the further the allocation is from the direct interests of the road users, the less support it receives. It is interesting to see that the, theoretically speaking, most elegant allocation of congestion pricing revenues, namely for the provision of road infrastructure capacity,[9] receives the highest average score. Given the second position of reductions in fixed yearly vehicle ownership taxes, it is clear that road users are relatively sympathetic towards such 'variabilization' of road charges: the median opinion for both allocations is 'good'. Since a certain part of the Dutch road investments is now financed with revenues from vehicle taxation, such variabilization may

---

[9]Under certain assumptions, in particular constant returns to scale in user cost and capacity construction, it can be shown that the revenues of optimal congestion pricing are just sufficient to cover the cost of optimal capacity supply (Mohring and Harwitz, 1962).

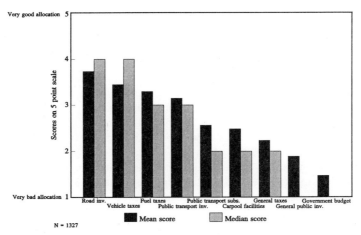

*Figure 10.6 Morning peak road users' opinions on various
allocations of revenues raised with road pricing*

indeed offer the government an important tool to overcome at least part of
the social resistance against road pricing. A shift from fuel taxes towards
congestion pricing seems less attractive; not only because fuel tax
reductions receive slightly less support than vehicle tax reductions, but in
particular also because fuel tax reductions will most likely stimulate road
usage outside peak hours, thus giving rise to additional environmental
externalities.

Switching to the less popular possibilities now, it is noteworthy that
investments in carpool facilities are viewed as a less desirable allocation
than public transport. Within the class of public transport, investments are
considered a more attractive allocation than subsidies in general. It is not
unlikely that this is closely related to the currently insufficient capacity of
public transport, notably rail, at peak hours in the Randstad area. General
purposes again receive less support than transport related purposes, with
general tax reductions being slightly preferred to general public
investments, and with the lowest scores obtained by the most general goal
specified, namely the government budget in general.

In order to obtain some insight into the factors that determine an
individual's opinion on the various possible allocations of revenues, the
scores were regressed with an ordered probit model. The explanatory
variables include the variables used in sub-model 4 above, as well as the
road user's opinion on road pricing as analysed in that sub-model, and a
dummy variable capturing the question of whether the respondent's
opinion on road pricing does depend on the allocation of revenues.
Because the outcomes were rather straightforward, and in order to save

space, the results are not presented in tabular form. The main conclusions are as follows.

First of all, respondents with a more positive opinion on road pricing also have a more positive opinion on most of the alternative allocations mentioned. This, in itself, is not surprising. Only the allocation of revenues for road investments is considered a significantly less attractive opinion by these groups; apparently because they think that road usage as such should be reduced. Looking at this from the other side, it means that people who have the strongest objections to road pricing are relatively strong in favour of using the revenues for infrastructural investments. This goal, therefore, may have a postive impact on the social feasibility of road pricing in particular also for this 'most problematic' group. Next, respondents who do not find the allocation of importance only to a limited extent have different opinions on the various alternatives. They are slightly less positive about reductions in fuel and vehicle taxes, and a bit more positive about the most general goal of the government budget. In other words, they are indeed a bit more 'indifferent' on the allocation of revenues.

Next, people who see congestion as a general problem are less positive about using the revenues for general and fuel tax reductions, and more positive about measures that may have an additional positive effect on congestion, such as investments in roads and carpool facilities.

Higher income groups are less in favour of general and fuel tax reductions, and more sympathetic towards road investments. This is consistent with the earlier findings on the importance of financial considerations, especially for lower income groups. The impact of the expectation to be compensated for the road price is as expected. These respondents are less positive about reductions in vehicle and fuel taxes, for which they are often compensated already, and more positive about allocations that may yield them additional benefits, such as road investments and public transport subsidies.

Finally, the considered alternatives for current behaviour to some extent influence preferences over various revenue allocations. It is for instance interesting that current carpoolers are not significantly more in favour of using the revenues for carpool facilities, whereas respondents who consider carpooling as an alternative to current behaviour are. Presumably, the latter do not carpool in the current situation because there are some prohibitive practical obstacles that prevent them from doing so. Respondents who will reschedule their trips are less in favour of road investments, from which they will probably hardly benefit after rescheduling. Respondents considering public transport as an alternative, not surprisingly, more strongly feel that revenues from road pricing should be used for public transport purposes. It is in this respect noteworthy that respondents with a currently bad public transport connection (a high lnPT/CO) are significantly less in favour of these measures. Apparently, these people seriously doubt the possibility of public transport ever becoming a reasonable alternative for their travelling during the morning peak.

In conclusion, the respondents indeed may have different preferences over the various alternative allocations of the revenues from road pricing, most of which are conform the expectations.

10.6   Conclusion

Road pricing, although being the theoretically speaking first-best economic solution to reduce excessive road traffic congestion, has so far not received much support outside the academic world. The foregoing analysis addressed this issue of limited social feasibility by analysing and discussing the results of a questionnaire that was held among morning peak road users in the Randstad area.

Road pricing as such was found not to be completely socially unacceptable. In the first place, people were found to be able to express some positive valuation of time gains through road pricing, with an average of nearly DFl 11 per hour. Secondly, about 25% of the respondents indicated finding road pricing a good idea, although most of these admit not to be keen on paying for morning peak road usage.

A recursive analysis revealed a number of factors that determine the disutility that road users attach to congestion, their willingness to pay for time gains, their considered alternatives for current behaviour, and finally their opinions on road pricing. As anticipated, it is mainly the financial transfers due to road pricing, and therewith its redistributive impacts, that determine road users' opinions on road pricing. This is in sharp contrast with the traditional economists' focus on allocative efficiency, for which it is only the sum of net benefits of road pricing − not the distribution − that counts. The analysis revealed that income, and in particular the narrowly related WTP for time gains, as well as the expectation to be compensated for road prices, dominate road users' opinions on road pricing. In addition, respondents who suffer from severe congestion, and, partly for that reason, see congestion as a general problem, do have more positive attitudes, both in terms of higher WTPs for time gains, and directly in terms of more positive opinions on road pricing. An implication is that the introduction of road pricing is likely to provoke less resistance when it is made explicitly clear to the public that it indeed serves a good and important social goal, and if road pricing is to be restricted to areas suffering from serious congestion.

The regressive impact of road pricing, which is often mentioned in the literature as a potential obstacle for its introduction, was clearly reflected in the various sub-models. It is, however, questionable whether this really provides a strong case against road pricing, as it has to be decided whether the progressive incidence of welfare losses due to unregulated congestion provides a sound basis for leaving this inefficiency in existence. Still, the allocation of revenues can be used to minimize resistance on income distributional grounds. The respondents indicated, with an overwhelming majority, finding the allocation of revenues of importance. Both for theoretical reasons, and given the response to the questions relating to various alternative allocations, it seems preferable to use a large share of the revenues for replacing the current fixed vehicle ownership taxes in financing the construction of additional road infrastructure. The regressive incidence of road pricing itself can then be dampened by larger reductions in such taxes for smaller and cheaper vehicles, providing lower income groups an opportunity to remain relatively well off. This, in turn, may prove to have a positive impact on average fuel efficiency of the car fleet. In addition, such a redefinition of the vehicle ownership tax structure may of course include additional benefits for cleaner cars *per se*. Finally, reductions in vehicle taxes may take away potential feelings of injustice concerning road users who are in the position of having their road prices and other expenditures on road usage compensated.

Other possible allocations are investments in public transport and perhaps in carpool facilities. Although the latter is not extremely popular among road users, it turned out that this option was preferred by those who consider carpooling, which may indicate the current existence of barriers to carpooling. Allocations of revenues outside the transport sector do not seem to be a good idea, and may stimulate existing prejudices of road users, considering themselves as being one of the government's favourite 'cash cows' — witness also many 'other remarks' made on the returned questionnaires.

It turned out that the most popular behaviourial response to congestion pricing, after the no-alternative option, is rescheduling. In the long run, additional positive impacts on congestion can be expected because road pricing stimulates the search for new jobs and residences. Also alternatives as public transport (strongly dependent, of course, on availability) and carpooling (especially for road users making the same trip each morning), and even trip abandonment are frequently mentioned. This suggests that road pricing surely needs not be frustrated by a completely inelastic demand for road transport in the morning peak.

In conclusion, road pricing will never become a popular policy among road users. However, it is not as unpopular as suggested by the most basic economic model of its welfare impacts, and may even pass the test of democratic control provided it is embedded in a transparent policy package, including supply-side measures to reduce congestion, and clear tax reduction schemes that should both take away some of the road users' scepticism on road and vehicle taxes in general, and provide lower income groups with enough benefits to take away the most urgent feelings of injustice.

Appendix 10.A   List of variables

Variable	**Description**
Opinion	4 point scale measuring the opinion on road pricing, with the following categories: 'bad idea'; 'moderate idea'; 'of course I do not feel like paying road charges but still I think it is a good idea'; and 'good idea'
lnWTP	The natural logarithm of the average of implied maximum WTP's for time gains
DC	Disutility of congestion: 4 point scale measuring the extent to which the respondent dislikes road usage in congested situations
DC34	Dummy variable; takes on the value of 1 if DC = 3 or 4, and 0 otherwise
DCT	5 point scale measuring the extent to which the respondent dislikes congestion because of time losses
DCT45	Dummy variable; takes on the value of 1 if DCT = 4 or 5, and 0 otherwise
DCU	5 point scale measuring the extent to which the respondent dislikes congestion because of uncertainty
DCU45	Dummy variable; takes on the value of 1 if DCU = 4 or 5, and 0 otherwise
DCD	5 point scale measuring the extent to which the respondent dislikes congestion because of driving conditions
DCD45	Dummy variable; takes on the value of 1 if DCD = 4 or 5, and 0 otherwise
DCM	5 point scale measuring the extent to which the respondent dislikes congestion because of higher out-of-pocket costs
DCM45	Dummy variable; takes on the value of 1 if DCM = 4 or 5, and 0 otherwise
DCF	5 point scale measuring the extent to which the respondent dislikes congestion because of the behaviour of fellow road users
DCF45	Dummy variable; takes on the value of 1 if DCF = 4 or 5, and 0 otherwise
CGP	Congestion as a general social problem: 4 point scale measuring the extent to which the respondent thinks congestion is a general social problem, for instance for environmental reasons or the impact on the economy
CGP34	Dummy variable; takes on the value of 1 if CGP = 3 or 4, and 0 otherwise
Income	Monthly net household income
Inc1	Dummy variable (reference group); takes on the value of 1 if Income ≤ DFl 2500
Inc2	Dummy variable; takes on the value of 1 if DFl 2500 < Income ≤ DFl 4500
Inc3	Dummy variable; takes on the value of 1 if Income > DFl 4500
HHS	Household size
HHSR	Dummy variable (reference group); takes on the value of 1 if HHS > 2
HHS2	Dummy variable; takes on the value of 1 if HHS = 2

HHS1   Dummy variable; takes on the value of 1 if HHS = 1

Carpool   Dummy variable; takes on the value of 1 if the respondent drives on average with more than 1 person in the morning peak when using the car, and 0 otherwise

Compensation Does the respondent expect to be compensated for a road price?
Compn   Dummy variable (reference group); takes on the value of 1 if Compensation = no
Compdk   Dummy variable; takes on the value of 1 if Compensation = don't know
Compy   Dummy variable; takes on the value of 1 if Compensation = yes

Purpose   Trip purpose when travelling on the road during morning peak hour
Purpc   Dummy variable (reference group); takes on the value of 1 if Purpose = commuting
Purpb   Dummy variable; takes on the value of 1 if Purpose = business
Purpm   Dummy variable; takes on the value of 1 if Purpose = multi-purpose — usually business and commuting
Purpo   Dummy variable; takes on the value of 1 if Purpose = other

Morning   Average number of mornings per week that the respondent drives in congestion
Morno3   Dummy variable (reference group); takes on the value of 1 if Morning > 3
Morn23   Dummy variable; takes on the value of 1 if Morning = 2 or 3
Mornle1   Dummy variable; takes on the value of 1 if Morning ≤ 1

Education   Highest educational degree obtained
Educ1   Dummy variable (reference group); takes on the value of 1 if Education = Basis, LBO, LAVO or MAVO (primary school, lower vocational, and lower and middle level of highschool)
Educ2   Dummy variable; takes on the value of 1 if Education = HAVO, VWO, or MBO (higher levels of highschool and middle level of vocational education)
Educ3   Dummy variable; takes on the value of 1 if Education = HBO (various polytechnics and higher level of vocational education)
Educ4   Dummy variable; takes on the value of 1 if Education = university

Occupation   Main occupation
Occft   Dummy variable (reference group); takes on the value of 1 if Occupation = full time employed
Occuent   Dummy variable; takes on the value of 1 if Occupation = entrepreneur
Occuo   Dummy variable; takes on the value of 1 if Occupation = other (part-time worker, unemployed, housewife/man, retired, etc.)

Age   Age (in years)
Age1   Dummy variable (reference group); takes on the value of 1 if Age ≤ 35
Age2   Dummy variable; takes on the value of 1 if 35 < Age ≤ 45
Age3   Dummy variable; takes on the value of 1 if Age > 45

Gender   Dummy variable; takes on the value of 1 if the respondent is female, and 0 if male

Sametrip   Dummy variable; takes on the value of 1 if the respondent makes more than 50% of the times the same trip (time, origin-destination, etc.) when travelling by car in the morning peak and 0 otherwise

lnCO/FR*   The natural logarithm of the ratio between travel time under congestion and free-flow travel time

lnPT/CO*   The natural logarithm of the ratio between travel time with public transport and by car under congestion

lnLength*   The natural logarithm of the travel distance by road

*   lnCO/FR, lnPT/CO and lnLength hold for the average trip if Sametrip = 1 and for the specific trip made when receiving the questionnaire otherwise

Alternative   Which alternative(s) does the respondent consider in case of prohibitively high road pricing?

NO-ALT   Dummy variable (reference group); takes on the value of 1 if the respondent sees no alternative to current behaviour in case of prohibitively high road prices

ALTOT   Dummy variable; takes on the value of 1 if Alternative = other private transport

ALTPT   Dummy variable; takes on the value of 1 if Alternative = public transport

ALTAT   Dummy variable; takes on the value of 1 if Alternative = trip abandonment

ALTCR   Dummy variable; takes on the value of 1 if Alternative = look for another residence

ALTCJ   Dummy variable; takes on the value of 1 if Alternative = look for another job

ALTCP   Dummy variable; takes on the value of 1 if Alternative = go carpooling (more often)

ALTR   Dummy variable; takes on the value of 1 if Alternative = reschedule the trip

ALTO   Dummy variable; takes on the value of 1 if Alternative = other

YC   The number of years the respondent has a car at his or her disposal

YC1   Dummy variable (reference group); takes on the value of 1 if YC ≤ 5

YC2   Dummy variable; takes on the value of 1 if 5 < YC ≤ 10

YC3   Dummy variable; takes on the value of 1 if YC > 10

YKM   The number of kilometres the respondent drives him-(her-)self in a car

YKM1   Dummy variable (reference group); takes on the value of 1 if YKM ≤ 20 000

YKM2   Dummy variable; takes on the value of 1 if 20 000 < YKM ≤ 40 000

YKM3   Dummy variable; takes on the value of 1 if YKM > 40 000 kilometres

11 THE SOCIAL FEASIBILITY AND EFFECTIVENESS OF REGULATORY PARKING POLICIES: A CASE STUDY AT THE FIRM LEVEL[1]

11.1 Introduction

This chapter studies the social feasibility and effectiveness of regulatory parking policies at the firm level. It thus investigates road transport policies at probably the lowest organizational and spatial level possible; apart, perhaps, from voluntarily 'self-regulation' of road users.

The analysis is directly related to two main 'policy tracks' mentioned in the Dutch Second Structure Scheme on Traffic and Transport (*SVV-II*; Tweede Kamer der Staten-Generaal, 1989−90), which proposes a rather broad and ambitious policy package for the transport sector, with an emphasis on curbing road transport externalities. Although many plans announced have not yet been implemented or even initialized, some plans did materialize; at least to some extent.

One of the main pillars of the SVV-II report is the emphasis on regulatory parking policies as a means of reducing urban road traffic (see also Chapter 6). According to the Dutch government, regulatory parking policies are an "indispensable part of an integral transport policy aiming at the reduction of the growth of road traffic" (Tweede Kamer der Staten-Generaal, 1991−92). Accordingly, parking policies are now increasingly being used in many Dutch cities. Also in various recent academic writings on the regulation of road transport externalities, parking policies as a second-best alternative to road pricing has received attention (Arnott, De Palma and Lindsey (1991a), Glazer and Niskanen (1992), and Chapter 6). In these studies, the second-best characteristics of parking policies, as an alternative to road pricing in the regulation of road traffic congestion, are analysed from different theoretical perspectives. Others have focused on the impacts and effectiveness of parking policies based on empirical evidence; see Willson and Shoup (1990) and Small (1992a) for overviews of experiences with employers' parking policies in the US and Canada.

---

[1]This chapter is based on an article that will appear in *Environment and Planning C (Government and Policy)* (Verhoef, Nijkamp and Rietveld, 1996c).

A second strategy (so-called 'track') in the SVV-II policy package, specifically directed to commuting behaviour, presupposes an active participation of firms. Firms exceeding the size of 50 employees are obliged to prepare so-called 'transport plans', in which a description should be given of the current commuting patterns of their employees, and initiatives should be launched concerning the reduction of car usage in the employees' commuting behaviour.

This chapter is related to both types of policy. It takes as an empirical application parking policies at the firm level in the case of the Free University (FU) in Amsterdam, including its Academic Hospital. Within the context of a general survey conducted for the preparation of the transport plan for the FU, an additional survey on parking behaviour was held. Its aim was twofold: (1) an assessment of the social feasibility of regulatory parking policies conducted at the firm level; and (2) an assessment of the effectiveness and viability of such a policy. This study is probably the first to investigate the social feasibility of regulation in the context of (employers') parking policies. Still, it is evident that employees' opinions are an important factor for the successful introduction and application of such policies. The second topic has been the subject of various studies discussed in Willson and Shoup (1990), and Small (1992a). However, these are all studies from the US and Canada, and, as will become clear, need therefore not be representative for the Dutch or European situation.

The study thus aims at providing insight into two main criteria for the evaluation of regulatory policies as discussed in Chapter 9: the social feasibility and the effectiveness of regulation. Hence, although the outcomes of the survey may to some extent be specific to the situation for the FU, the general issues considered are not, and the outcomes can in many respects be taken as illustrative for issues and obstacles encountered in the formulation of firm policies aiming at reducing car usage in commuting, for many firms at many locations.

The chapter has the following structure. The social feasibility of regulatory parking policies at the firm level is discussed in Section 11.2, where some general results are presented, and in Section 11.3, containing a more thorough statistical analysis of the opinions on such policies. The expected effectiveness of regulatory parking policies is discussed in Section 11.4. Section 11.5 investigates the possibility of a strategic bias in the response to the 'willingness to pay for parking space' questions. Finally, Section 11.6 contains the conclusions.

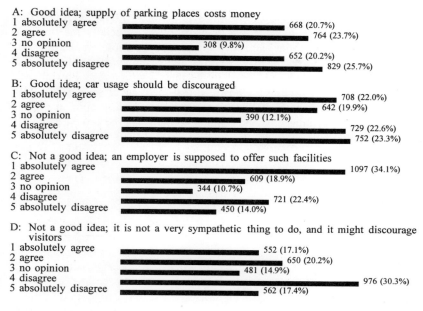

A: Good idea; supply of parking places costs money
1 absolutely agree — 668 (20.7%)
2 agree — 764 (23.7%)
3 no opinion — 308 (9.8%)
4 disagree — 652 (20.2%)
5 absolutely disagree — 829 (25.7%)

B: Good idea; car usage should be discouraged
1 absolutely agree — 708 (22.0%)
2 agree — 642 (19.9%)
3 no opinion — 390 (12.1%)
4 disagree — 729 (22.6%)
5 absolutely disagree — 752 (23.3%)

C: Not a good idea; an employer is supposed to offer such facilities
1 absolutely agree — 1097 (34.1%)
2 agree — 609 (18.9%)
3 no opinion — 344 (10.7%)
4 disagree — 721 (22.4%)
5 absolutely disagree — 450 (14.0%)

D: Not a good idea; it is not a very sympathetic thing to do, and it might discourage visitors
1 absolutely agree — 552 (17.1%)
2 agree — 650 (20.2%)
3 no opinion — 481 (14.9%)
4 disagree — 976 (30.3%)
5 absolutely disagree — 562 (17.4%)

Figure 11.1 Employees' opinions on the charging of parking levies

11.2   Employees' opinions on parking charges: some general results

The parking survey[2] started with four propositions concerning a possible charging of parking fees by the Free University (abbreviated FU hereafter), for which respondents were asked to indicate on a 5 point scale to what extent they agree. The propositions were the following:

A.   *I think it is a good idea for the FU to charge for parking places: it costs money to supply parking space*
B.   *I think it is a good idea for the FU to charge for parking places: car usage should be discouraged*
C.   *I think it is not a good idea for the FU to charge for parking places: an employer is supposed to offer such facilities*
D.   *I think it is not a good idea for the FU to charge for parking places: it is not a very sympathetic thing to do, and it might discourage visitors*

---

[2] The total response to the complete survey was 1773 (52%) for the Academic Hospital and 1803 (43%) for the University, and hence 3582 (46%) in total. The University and the Hospital are located side to side, outside the city centre of Amsterdam, near a residential area. About 40% of the respondents usually use the car, and 30% the bicycle, in commuting. The remainder of the respondents uses public transport or other modes (walking, mopeds, etc.). From the respondents, 3221 persons filled out the parking survey partly (only the question related to attitudes), or completely.

The response to these four propositions is given in Figure 11.1. At first sight, the opinions seem quite evenly distributed. Especially the first two propositions receive about as much support as opposition. Concerning the other two propositions, the first receives more support than the second. Apparently, people do admit that they let their own interests prevail over others' interests. Finally, it may be noted that the issue as such is generally believed to be sufficiently important to formulate a clear opinion on: for each of the propositions, the 'no opinion' option has the lowest score.

	B	C	D
A	0.59 (51.49)	−0.67 (−65.03)	−0.27 (−17.86)
B		−0.58 (−51.59)	−0.21 (−13.86)
C			0.25 (16.38)

Table 11.1   Rank correlations of attitudes: Kendall's τ (t-value)

Table 11.1 gives the rank correlations between the responses to these four propositions. It is clear that the responses are strongly correlated. This shows that respondents often consistently indicate either to be in favour of, or opposed to parking policies. However, the response to proposition D (the impact on visitors) is less strongly correlated to the responses on the other propositions.

To obtain some insight into the general opinions on the charging of parking levies by the FU, the scores on each of the four propositions were assigned values from 1 (absolutely agree) to 5 (absolutely disagree). By adding the scores for A and B, and subtracting those for C and D, a 17-points scale is created. A value of −8 indicates an extreme preference for the levying of parking charges, while a value of +8 indicates the opposite.

Of course, this procedure has some theoretical drawbacks. First, the scores measured on the four questions are of an ordinal rather than a cardinal nature, implying by definition that they cannot be added. Secondly, this procedure ignores possible arguments in favour of or against parking levies that have not been asked for in the survey. Notwithstanding these drawbacks, the procedure yields a convenient summary statistic, which − if handled with caution − may be expected to reflect the general opinion on parking charges in a sufficiently accurate way. Also the high rank correlations in Table 11.1 to some extent support the assumption of the existence of a general opinion towards parking policies. Figure 11.2 gives the distribution of the generalized opinion, which is again remarkably evenly distributed: the median value is at the opinion of 0 (implying indifference towards the levying of parking charges). The peaks in Figure

11.2 are presumably due to people being inclined to indicate either extreme, or moderate opinions.

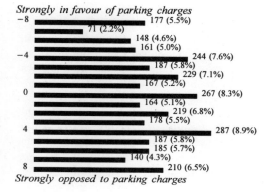

Figure 11.2 Generalized opinions on the charging of parking levies

The seemingly even distribution in Figure 11.2 is disturbed quite drastically when the respondents are classified along relevant distinct criteria. In Figure 11.3, the respondents are divided into two groups: those who most often use the car for commuting ('regular car users' in the sequel), and those who most often use alternative transport, such as public transport or bicycles.

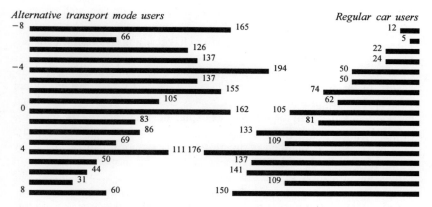

Figure 11.3 Generalized opinions on the charging of parking levies; alternative transport mode versus regular car users

Figure 11.3 clearly demonstrates that respondents usually commuting by car are generally opposed to the usage of parking charges, whereas the opposite holds for those usually commuting by alternative transport modes. Indeed, the right-hand side of Figure 11.3 more or less repeats the pattern depicted in Figure 10.3 for the social feasibility of road pricing. Of course, there is nothing unexpected about this result. However, it is in some respects revealing. When considering the social feasibility of regulation of road transport externalities, the attention is usually focused on (certain groups of) road users (see also Chapter 10). Of course, this is an important issue. Moreover, when studying the regulation of an intra-sectoral externality such as congestion, it is likely to be sufficient to study road users' opinions only, as both the benefits and the costs of such policies will generally remain within the population of road users − although this needs not hold for the allocation of contingent regulatory tax revenues. However, as far as the regulation of environmental externalities is concerned, consideration of merely road users' opinions may indeed give an overly pessimistic view of the social feasibility of such policies. This implies in the first place that a government wishing to assess a society's 'demand for environmental regulation' may underestimate the benefits that other groups may derive from environmental policies. These other groups will generally not be indifferent. Secondly, the overall social feasibility of environmental regulation may certainly benefit from making the public at large aware of the favourable impacts of such policies, hence creating a larger social momentum for environmental regulation.

Apparently, the respondents' mode of transport is an important element explaining their opinions on parking charges; but presumably, it is not the only relevant variable. The next section aims at providing a more complete picture of the underlying factors determining the opinions on such policies.

11.3   Employees' opinions on parking charges: a multinomial ordered probit analysis

A statistical analysis of 'soft' data such as opinions on a certain policy is, because of the subjectivity of the data, not a very easy task. An additional problem in the present data set is the absence of some individual characteristics that may be relevant as explanatory factors for the opinions studied (such as age, gender, type of job, income, or number of years employed). Still, a number of interesting observations can be made by means of statistical analysis. This is in particular important because it enables identification of the characteristics that cause a commuter to be more, or less, opposed to parking policies. This information on opinions, in turn, although perhaps not readily translatable into actual behaviour, may help the employer in deciding whether to use parking policies, and − if so − to introduce parking policies in such a way that the resistance among employees is minimized.

Because of the nature of the dependent variable, an ordered probit model was used (see Section 10.4.5). The model aims to determine the impact of the following variables on the response to the four propositions (where italics indicate the terms used in the sequel when referring to these variables): (1) the question of whether the respondent has a car at her/his *disposal* for commuting; (2) the question of whether the respondent is a *regular car user* when commuting; (3) the physical *distance* between home and work (measured in road-kilometres); (4) the *travel time ratio* of public transport/road transport; (5) the number of days per week that the respondent is actually working at the FU (*# working days*); (6) the question of whether the respondent indicated that she/he sees parking as a major problem of car usage in commuting (*parking problem*); (7) the question of whether the respondent currently uses a *parking place* provided by the employer; and finally (8) two dummy variables, distinguishing employees at the *university* and *elsewhere* (a very small group) from those in the reference group working at the hospital. Except for *distance, travel time ratio* and *# working days*, each of these explanatory variables are dummy variables, with a value of 1 denoting a confirmative response.

The first two variables capture the respondents' 'car-mindedness'. Variables 3 and 4 indicate to what extent respondents are (or think they are) dependent on the car for their commuting. Finally, variables 5−7 capture the extent to which one is dependent on the FU's parking policy. For each of the variables, a negative relation between its value and the extent to which a respondent agrees with the usage of parking fees can be expected, except for the *university* and *elsewhere* dummies, for which there is no *a priori* expectation. Hence, positive ß's are expected for the 'good idea' propositions A and B, and negative ß's for the 'not a good idea' propositions C and D.

Clearly, most of the above mentioned variables will have a potential impact on the opinions only if the respondent is a 'choice commuter'; that is, if he or she can choose between the car and alternative transport modes for commuting. Therefore, the model was estimated only for those respondents who do have a car at their disposal for the morning commute, and for whom *disposal* is therefore equal to 1. In order to show the impact of this dummy itself, it can be reported here that the difference between the average opinion of the 2209 respondents with a car at their disposal and that of the 938 others is (3.33−2.46=) 0.87 for proposition A; (3.41−2.25=) 1.16 for proposition B; (2.36−3.26=) −0.90 for proposition C; and (3.03−3.28=) −0.25 for proposition D. These differences are conform expectations, and the t-tests have shown that they are all significant at the 0.001 level.

A complication for the statistical analysis of the choice travellers' opinions is caused by the *regular car user* dummy, which was shown to be an important explanatory variable for the generalized opinions in Figure 11.3. When including this variable in the estimation, one has to take account of the possibility that it might 'absorb' some of the explanatory

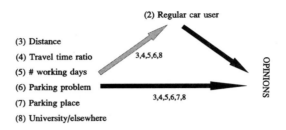

(2) Regular car user

(3) Distance
(4) Travel time ratio   3,4,5,6,8
(5) # working days
(6) Parking problem
(7) Parking place   3,4,5,6,7,8
(8) University/elsewhere

OPINIONS

Figure 11.4   The full recursive model for choice commuters'
opinions on parking policies

power of other independent variables, such as *distance* or *travel time ratio*, because of the expected impact of these variables on modal choice itself. In order to be able to check whether this is the case, a logit estimation was performed first, identifying the impact of the other explanatory variables on the *regular car user* dummy. The full recursive model then becomes as depicted in Figure 11.4. The black arrows represent the multinomial ordered probit analysis of the choice travellers' opinions on parking policies. The shaded arrow represents the additional logit analysis, the results of which might help in understanding the explanatory power of the various variables in the ordered probit estimation.

The results of the logit estimation are given in Table 11.2. It turns out that, apart from the *university* and *elsewhere* dummies, it is in particular the *travel time ratio* that is a significant factor in explaining why FU employees become a regular car user in commuting. Furthermore, respondents who see parking as a problem when commuting by car are significantly less likely to be a regular car user. Both findings conform the expectation. *Distance* as such is an insignificant explanatory factor in this estimation, which is due to a relatively weak presence of regular car users for both the relatively short (cyclists) and the relatively long distances (train). The *parking place* dummy was not included here, as the causality of any significant correlation would be disputable.

Tables 11.3a and 11.3b give the results of the multinomial ordered probit analysis of the choice commuters' response to the four propositions. The question of whether the respondent is a *regular car user* turns out to be the most significant factor in the explanation of opinions on parking levies for the first three propositions, with the expected signs. Moreover, the strongest discrepancy between regular car users' and others' opinions is found for the proposition that car usage should be discouraged (B), indicating that there is little hope for a voluntary reduction of car usage in commuting.

	ß	t-value	sign. t[#]
Distance	0.00	0.62	0.541
Travel time ratio[***]	0.58	7.13	0.000
# working days	−0.05	−1.08	0.281
Parking problem[***]	−0.77	−7.80	0.000
University[***]	−1.10	−10.60	0.000
Elsewhere[**]	−0.43	−2.57	0.010
Constant	0.43	1.39	0.166
Measures of fit:			
likelihood ratio χ^2 (sign.)	213 (0.000)		
−2 log likelihood full model	2610		
−2 log likelihood restricted model	2823		
pseudo R^2	0.08		

N = 2209
[#] Two sided test for significance of t
[*] Significant at the 0.1 level
[**] Significant at the 0.05 level
[***] Significant at the 0.01 level

*Table 11.2   Logit estimation of the choice for car
(for 'choice commuters')*

Secondly, it is remarkable that for each of the four propositions, there exist significant differences between respondents working at the hospital (the reference group), the *university*, and *elsewhere*. In cases A−C, those working at the hospital appear to be significantly more opposed to parking charges than the rest of the respondents. However, in the case of proposition D (the impact on visitors), the opposite occurs. The general relative opposition against parking policies at the hospital most probably reflects that it is more difficult for employees at the hospital to find a parking place near their work location, partly due to the visitors of the hospital using the available space. This could also be the reason for their smaller concern with visitors (proposition D). The hospital attracts more visitors than the university, which may cause its employees to feel as if they are having to compete for parking space with visitors more strongly than at the university. If anything, these differences demonstrate that the opinions on the type of measures considered may certainly vary from organization to organization, depending on more characteristics, which may be of a social, cultural and presumably also organizational nature, than just those directly related to car ownership and usage. In addition to the differences in opinions, Table 11.2 shows that employees at the hospital are more inclined to be a regular car user than others.

	Opinions on proposition A: Good idea; costs money[A]			Opinions on proposition B: Good idea; car use[B]		
	ß	t-value	sign. t[#]	ß	t-value	sign. t[#]
Regular car user	0.743	14.08	***0.000	1.053	20.18	***0.000
Distance	0.002	2.36	**0.018	0.004	4.03	***0.000
Travel time ratio	0.012	0.29	0.770	−0.007	−0.17	0.867
# working days	0.052	1.92	*0.055	0.062	2.33	**0.020
Parking problem	0.174	3.54	***0.000	0.103	2.10	**0.036
Parking place	−0.017	−0.28	0.782	0.051	0.80	0.423
University	−0.408	−7.54	***0.000	−0.406	−7.53	***0.000
Elsewhere	−0.261	−3.14	***0.002	−0.219	−2.73	***0.006
Constants:						
α_1	−0.441	−2.62	0.009	−0.436	−2.62	0.009
α_2	0.336	2.00	0.046	0.359	2.18	0.029
α_3	0.557	3.31	0.001	0.740	4.49	0.000
α_4	1.206	7.10	0.000	1.544	9.24	0.000
Measures of fit:						
lik. rat. χ^2 (sign.)	350 (0.000)			576 (0.000)		
−2 log. lik. full	6139			6013		
−2 log. lik. rest.	6489			6589		
pseudo R^2	0.05			0.09		

N = 2128

[A] I think it is a good idea for the FU to charge for parking places: it costs money to supply them
[B] I think it is a good idea for the FU to charge for parking places: car usage should be discouraged
[#] Two sided test for significance of t
[*] Significant at the 0.1 level
[**] Significant at the 0.05 level
[***] Significant at the 0.01 level

Table 11.3a Results of the multinomial ordered probit analyses of the choice commuters' opinions on parking policies for propositions A and B

	Opinions on proposition C: Not a good idea; employer[C]			Opinions on proposition D: Not a good idea; not sympathetic[D]		
	ß	t-value	sign. t[#]	ß	t-value	sign. t[#]
Regular car user	−0.756	−14.13	***0.000	−0.199	−3.88	***0.000
Distance	−0.004	−3.53	***0.000	−0.000	−0.42	0.673
Travel time ratio	−0.003	−0.07	0.941	−0.031	−0.80	0.424
# working days	−0.059	−2.14	**0.032	−0.084	−3.38	***0.001
Parking problem	−0.166	−3.34	***0.001	0.015	0.32	0.752
Parking place	−0.091	−1.38	0.166	0.062	0.98	0.326
University	0.588	10.65	***0.000	−0.335	−6.32	***0.000
Elsewhere	0.356	4.25	***0.000	−0.290	−3.52	***0.000
Constants:						
α_1	−0.925	−5.45	0.000	−1.606	−10.03	0.000
α_2	−0.324	−1.92	0.055	−0.962	−6.10	0.000
α_3	−0.056	−0.33	0.739	−0.596	−3.79	0.000
α_4	0.799	4.70	0.000	0.334	2.11	0.035
Measures of fit:						
lik. rat. χ^2 (sign.)		437 (0.000)			61 (0.000)	
−2 log. lik. full		5736			6619	
−2 log. lik. rest.		6173			6680	
pseudo R^2		0.07			0.01	

N = 2128

[C] I think it is not a good idea for the FU to charge for parking places: an employer is supposed to offer such facilities

[D] I think it is not a good idea for the FU to charge for parking places: it is not a very sympathetic thing to do, and it might discourage visitors

[#] Two-sided test for significance of t

[*] Significant at the 0.1 level

[**] Significant at the 0.05 level

[***] Significant at the 0.01 level

Table 11.3b Results of the multinomial ordered probit analyses of the choice commuters' opinions on parking policies for propositions C and D

Next, the travel *distance* is significant, and has the expected sign, for propositions A−C. The same holds, for each of the propositions, for the respondents' *number of working days*. Given the statistical insignificance of these variables in the logit model, it turns out that they only have a direct impact on the opinions on parking policies, and no significant impact on modal choice. The *travel time ratio*, in contrast, is not significant in any of the cases. Apparently, the relative advantage of car use compared to public transport is already fully captured by its impact on modal choice (see Table 11.2), and has no additional effect on the opinions.

The dummy *parking problem* is significant, with the sign according to the prior expectation, for propositions A−C. This shows that those who face difficulties finding a parking place in the morning commute are quite reluctant to pay for such a parking place, presumably because they feel they already face 'time costs' in the process of having their cars parked. The logistic regression in addition shows that people who see parking as a problem in commuting by car are less inclined to be a regular car user (see Table 11.2). It is remarkable that this dummy is completely insignificant for proposition D. Apparently, these respondents are concerned with their own difficulties of finding a parking place, and do not at all distinguish themselves from other respondents when it comes to the impact of parking charges on the FU's visitors. Surprisingly, the dummy representing the current usage of a *parking place* offered by the FU has no significant impact.

Finally, when comparing the measures of goodness of fit, it turns out that the response to proposition B ('car usage should be reduced') produces the best results; whereas the response to proposition D ('impact on visitors') is the most difficult to explain statistically. For each of the four propositions, the likelihood ratios indicate that the estimated models do make sense; although, as in the previous chapter, the overall fit is not impressive. Again, it is only the parameter estimates, and significance, that is relevant in these estimations.

In summary, the results in the first place indicate that respondents who do have a car at their disposal for commuting are more opposed to parking policies than others. Next, for the choice commuters, the most significant explanatory variable for their opinions on parking policies is the *regular car user* dummy. *Distance* and *# working days* are also significant factors, whereas they are not significant in determining whether one becomes a regular car user. The opposite holds for *travel time ratio*, where the contingent impact on opinions is fully captured by its effect on modal choice. The *parking problem*, *university* and *elsewhere* dummies are significant factors in both estimations, showing that apart from their impact via modal choice, they have additional explanatory power for the opinions. Therefore, from the viewpoint of feasibility, a quite pessimistic picture

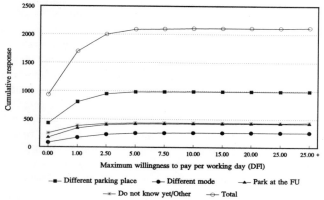

Figure 11.5 Cumulative maximum willingness to pay per working day for a parking place offered by the FU, and second-choice alternatives (total population, unweighted)

emerges: those commuters who are responsible for the highest numbers of car-kilometres per week (regular car users, located relatively far away and commuting relatively many times a week) have the strongest opposition against parking charges at the FU. In order to assess whether it is still worthwhile to pursue such policies, the next section will discuss the expected effectiveness of regulatory parking policies at the FU.

11.4   The effectiveness of regulatory parking policies at the FU

This section addresses the potential effectiveness of regulatory parking policies conducted by the FU in reducing car usage in its employees' commute. For that purpose, respondents who do at least sometimes use the car in the morning commute were asked for their maximum willingness to pay (WTP) for a parking place offered by the FU, assuming that no restitution is possible. A simple payment card method was used, with prices ranging from DFl 0.00 up to DFl 25.00 or more per working day (see Figure 11.5 for the exact values used).[3] In addition, respondents were asked to indicate their most likely behaviourial response in case of parking fees exceeding their WTP. This question was completed by 2116 respondents.

Figure 11.5 shows the unweighted cumulative response: for each parking fee, along the horizontal axis, the curve labelled 'Total' gives the

---

[3]The exchange rate of the Dutch guilder (DFl) is DFl 2.06 = 1 ECU.

number of respondents for whom that fee is equal to, or larger than, the maximum WTP indicated on the payment card. Hence, if each of the 2116 respondents would be present at the FU at a certain day, an anti-clockwise 90° rotation of this upper curve would, after replacing the values y along the vertical axis of Figure 11.5 by $(2116 - y)$, give the inverse demand curve for parking places offered by the FU (postponing the issue of biased WTP response to Section 11.5). In Figure 11.6 (Section 11.5), such a transformation is depicted for the demand for parking places per week, which is a more meaningful base for a demand curve than the unweighted response. The upper curve in Figure 11.5 thus gives an indication of the monetary value of the respondents' surpluses derived from commuting by car and parking at the FU for free, compared to choosing their second-choice alternatives, since the derived demand curve for parking places is simply the demand for trips minus the marginal private costs for travelling, hence representing consumers' surplus in case parking costs are equal to zero (Chapter 6).

The nature of the second-choice alternatives is given in the other curves in Figure 11.5. The shares of the four options distinguished remain rather constant along the horizontal axis. About 50% of the respondents indicate that they will look for a different parking place in the neighbourhood of the FU when the parking fee exceeds their WTP. Given the location of the FU, near a large residential area, a considerable share of these respondents will presumably indeed succeed in finding a parking place in the area around the FU. Only 12% of the respondents will choose an alternative transport mode, usually cycling or public transport. The other 40% is evenly distributed among those who do not know yet what to do in such a case, and those who will park their car at the parking facilities of the FU despite the excessive price. These latter respondents either have a WTP which is very carefully chosen between two values given on the payment card, or did not understand the question correctly: they apparently have a WTP higher than what they indicated on the payment card.

The results in Figure 11.5 cast serious doubt on the effectiveness of regulatory parking policies at the FU. The picture becomes even more dramatic when considering the impact of parking fees on car mobility, measured in weekly vehicle-kilometres. When considering the regular car users only, and after weighting their response by the number of working days at the FU and twice the commuting distance to account for round trips, it turns out that only 3.5% of the affected regular vehicle-kilometres will be diverted to alternative transport modes. About 50% of the affected regular vehicle-kilometres is generated by respondents who will look for a different parking place.[4] As far as the remaining regular vehicle kilometres are concerned (the categories 'Park at the FU' and 'Do not know yet/Other'), the intended reaction to prohibitive parking fees is not clear. After proportionally dividing these respondents among the two ultimate options, it is found that 93.5% of the affected regular vehicle-kilometres will be diverted to different parking places, and 6.5% to alternative transport modes, including carpooling. These figures are quite insensitive to the value of the parking fee considered. This measure of 'relative effectiveness' of 6.5% is very low, and this is a direct consequence of the fact that the policy is easily avoided by choosing another parking place. It may be noted that an unavoidable financial incentive by the FU, such as relative reductions of commuting allowances for solo-driving car users compared to allowances for carpoolers and public transport users, would have a much higher relative effectiveness in affecting the number of vehicle-kilometres.

As noted before, the WTP response can be used to derive various demand relations. An important summary statistic associated with demand relations is the elasticity of demand η, defined as the percentual change in demand (N) due to a one percent change in price P: $\eta = \partial N/\partial P \cdot P/N$. The elasticity of demand is usually specific to the particular point of the demand curve that is evaluated. For instance, for a constant slope (linear) demand function, demand elasticity runs from zero at the intercept with the horizontal axis to minus infinity at the intercept with the vertical axis.

	1 Unweighted	2 Parking places at FU	3 Parking places at FU[1]	4 Car trips	5 Car trips[1]	6 Veh. kms.	7 Veh. kms.[1]
Total	−1.156	−2.111	−2.055	−0.027	−0.037	−0.018	−0.029
Subgroups: Alternative transport	−0.737	−1.909	−1.759				
Alternative parking place	−1.255	−2.035	−1.798				
Other	−1.321	−2.240	−2.386				

[1]   Corrected for strategic bias (see Section 11.5)

Table 11.4   Demand elasticities implied by the WTP response

In Table 11.4, the elasticities of demand implied by the WTP response is given for a number of demand relations, evaluated at the parking fee level

---

[4]The extent to which the associated search processes in themselves will subsequently lead to more vehicle-kilometres is then of course an interesting side issue; but it is difficult to consider without speculation given the available information.

of DFl. 1. The first column gives the elasticities of the 'demand curve' based on the unweighted data (Figure 11.5), and the second column after weighting by the number of working days, thus giving the weekly demand for parking places at the FU. Both for total demand and for the three sub-groups distinguished, it turns out that demand is more elastic after weighting by the number of working days. This is plausible, as it merely indicates that more frequent commuters would respond more strongly to price changes than others.

Turning to the sub-division in user groups, those who have indicated switching towards alternative transport modes have the most inelastic demand, followed by those who will seek a different parking spot and finally those who belong to the joint rest category for which the second choice is not known (don't know yet/other/park at the FU). This suggests that the switch to alternative transport, even when it is preferred to seeking another parking place as a second alternative, is considered a more difficult one, requiring a larger financial incentive, than the switch to another parking place. The elasticities for the rest group can presumably be explained by the fact that these respondents did not seriously consider the alternative choice they will have to make, hence overstating their elasticity of demand.

Since the group that will choose alternative transport is relatively small, it should be no surprise that the demand for car trips with respect to parking charges, in the fourth column of Table 11.4, is quite inelastic (to derive this elasticity, the respondents for whom the second choice is not known are again proportionately divided among alternative transport and alternative parking place). Even more inelastic is the demand for vehicle-kilometres with respect to parking charges in the sixth column, which is in accordance with the findings for opinions discussed in the previous section.

The elasticities in the fourth and sixth column in Table 11.4 paint a far less favourable picture than do those in the studies reviewed by Willson and Shoup (1990), which range from -0.1 to -0.68 for car trips. There is a number of potential reasons for this discrepancy. The most important one is undoubtedly related to neighbourhood parking. As this phenomenon is only briefly mentioned by Willson and Shoup (1990), it is presumably not a relevant option for the case studies reviewed in their paper. Secondly, it may be hypothesized that some differences between the present case and the typical North American situation may play a role. For instance, whereas in the studies reviewed in Willson and Shoup (1990) the single most important alternative is carpooling, only 0.6% of the FU employees mention this as their second alternative. This may be due to various specific circumstances, such as a relatively flexible working hours regime, especially at the university, and the relative attractiveness of other transport modes (public transport, cycling). Furthermore, it should be borne in mind that in the initial situation, only 40% of the respondents are regular car commuters. Presumably, this figure is much higher in the typical North American situation. As a consequence, one might suspect that in the initial situation at the FU, a considerable pre-selection process has already taken place, which causes the current group of regular car users to be those who indeed have a relatively strong need or desire to commute by car. Thirdly, the elasticities may be biased because of strategic response. This possibility will be dealt with in the next section.

In summary, it does not seem to be a good idea to stimulate the intended shift in the modal split of the FU's employees from car to alternative transport modes by means of regulatory parking policies. Apart from a very modest reduction in vehicle-kilometres, this will mainly result in a considerable shift of the 'parking burden' from the FU onto the surrounding area, with an expectedly negative impact on the FU's local image. Unless more stringent parking policies are to be implemented in the FU's neighbourhood, such a policy seems no fruitful option. However, the fact that regulatory parking policies by the FU cannot be used as a 'stick' in affecting the employees' commuting behaviour does of course not imply that it could not be used as a 'carrot'. The most logical option in this respect, unfortunately not covered by the survey, seems to offer cheap or free, and perhaps guaranteed, parking places for carpoolers. Since 44% of the regular car users indicated that they see parking as a major problem of car usage, such a measure may have some potential, especially since the practically unavoidable time loss associated with carpooling could in that way at least to some extent be compensated.

11.5 An analysis of the willingness to pay for a parking place

WTP data such as those discussed above always contain some particular inherent unreliability, as they are not based on actual behaviour. At best, WTP data reflect intended market behaviour; however, the data may additionally be biased when respondents exhibit strategic behaviour. Strategic responses can for instance be expected when respondents foresee that the outcomes of the survey may be used in actual policy formulation. In the present context, this would lead respondents to give a low bid when they foresee the FU basing their parking charges on the outcomes of this study. A specific form of biased bidding arises when respondents express their dislike of paying for the good in question by giving a very low WTP, which would lead to an additional downwards bias in the WTP estimates. This phenomenon is usually referred to as 'protest bidding'. This section investigates the plausibility of the WTP responses discussed above. As the two sources of downwards bias in the WTP response just mentioned are hard or even impossible to disentangle, the response will be tested for a general downwards strategic bias, which may be caused by protest bidding, or by an attempt to make the employer set lower parking fees, or both.

This exercise is interesting not only for the primary reason of assessing the impact of a number of potential explanatory variables on the willingness to pay for a parking place. It may also give some indication of the role of strategic response and protest bidding in studies based on contingent valuation methods (CVM) in general. CVM surveys are often used for the valuation of environmental amenities (see Mitchell and Carson, 1989). In contrast to many other studies, here the stated preference results can be compared with revealed preference data for a specific subset of the respondents.

In order to obtain some insight into the factors determining the willingness to pay for a parking place, including the role of strategic bidding, the WTP responses were regressed on a number of potential explanatory variables. The strategic bidding effect was captured by including the generalized opinion (see Figure 11.2) as one of the explanatory variables. The hypothesis is that the impact of this generalized opinion on biased bidding is not symmetric. Whereas a strong opposition against parking charges may indeed cause respondents to mention a lower than their true WTP, the opposite of respondents boosting their true WTP, because they agree with the instrument of parking charges, seems far less plausible. The reverse causality is more likely in these cases: the fact that one can afford a relatively high bid for a parking place may lead such respondents to be in favour of parking charges, because this might increase their chances of receiving a parking place for the money they are willing to pay for it. This however, is not strategic bidding, as the bid then still reflects true WTP. For this reason, the generalized opinion was rescaled to what will be called the opposition index. This index is equal to the generalized opinion for values greater than or equal to zero, and is kept equal to zero for negative values of the generalized opinion. With ordinary least squares, the following relation was subsequently estimated for the regular car users (with two-sided t-statistics and significance between parentheses):

$$
\begin{aligned}
\text{WTP} = \quad & -0.166 \cdot \text{Opposition index } (-12.38,\ 0.000) + 0.001 \cdot \text{Distance } (0.54;\ 0.590) \\
& + 0.052 \cdot \text{Travel time ratio } (0.84;\ 0.403) - 0.188 \cdot \# \text{ working days } (-4.63; \\
& 0.000) - 0.169 \cdot \text{Parking problem } (-2.15;\ 0.032) + 0.400 \cdot \text{University } (4.75; \\
& 0.000) + 0.298 \cdot \text{Elsewhere } (2.30;\ 0.022) + 1.948 \ (7.62;\ 0.000) \\
& R^2 = 0.16^5
\end{aligned}
$$

---

[5] A regression of the, from a theoretical point of view, less attractive model with the *generalized opinion* instead of the *opposition index* yields comparable results. The coefficient of the generalized opinion is somewhat lower (-0.153); the t-value raises to -15.89. The R^2 increases up to 0.21. The better statistic fit is presumably caused by correlation due to the reversed causal relation described in the main text, with high WTP respondents being in favour of parking charges because they expect to increase their chances of finding a parking place.

This simple regression offers some surprising insights. First of all, the opposition index turns out to be a very important factor for the explanation of the stated preference WTP. The more one is opposed to parking policies, the lower the bid. This strongly suggests the presence of biased WTP responses.[6]

The idea of biased bidding is further supported by the sign and significance of the *parking problem* dummy. Respondents who have indicated that they face difficulties finding a parking place in the morning commute have a signicantly lower willingness to pay for a parking place. This, of course, is at odds with any economic logic, which would predict a higher willingness to pay for a good with a higher value (a parking place if one generally finds it hard to find one) than for a good with a lower value (a parking place if one generally finds it easy to find one). Apparently, the regular car user does not consider a parking place as a normal economic good. Rather, these results, and those in Section 11.3, indicate that the regular car user, although needing a parking place for her/his commute, actually finds the supply of parking space mainly to be the employer's responsibility, and is not willing to pay (much) for its usage.

Next, the impact of the variables *distance* and *travel time ratio*, although having the expected sign, is not significant in the determination of the WTP. The # *working days* is significant, and has a negative sign: the more often one is present at the FU, the less one is willing to pay, per working day, for a parking place. This is presumably due to some budget effect. Unfortunately, incomes are not included in the data set. However, the sign of this parameter suggests that the number of working days at the FU is more related to the question of whether respondents work at home or somewhere else on other working days, than that it is related to overall income, in which case the sign of the parameter might also have been positive. Finally, in line with the findings mentioned in Section 11.3, the WTP is significantly lower for respondents at the hospital than for those working at the *university* and *elsewhere*.

---

[6]It is of course not unambiguous whether the relation between the opposition index and the WTP is entirely due to strategic bias. For the same reason mentioned above when explaining the choice for the opposition index instead of the full range generalized opinion, also here the causality could actually be of the reverse nature. Then, a small budget would lead respondents to be able to make only a small bid, and the opposition against parking charges could then reflect the fear of being priced off the parking market. Then, the bid would reflect the true WTP, and would not be biased because of protest bidding. However, given the generally low levels of the WTPs (see Figure 5.4), and the fact that free parking space is available in the area around the FU, this does not seem to be very likely.

It is perhaps worth mentioning here that estimations with the respondents subdivided according to their second-favourite alternatives to parking at the FU did not yield any significantly better results. In other words, the WTP response does not vary with the alternative that respondents have in mind.

Apart from the regression discussed above, there is a second possibility of checking the WTP responses for strategic bidding. In particular, it is possible to compare the WTP reported by respondents who have indicated that they usually park at a parking place at the FU with the prices actually charged. When the survey was held, these prices were DFl 2.50 per day; DFl 12.50 for a monthly ticket and DFl 120 for a yearly ticket. The latter two would, for full-time workers working on average 20 days a month and 240 days a year, result in daily prices of DFl 0.63 and DFl 0.50, respectively. Logically speaking then, respondents with a WTP of DFl 0.00 will not park at this parking place. However, it turns out that, among the 421 respondents regularly using these parking places, no less than 159 (38%) report a maximum willingness to pay for a parking place of DFl 0.00. Clearly, also this observation strongly suggests the presence of a strategic bias in the WTP responses.

It is tempting somehow to try and correct the WTP responses for this strategic bidding bias. The most straightforward way of doing so is by adding a sum of 0.166 times the opposition index to the reported maximum willingness to pay, on basis of the above mentioned parameter estimate. In that case, the number of unexplainable parkers at the specific parking place reduces to 47 (11.2%), which is a significant improvement when compared to the 38% obtained with the uncorrected data. In Table 11.4, the impacts of this correction on demand elasticities is given. For the demand for parking places (columns 2 and 3), the impact is a slight decrease of the demand elasticity. For the demand for car trips and vehicle-kilometres, the elasticities with respect to parking charges increase.[7] Hence, this correction indeed boosts the elasticity of the demand for trips a bit further up to the order of magnitude mentioned by Willson and Shoup (1990), but the 'neighbourhood parking leak' remains considerable.

---

[7]The reader may wonder why, due to the correction, the elasticities of demand for car trips and vehicle-kilometres *increase*, while the elasticity of demand for parking places at the FU *decreases*. This has to do with the definition of demand elasticity. Each of the demand curves considered gets flatter at DFL 1.00 due to the correction, as the number of respondents with a zero WTP reduces after the correction (compare Figure 11.6). However, for the elasticity of demand for parking places, this effect is dominated by the higher 'corrected' level of demand at DFl 1.00, leading to a smaller elasticity. For the demand for trips and vehicle-kilometres, the relative decline in demand at DFl 1.00 due to the correction is much smaller, and the impact of the flatter slope of the demand curve dominates.

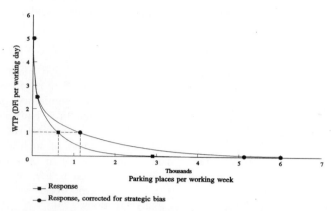

Figure 11.6 Demand curves for parking places at the FU: WTP response, and WTP after simple correction for protest response; regular car users weighted by presence

The regular car users' corrected and uncorrected demand curves for parking places at the FU are sketched in Figure 11.6. One should be cautious with the interpretation of these curves, not only because they are based on WTP data only, but also because the data are obtained in a context where car users are able to use alternative, free parking places in the neighbourhood of the employer. Nevertheless, it is clearly interesting to confront these two curves with the cost of supplying parking places.

Given the heavily regulated nature of the land market, it is difficult to determine the actual value of land in the neighbourhood of the FU. In a recent publication of the Dutch government (Tweede Kamer der Staten-Generaal, 1991–92), an average land value for parking space of DFl 250 per square meter (m²) for The Netherlands is used. The land used for a parking place of 12 m² would then represent a yearly value of DFl 240 (at an interest rate of 8%). With 250 working days a year, a daily price of about DFl 1 would compensate only for the land costs embodied in the parking place, excluding costs of construction and maintenance. Presumably, land values will be higher than the Dutch average in the area around the FU. Still, even with this conservative estimate, only 10% of the 'average' (weighted with the number of working days) regular car users are willing to pay these implicit costs of their modal choice according to the uncorrected stated preference data. After the simple correction for strategic bidding outlined above, this percentage increases to about 18%.

Therefore, proper pricing of parking space in itself may already have a considerable impact on the respondents' modal split decisions, before any additional regulatory fee aiming at a reduction in car use is included in such levies. However, it is clear that the success of such policies will strongly depend on the question of whether they are conducted on a sufficiently large spatial scale.

11.6 Conclusion

The foregoing analysis concerned the intersection of two main policy 'tracks' followed in The Netherlands for the containment of road transport externalities: transport plans at the firm level, and regulatory parking policies. The outcomes of a survey conducted at the Free University in Amsterdam were used to discuss the employees' opinions on regulatory parking policies at the firm level, and the effectiveness of such a policy. The outcomes of this survey can in many respects be taken as illustrative for comparable issues and obstacles to be encountered in the formulation of firm policies aiming at reducing car usage in the employees' commuting behaviour, for many organizations at many locations.

Concerning the social feasibility of regulatory parking policies by the FU, it was found that, although the overall generalized opinions are remarkably evenly distributed, regular car users are relatively strongly opposed to such measures, whereas the opposite holds for those usually commuting by alternative transport modes. Therefore, as far as the regulation of environmental externalities of road usage is concerned, consideration of merely road users' opinions may give an overly pessimistic picture of the social feasibility of such policies.

Section 11.3 presented a more refined statistical analysis of the factors determining employees' opinions. Such an identification of characteristics that cause a commuter to be more, or less, opposed to parking policies may help the employer in deciding whether to use parking policies in affecting the employees' modal choice, and − if so − to introduce it in such a way that the resistance among employees is minimized.

A first finding was that respondents who do have a car at their disposal for commuting are more opposed to parking policies than others. Current modal choice is the most significant variable in determining the choice commuters' opinions on parking policies. The recursive model of the opinions in addition revealed that it is in particular the relative attractiveness of modes (travel time ratio, the perceived difficulties in finding a parking place) that determines modal choice, whereas absolute characteristics of commuting behaviour, such as distance and the number of working days, have additional explanatory power for the opinions on parking policies. Hence, the data strongly suggest that commuting behaviour can be diverted into more favourable directions by supplying good quality alternatives. The analysis further indicates that employees' opinions on the type of measures considered may vary strongly between different organizations, depending on more characteristics, which may be of a social, cultural and presumably also organizational nature, than just those directly related to car ownership and car usage. The strongest discrepancy between regular car users' and the others' opinions is found for the proposition that car usage should be discouraged. This suggests that there is little hope for a voluntary reduction of car usage in commuting, and that hence stronger policies are needed to realize a favourable change in the existing commuting patterns.

However, although parking policies at larger spatial scales may be an effective means for reducing car usage, it does not seem a good idea for an individual firm to engage in more stringent parking policies. The analysis indicates that this may result in a considerable shift of the 'parking burden' from the firm onto the surrounding area, with an expectedly negative impact on the firm's local image. The implied demand elasticities of car trips and vehicle-kilometres with respect to parking charges are, accordingly, very low. Still, the fact that regulatory parking policies by the firm cannot be used as a 'stick' in affecting the employees' commuting behaviour does of course not imply that it could not be used as a 'carrot'. The most logical option in this respect seems to offer cheap or free, and perhaps guaranteed, parking places for carpoolers. Since the majority of the regular car users indicated that they see parking as a major problem of car usage, such a measure may have some potential, especially since the practically inevitable time loss associated with carpooling might then at least to some extent be compensated for. Individual firms wishing to use financial incentives for affecting their employees' commuting behaviour should look for unavoidable measures, for instance in the sphere of mode-specific commuting allowances, such as reductions of allowances for car users.

In Section 11.5, evidence for a considerable strategic bias in the WTP response for a parking place was found, which necessitates a correction procedure before using these data. This underlines the care that should be taken when dealing with hypothetical WTP data. Another conclusion from this section is that car users do not at all consider parking space, at least at the work location, as a normal economic good. They are in general opposed to the pricing of parking space; they also have a lower WTP when the actual value of a parking place is higher. Most regular car users have a WTP for a parking place that even falls short of its conservatively estimated land value. In accordance with the theory of externalities, individuals apparently do not regard unpriced economic goods from a scarcity perspective, and indeed may have to be 'trained' to do so. Given the finding that this is the case for land use, which is actually priced in many other situations, this may certainly be expected to hold true for environmental goods. Since favourable voluntary adaptations in commuting behaviour are not likely to materialize, it seems that such training is indeed needed in policies aiming at a reduction of road transport externalities.

PART IV

CONCLUSION

12 TOWARDS AN EFFICIENT AND SOCIALLY FEASIBLE REGULATION OF ROAD TRANSPORT EXTERNALITIES

The regulation of road transport externalities has come to the forefront as one of the most important issues in contemporary transport policies. Both intra-sectoral externalities of road transport, notably congestion and accidents, and inter-sectoral externalities, such as accidents, noise annoyance and environmental pollution, cause excessive social pressures, and only a few optimists would advocate a *laissez-faire* approach to these problems. More stringent regulation of these externalities seems both desirable and necessary; however, the design of such policies is often not straightforward and may therefore be the subject of heated debate. In the foregoing chapters, the regulation of road transport externalities was studied from the economic perspective. This chapter summarizes the most important findings, and will subsequently discuss a number of policy implications.

Chapter 2 discussed some conceptual issues concerning the external effects of road transport. Starting with the definition of externalities, it was assessed that transport does not yield any significant external benefits, whereas considerable external costs are involved, in particular in road transport. These externalities, as well as their regulation, can be considered from the equity as well as the allocative efficiency perspective. Unfortunately, there is no straightforward one-to-one mapping between these two viewpoints, which often gives rise to fuzzy discussions in policy debates. This distinction between allocative efficiency and equity is dealt with in the remainder of the book, where Part II primarily considered allocative efficiency of regulation, while Part III was dedicated to the equity aspects and social feasibility of regulation.

Part II of the book paid attention to a number of peculiarities of road transport that make the sector differ from others, and therefore render common economic wisdom on the regulation of externalities of only limited use. In particular, only under rather stringent assumptions − such as first-best conditions elsewhere in the (spatio-) economic system, perfectly flexible regulatory policies for all road users and on the entire road network, and with full information − would the standard Pigouvian solution of marginal external cost pricing be sufficient to achieve optimality in externalities generated by road transport. Needless to say, these assumptions are usually not met in reality. Some consequences for the efficiency of regulation were investigated in Part II.

Chapter 3 focused on second-best alternatives to the first-best Pigouvian bench-mark policy, which do not allow to fully capture the heterogeneity that is likely to exist among road users, or to charge every single road user involved. Such crudeness in regulatory fees is likely to arise with many practical pricing strategies that have been advocated for the regulation of road transport externalities, such as parking fees, fuel taxes, peak hour permits, cordon charges or area licenses. The optimal second-best fees for such situations were derived and discussed, and a so-called 'index of relative welfare improvement' showed the impact of demand structures and marginal external cost differences across user groups on the efficiency of such second-best regulation.

Chapter 4 explicitly acknowledged the network environment in which road transport externalities arise, by studying the situation where regulation on a part of the network causes spill-overs on an unregulated part. In this case, the regulator has to trade off a number of 'sub-goals' contributing to the overall goal of efficient usage of the network, comprising overall demand as well as route split effects. As a consequence, the optimal second-best fee may actually turn out to be a subsidy. A simulation model showed the impact of a number of key parameters on the relative efficiency of such policies. Also private revenue maximizing tolling, not an unlikely situation in the future supply of road infrastructure, was considered. It was found that the intuitive expectation that it is 'good' for overall economic efficiency to restrict monopolistic power does certainly not necessarily hold for the control of congested networks.

Road traffic congestion is often only predictable to a limited extent. In such cases, information provision, for instance with ATIS (advanced travellers' information systems) may be used as a user friendly means of improving road network efficiency. Chapter 5 studied the relative efficiency of, and interaction between various information and pricing instruments for the regulation of stochastic congestion. Especially now that both the introduction of high quality information systems and the application of road pricing schemes may become reality in the foreseeable future, these are important matters that deserve careful evaluation. It was found that information provision and 'flat' tolling, based on expected rather than actual congestion, are highly complementary: the combination of these two instruments performs almost as well as the theoretical first-best solution of 'fine' tolling, based on actual congestion. Given the psychological advantages of flat tolling, related to the predictability and transparency of tolls, such a combination is likely to be more attractive than the use of fine tolls. The efficiency gains of flat tolling and information provision were found to be sub-additive in most cases, implying 'diminishing returns of regulation'.

Chapter 6 presented an economic analysis of parking policies, which is one of the main policies used in the Netherlands for the regulation of road transport. A simple diagrammatic model was used to illustrate three main advantages of parking fees compared to physical restrictions in parking space supply: an information argument, a temporal efficiency argument, and an inter-temporal efficiency argument. An urban model was subsequently presented which studied the spatial ins and outs of parking policies. In particular, it was studied in the context of the traditional mono-centric urban economic model how parking policies can be optimized by using spatially differentiated fees.

This spatial dimension of transport was explored further in Chapter 7, containing a spatial price equilibrium model for studying the interdependencies between transport, infrastructure and spatial economy in the formulation of environmental policies aiming at global sustainability targets. First-best and second-best policies were considered, allowing for endogenous environmental technologies. An endogenous 'shadow price of sustainability' arose from this model, which not only depends on the extent to which non-intervention emissions exceed the target, but also on the 'quality' of the environmental policies pursued to meet this target. Hence, this shadow price partly reflects the social costs of inefficient regulation.

Although the goal of allocative efficiency is an important one for the economic evaluation of the regulation of road transport externalities, the distributional aspects and social feasibility of regulation have proven to be at least as important in the practice of policy formulation. These issues were dealt with in Part III of the book.

Chapter 8 considered the welfare effects of an externality and its regulation for both the generators and the receptors. The analysis concentrated on the compatibility of optimization and compensation of external costs. An important implication of the external cost approach to environmental issues was stressed, namely that equal exposures to a physical effect imply, *ceteris paribus*, larger external costs for higher income groups. The unattractive policy implications of this often ignored feature are evident: an externality generating activity should, from the allocative efficiency point of view, preferably be located near lower income groups. The analysis subsequently focused on equity aspects between generator(s) and receptor(s) of external costs. In a static context, the compensation and optimization of an external cost are more likely to be compatible as long as the receptors are actively engaged in direct negotiations over this compensation, since otherwise they will not face the optimal incentive to undertake defensive measures. In a localized-dynamic context, however, compensation is incompatible with optimization. Victims in that case should even be charged for being a victim. Interestingly, Coasian negotiations, often thought of as relevant for small-number cases, were seen to be seriously undermined by induced strategic or free-rider behaviour in this case, rendering the Coasian solution non-optimal for the long-run regulation of localized undepletable externalities.

Chapter 9 studied the discrepancy between economic theory and practice of regulating road transport externalities from the viewpoint of the trade-off between efficiency, effectiveness and social feasibility of regulation. Since there is a certain limit to the freedom of a democratic government in formulating their regulatory policies, this is a highly important, but yet hardly explored research area. Unfortunately, there appears to be some inverse relation between the efficiency and effectiveness of regulation on the one hand, and its social feasibility on the other. However, the regulator is not merely restricted to making a negative trade-off between efficiency, effectiveness and social feasibility of regulation. From a more positive perspective, there appears to be room for strategies aiming at increasing the efficiency and effectiveness of regulation, given a certain social feasibility, and *vice versa*. Four important trajectories in this respect may be (1) the usage of tradable permits; (2) the usage of 'feebates'; (3) the formulation of well balanced mixes of second-best and third-best policies, approaching first-best standards as much as possible; and (4) 'ear-marking' of regulatory tax revenues.

Road pricing, for the purpose of managing road traffic congestion, is a striking example of the above mentioned tension between efficiency and social feasibility of regulation. Although being the theoretically speaking first-best solution to reduce excessive congestion, it has so far not received much support outside the academic world. Chapter 10 addressed the limited social feasibility of road pricing by analysing and discussing the results of a questionnaire that was held among morning peak road users in the Randstad area. As one might anticipate, it is mainly the financial redistributive impact of road pricing that determines road users' opinions on road pricing. This is in sharp contrast with the traditional economists' focus on allocative efficiency. Although road pricing will never become a popular instrument among road users, a number of encouraging findings for its social feasibility can be mentioned. In the first place, this feasibility increases with the severity of congestion, indicating that road pricing gets more acceptable to the public, the more it is needed. Moreover road pricing stands a greater chance of passing the test of democratic control provided it is embedded in a transparent policy package, including supply-side measures to reduce congestion, and clear tax reduction schemes that should both take away some of the road users' scepticism on regulatory taxation in general, and provide in particular lower income groups with enough benefits to take away some of the most urgent feelings of injustice. For instance, the regressive incidence of road pricing can be dampened by larger reductions in vehicle taxes for smaller vehicles; this, in turn, may prove to have a positive impact on the average fuel efficiency of the car fleet. Of course, additional benefits for cleaner cars *per se* could also be considered for such environmental purposes.

Moreover, the analysis in Chapter 11, concerning regulatory parking policies at the firm level, showed that consideration of road users' opinions only may give an overly pessimistic picture of the overall social feasibility of regulation. This is in particular relevant for environmental externalities, where the government may seek to increase the feasibility by convincing the public at large of the beneficial effects of such regulation. Another conclusion was that escaping behaviour may indeed seriously undermine the effectiveness of regulation. In the case considered, parking fees at the firm level will simply induce employees to park their cars in adjacent areas. As a large majority of road users turned out to have a willingness to pay for a parking place that even falls short of its land value, it was concluded that individuals indeed do not consider unpriced economic goods from a scarcity perspective. This may certainly hold true for environmental 'goods'.

Throughout the book, the complexity of regulating road transport externalities has been stressed. Numerous problems were found to be hidden by the most simple textbook representation of the Pigouvian solution to road transport externalities. These problems have given rise to the diversity in issues studied in this book. Although this diversity renders a general conclusion impossible, as it would necessarily lead to the sort of simplification that was proven inappropriate by the foregoing analyses, a number of more or less general policy lessons can be drawn on basis of the research discussed.

Road transport externalities pose excessive pressures on contemporary life in terms of congestion, emissions, accidents and noise annoyance; and more stringent regulation seems necessary. Given the derived demand for transport, this is not only so because of the current size of road transport externalities, but also because current mobility patterns provoke and facilitate shifts in the factors behind the demand of transport (for instance, in terms of spatial organization) that will undoubtedly negatively affect the effectiveness and social feasibility of future regulation. *Laissez-faire*, therefore, not only shifts the burden of some of the environmental externalities to future generations, it also leaves them with a mobility intensive socio-economic and spatio-economic structure that increases the difficulties they will face in regulating road transport externalities.

An important trade-off that has to be made is between the efficiency and social feasibility of regulation. A democratic government faces strong incentives to let the latter prevail over the former, and consequently, so far the record of policy achievements in terms of containing road transport externalities is not impressive. However, due to the size of the effects, and particularly due to various characteristics of the sector, any form of regulation other than based on economic principles, which is socially the least feasible type of regulation, is bound to lead to considerable economic losses. However disputable and limited the concept of Pareto efficiency for the overall evaluation of regulatory policies may be, it does guarantee least cost (or actually, maximum net benefit) solutions to externality regulation, and therefore avoids wasteful usage of scarce resources. It was found at various places that, the less close a regulatory policy is to the bench-mark of marginal external cost pricing, the larger such welfare losses will be. Governments seriously wanting to significantly reduce road transport externalities against any reasonable social cost therefore cannot do without financial incentives, and should carefully keep an eye on the first-best bench-mark in designing such policies in practice. In addition, more efficient regulation may turn out to be more socially feasible in the longer run, simply because achievements are made against lower social costs.

When formulating regulatory road transport policies, it should never be forgotten that the demand for road transport is a derived demand. Unless sufficient adaptations take place in the factors behind that demand, possibly stimulated by what was called 'indirect demand management' in Chapter 9, direct regulation of road transport is likely to be frustrated by inelasticity of demand, which lowers the social feasibility by increasing the distributive impact of regulatory taxation relative to the efficiency impact.[1] Likewise, supply-side measures, often the responsibility of governments themselves owing to the publicness of the goods concerned, should be used to mutually increase the efficiency and social feasibility of regulation.

A number of strategies to simultaneously meet certain standards of efficiency and social feasibility of direct demand regulation have been put forward. For regulatory taxes, ear-marking, such as tax variabilization and allocation of revenues for supply-side measures, seems to be an important strategic weapon; both on theoretical and empirical grounds. Apart from that, financial incentives with considerably smaller distributional impacts than Pigouvian taxes can be envisaged. Two of these are tradable permits and feebates. These instruments certainly deserve attention in future research on the regulation of road transport externalities.

This brings us to some possible directions for future research. It is clear that many of the analyses only provide a first step to considering the regulation of road transport externalities in more realistic settings than the simple textbook model. Many of the analyses in Part II could for instance be carried out on larger and more realistic networks. Although this is likely to result in models that cannot be solved analytically, it would clearly be

---

[1]However, in such cases, it will provide relatively stronger incentives to adopt, for instance, technological solutions (see Chapter 7).

interesting to apply the findings in Part II in simulation models of more complex networks. Apart from that, it may certainly prove worthwhile to repeat some of the simulations in Part II with differently shaped cost and demand curves. Empirical research into the nature of these curves may serve as a basis for such exercises.

Furthermore, on a more theoretical level, the modelling of congestion as such deserves more attention. Both the economically oriented rising cost curves approach followed in this book, and the more or less competing bottleneck approach, appear to have their own specific shortcomings. The approach followed in this book could be criticized on its static nature, whereas congestion obviously is a dynamic process. The bottleneck model, in contrast, has remarkable implications in that the optimal level of congestion is zero, and that the social feasibility of congestion pricing should not be a problem, because everybody is equally well off without and with optimal pricing before any redistribution of toll revenues has occurred. The integration of these two approaches would undoubtedly offer a fascinating challenge.

Next, it may prove worthwhile to introduce heterogeneity among road users in most of the models presented in Part II, where both efficiency and equity aspects of regulation could then be studied in more depth on basis of theoretical models.

The analysis in Chapter 7 on the issue of transport and sustainable development of course only provides a first theoretical framework. Dynamics, in this case, is the first enrichment that springs to mind. Apart from that, the whole issue of inter-sectoral and spatial interdependencies in the context of externality regulation clearly offers a field that requires many further research efforts.

Finally, the empirical investigation of the feasibility of regulation, such as presented in Chapters 10 and 11, also deserves much more attention, particularly as it may turn out to be the crucial success factor for regulatory policies. As a first step, feasibility concepts other than the narrowly defined social feasibility (the economic, technical, institutional, legislative, political and broad social feasibility; see Chapter 9) could be investigated.

Undoubtedly, the reader will be left with more open questions than these. Nevertheless, I sincerely hope that this book has answered more questions than it has raised but kept unanswered.

REFERENCES

Acutt, M.Z. (1996) "Modelling greenhouse gas emissions from cars in Great Britain" *Transportation Planning and Technology* forthcoming.

Arnott, R.J. (1979) "Unpriced transport congestion" *Journal of Economic Theory* **21** 294−316.

Arnott, R., A. de Palma and R. Lindsey (1990a) "Departure time and route choice for the morning commute" *Transportation Research* **24B** (3) 209−228.

Arnott, R., A. de Palma and R. Lindsey (1990b) "Economics of a bottleneck" *Journal of Urban Economics* **27** 11−30.

Arnott, R., A. de Palma and R. Lindsey (1991a) "A temporal and spatial equilibrium analysis of commuter parking" *Journal of Public Economics* **45** 301−335.

Arnott, R., A. de Palma and R. Lindsey (1991b) "Does providing information to drivers reduce traffic congestion?" *Transportation Research* **25A** (5) 309−318.

Arnott, R., A. de Palma and R. Lindsey (1992) "Route choice with heterogeneous drivers and group-specific congestion costs" *Regional Science and Urban Economics* **22** 71−102.

Arnott, R., A. de Palma and R. Lindsey (1993) "A structural model of peak-period congestion: a traffic bottleneck with elastic demand" *American Economic Review* **83** (1) 161−179.

Arnott, R., A. de Palma and R. Lindsey (1994) "The welfare effects of congestion tolls with heterogeneous commuters" *Journal of Transport Economics and Policy* **28** 139−161.

Atkinson, A.B. and J.E. Stiglitz (1980) *Lectures on Public Economics*. McGraw-Hill, London.

AVV (Adviesdienst Verkeer en Vervoer) (1995) *Verkeersgegevens; Jaarrapport 1994*. Ministerie van Verkeer en Waterstaat, DGR, Rotterdam.

Banister, D. and K.J. Button (1993a) "Environmental policy and transport: an overview". In: D. Banister and K.J. Button (eds.) (1993) *Transport, the Environment and Sustainable Development*. E & FN Spon, London.

Banister, D. and K.J. Button (eds.) (1993b) *Transport, the Environment and Sustainable Development*. E & FN Spon, London.

Barde, J.-P. and K.J. Button (1990) *Transport Policy and the Environment: Six Case Studies*. Earthscan, London.

Bator, F.M. (1958) "The anatomy of market failure" *Quarterly Journal of Economics* **72** 351−379.

Baumol, W.J. and W.E. Oates (1988) *The Theory of Environmental Policy*, second edition. Cambridge University Press, Cambridge.

Ben-Akiva, M., A. de Palma and I. Kaysi (1991) "Dynamic networks models and driver information systems" *Transportation Research* **25A** (5) 251−266.

Berechman, J. (1993) *Public Transit Economics and Deregulation Policy*. Studies in Regional Science and Urban Economics **23**. North-Holland, Amsterdam.

Bergstrom, T., L. Blume and H. Varian (1986) "On the private provision of public goods" *Journal of Public Economics* **29** 25−49.

Bernstein, D. and I. El Sanhouri (1994) "Congestion pricing with an untolled alternative" Draft, Massachusetts Institute of Technology, Cambridge.

Bleijenberg, A.N., W.J. van den Berg and G. de Wit (1994) *Maatschappelijke Kosten van het Verkeer: Literatuuroverzicht*. Centrum voor Energiebesparing en Schone Technologie, Delft.

Bonenschansker, E., M.G. Leijsen and H. de Groot (1995) *The Price of Mobility in The Netherlands*. Institute for Research on Public Expenditure (IOO), Den Haag.

Bonsall, P.W. (1992) "The influence of route guidance advice on route choice in urban networks" *Transportation* **19** (1) 1−23.

Borins, S.F. (1988) "Electronic road pricing: an idea whose time may never come" *Transportation Research* **22A** (1) 37−44.

Bovenberg, A.L. (1995) "Environmental taxation and employment" *De Economist* **143** (2) 111−140.

Boyce, D.E. (1988) "Route guidance systems for improving urban travel and location choices" *Transportation Research* **22A** (4) 275−281.

Braid, R.M. (1989) "Uniform versus peak-load pricing of a bottleneck with elastic demand" *Journal of Urban Economics* **26** 320−327.

Bruinsma, F.R. (1994) *De Invloed van Transportinfrastructuur op Ruimtelijke Patronen van Economische Activiteiten*. PhD dissertation, Free University, Amsterdam. NGS **175**, KNAG, Utrecht.

Buchanan, J.M. and W.C. Stubblebine (1962) "Externality" *Economica* **29** 371−384.

Buchanan, J. and G. Tullock (1975) "Polluters' profits and political response: direct controls versus taxes" *American Economic Review* **65** 139−147.

Button, K.J. (1992) "Alternatives to road pricing". Paper presented to the OECD/ECMT/NFP/GVF Conference on "The Use of Economic Instruments in Urban Travel Management", Basel.

Button, K.J. (1993a) *Transport Economics*. Edward Elgar, Aldershot.

Button, K.J. (1993b) *Transport, the Environment and Economic Policy*. Edward Elgar, Aldershot.

Button, K.J. and D. Pitfield (eds.) (1991) *Transportation Deregulation: An International Movement*. MacMillan, Basingstoke.

Button, K.J. and W. Rothengatter (1996) "Motor transport, greenhouse gases and economic instruments" *International Journal of Environment and Pollution* forthcoming.

Button, K.J. and E.T. Verhoef (eds.) (1996) *Road Pricing, Traffic Congestion and the Environment: Issues of Efficiency and Social Feasibility*. Edward Elgar, Aldershot (forthcoming).

Carraro, C. and A. Soubeyran (1995) "Environmental taxation and employment in a multi-sector general equilibrium model" EEE Nota di Lavoro 35.95, Fondazione Eni Enrico Mattei, Milan.

CBS (Centraal Bureau voor Statistiek) (1995) *Kwartaalbericht Milieustatistieken 1995-1*. Sdu, Den Haag.

Coase, R.H. (1960) "The problem of social cost" *Journal of Law and Economics* **3** (Oct.) 1−44.

Cropper, M.L. and W.E. Oates (1992) "Environmental economics: a survey" *Journal of Economic Literature* **30** 675−740.

Daganzo, C.F. (1995) "A Pareto optimum congestion reduction scheme" *Transportation Research* **29B** (2) 139–154.

Daly, H.E. (1989) "Steady-state and growth concepts for the next century". In: F. Archibugi and P. Nijkamp (eds.) (1989) *Economy and Ecology: Towards Sustainable Development*. Kluwer, Dordrecht, 73–87.

Dawson, J.A.L. and I. Catling (1986) "Electronic road pricing in Hong Kong" *Transportation Research* **20A** (2) 129–134.

De Palma, A. and R. Lindsey (1992) "The potential benefits of a combined route guidance and road pricing system: an economic analysis" Draft, Université de Genève, Département d'Economie Commerciale et Industrielle.

De Palma, A. and R. Lindsey (1995) "Information, welfare and usage of congestible facilities under different pricing regimes" Draft, Université de Genève, Département d'Economie Commerciale et Industrielle.

Diamond, P.J. (1973) "Consumption externalities and imperfectly corrective pricing" *Bell Journal of Economics and Management Science* **4** 526–538.

Diekmann, A. (1991) "Kosten en baten van de auto: poging tot een juiste afweging" *Mobiliteitschrift* **91** (7,8) 3–11. Stichting Weg.

Dodgson, J. (1996) "Issues in evaluating the long-term global impacts of transport policy" *International Journal of Environment and Pollution* forthcoming.

EC (Commission of the European Communities) (1992a) *White Paper on The Future Development of the Common Transport Policy: A Global Approach to the Construction of a Community Framework for Sustainable Mobility*. Brussels.

EC (Commission of the European Communities) (1992b) *Green Paper on The Impact of Transport on the Environment: A Community Strategy for Sustainable Development*. DGVII, Brussels.

EC (Commission of the European Communities) (1995) *Green Paper Towards Fair and Efficient Pricing in Transport: Policy Options for Internalising the External Costs of Transport in the European Union*. Directorate-General for Transport, Brussels.

El Sanhouri, I. (1994) *Evaluating the Joint Implementation of Congestion Pricing and Driver Information Systems*. PhD dissertation, Massachusetts Institute of Technology, Cambridge.

Else, P.K. (1981) "A reformulation of the theory of optimal congestion taxes" *Journal of Transport Economics and Policy* **15** 217–232.

Else, P.K. (1982) "A reformulation of the theory of optimal congestion taxes: a rejoinder" *Journal of Transport Economics and Policy* **16** 299–304.

Else, P.K. (1986) "No entry for congestion taxes?" *Transportation Research* **20A** (2) 99–107.

Emmerink, R.H.M., P. Nijkamp and P. Rietveld (1995) "Is congestion-pricing a first-best strategy in transport policy? A critical review of arguments" *Environment and Planning* **22B** 581–602.

Emmerink, R.H.M., E.T. Verhoef, P. Nijkamp and P. Rietveld (1995) "Information effects in transport networks with stochastic capacity and uncertainty costs". TRACE discussion paper TI 95-158, Tinbergen Institute Amsterdam–Rotterdam.

Emmerink, R.H.M., E.T. Verhoef, P. Nijkamp and P. Rietveld (1996a) "Information policy in road transport with elastic demand: some welfare economic considerations" *European Economic Review* forthcoming.

Emmerink, R.H.M., E.T. Verhoef, P. Nijkamp and P. Rietveld (1996b) "Endogenising demand for information in road transport" *Annals of Regional Science* forthcoming.

Emmerink, R.H.M., E.T. Verhoef, P. Nijkamp and P. Rietveld (1996c) "Information in road networks with multiple origin-destination pairs" *Regional Science and Urban Economics* forthcoming.

Emmerink, R.H.M., E.T. Verhoef, P. Nijkamp and P. Rietveld (1996d) "Information provision in road transport with elastic demand: a welfare economic approach" *Journal of Transport Economics and Policy* forthcoming.

Evans, Alan W. (1992) "Road congestion: the diagrammatic analysis" *Journal of Political Economy* **100** (1) 211−217.

Evans, Andrew W. (1992) "Road congestion pricing: when is it a good policy?" *Journal of Transport Economics and Policy* **26** 213−243.

Evans, Andrew W. (1993) "Road congestion pricing: when is it a good policy?: a rejoinder" *Journal of Transport Economics and Policy* **27** 99−105.

Foster, C. (1974) "The regressiveness of road pricing" *International Journal of Transport Economics* **1** 133−141.

Foster, C. (1975) "A note on the distributional effects of road pricing: a comment" *Journal of Transport Economics and Policy* **9** 186−187.

Freeman III, A.M. (1993) *The Measurement of Environmental and Resource Values: Theory and Methods*. Resources for the Future, Washington.

Fujita, M. (1989) *Urban Economic Theory: Land Use and City Size*. Cambridge University Press, Cambridge.

Gastaldi, M., J.-P. Pradayrol, E. Quinet and M. Rega (1996) "Valuation of environmental externalities: from theory to decision making" *Transportation Planning and Technology* forthcoming.

Geerlings, H. (1996) "Technological innovations in the transport sector: the need for cooperation to reach environmental interest" *Transportation Planning and Technology* forthcoming.

Giuliano, G. (1992) "An assessment of the political acceptability of congestion pricing" *Transportation* **19** (4) 335−358.

Glazer, A. (1981) "Congestion tolls and consumer welfare" *Public Finance* **36** (1) 77−83.

Glazer, A. and E. Niskanen (1992) "Parking fees and congestion" *Regional Science and Urban Economics* **22** 123−132.

Goddard, H.C. (1996) "Sustainability, tradeable permits and the world's large cities: a new proposal for controlling vehicle emissions, congestion and urban decentralization with an application to Mexico City" *International Journal of Environment and Pollution* forthcoming.

Gomez-Ibañez, J.A. and K.A. Small (1994) *Road Pricing for Congestion Management: A Survey of International Practice*. NCHRP Synthesis 210, Transportation Research Board, National Academy Press, Washington.

Goodwin, P.B. (1989) "The rule of three: a possible solution to the political problem of competing objectives for road pricing" *Traffic Engineering and Control* **30** (10) 495−497.

Hahn, R.W. (1989) "Economic prescriptions for environmental problems: how the patient followed the doctor's orders" *Journal of Economic Perspectives* **3** (2) 95−114.

Hau, T.D. (1991) "Economic fundamentals of road pricing: a diagrammatic analysis" Revised Draft, Transport Division, The World Bank, Washington.

Hau, T.D. (1992) "Congestion charging mechanisms: an evaluation of current practice" Preliminary Draft, Transport Division, The World Bank, Washington.

HCG (Hague Consulting Group) (1990a) *The Netherlands' 'Value of Time' Study: Final Report*. HCG, Den Haag.

HCG (Hague Consulting Group) (1990b) *Value of Travel Time Saved for Business Trips*. HCG, Den Haag.

HCG (Hague Consulting Group) (1992) *De Reistijdwaardering in het Goederenervoer: Rapport Hoofdonderzoek*. HCG, Den Haag.

Hicks, J.R. (1939) "The foundation of welfare economics" *Economic Journal* **49** 696−712.

Hills, P. (1993) "Road congestion pricing: when is it a good policy?: a comment" *Journal of Transport Economics and Policy* **27** 91−99.

Himanen, V., P. Nijkamp and J. Padjen (1992) "Environmental quality and transport policy in Europe" *Transportation Research* **26A** (2) 147−157.

Hoevenagel, R. (1994) *The Contingent Valuation Method: Scope and Validity*. PhD dissertation, Institute for Environmental Studies (IVM), Free University, Amsterdam.

Johansson, B. and L.-G. Mattsson (1995) *Road Pricing: Theory, Empirical Assessment and Policy*. Transportation Research, Economics and Policy 3. Kluwer, Boston.

Johansson, P.-O. (1987) *The Economic Theory and Measurement of Environmental Benefits*. Cambridge University Press, Cambridge.

Johansson, P.-O. (1991) *An Introduction to Modern Welfare Economics*. Cambridge University Press, Cambridge.

Jones, P. (1991) "Gaining public support for road pricing through a package approach" *Traffic Engineering and Control* **32** (4) 194−196.

Jones, P.M. and I. Salomon (1993) "Technological and social developments and their implications for in-home/out-of-home interactions". In: P. Nijkamp (ed.) (1993) *Europe on the Move: Recent Developments in European Communications and Transport Activity Research*. Avebury, Aldershot, 95−113.

Kågeson, P. (1993) *Getting the Prices Right: A European Scheme for Making Transport Pay its True Costs*. T&E 93/6, European Federation for Transport and Environment, Brussels/Stockholm.

Kaldor, N. (1939) "Welfare propositions of economics and interpersonal comparisons of utility" *Economic Journal* **49** 549−552.

Kanemoto, Y. (1980) *Theories of Urban Externalities*. North-Holland, Amsterdam.

Knight, F.H. (1924) "Some fallacies in the interpretation of social cost" *Quarterly Journal of Economics* **38** 582−606.

Koh, W.T.H. and D.K.C. Lee (1994) "The vehicle quota system in Singapore: an assessment" *Transportation Research* **28A** (1) 31−47.

Lave, C. (1994) "The demand curve under road pricing and the problem of political feasibility" *Transportation Research* **28A** (2) 83−91.

Lave, C. (1995) "The demand curve under road pricing and the problem of political feasibility: author's reply" *Transportation Research* **29A** (6) 464−465.

Layard, R. (1977) "The distributional effects of congestion taxes" *Economica* **44** 297−304.

Lévy-Lambert, H. (1968) "Tarification des services à qualité variable: application aux péages de circulation" *Econometrica* **36** (3−4) 564−574.

Maddala, G.S. (1983) *Limited-Dependent and Qualitative Variables in Econometrics*. Cambridge University Press, Cambridge.

Maddison, D., D. Pearce, O. Johansson, E. Calthrop, T. Litman and E. Verhoef (1996) *Blueprint for a Green Economy 5: The True Cost of Transport*. Earthscan, London.

Mahmassani, H.S. and R. Jayakrishnan (1991) "System performance and user response under real-time information in a congested traffic corridor" *Transportation Research* **25A** (5) 293−308.

Marchand, M. (1968) "A note on optimal tolls in an imperfect environment" *Econometrica* **36** (3−4) 575−581.

May, A.D. (1992) "Road pricing: an international perspective" *Transportation* **19** (4) 313−333.

Mayeres, I. and S. Proost (1995) "Optimal tax rules for congestion type of externalities" Paper presented at the 7th WCTR, Sydney, Australia.

Meadows, D.H., D.L. Meadows, J. Randers and W.W. Behrens III (1972) *The Limits to Growth*. Universe Books, New York.

Ministerie van Verkeer en Waterstaat (1995) *Jaarbericht Vervoerend Nederland 1994*. Den Haag.

Mishan, E.J. (1971) "The postwar literature on externalities: an interpretative essay" *Journal of Economic Literature* 9 1–28.

Mitchell, R.C. and R.T. Carson (1989) *Using Surveys to Value Public Goods: The Contingent Valuation Method*. Resources for the Future, Washington.

Mohring, H. (1989) "The role of fuel taxes in controlling congestion". In: *Transport Policy, Management and Technology Towards 2001: Proceedings of the Fifth World Conference on Transport Research* (Yokohama) 1 243–257.

Mohring, H. and M. Harwitz (1962) *Highway Benefits*. Northwestern University Press, Evanston Il.

Mokhtarian, P.L., S.L. Handy and I. Salomon (1994) "Methodological issues in the estimation of the travel, energy and air quality impacts of telecommuting". Draft, University of California.

Nash, C.A. (1982) "A reformulation of the theory of optimal congestion taxes: a comment" *Journal of Transport Economics and Policy* 26 295–299.

Nijkamp, P. (1994) "Roads towards environmentally sustainable transport" *Transportation Research* 28A (4) 261–271.

Nijkamp, P. and S. Rienstra (1995) "Private sector involvement in financing and operating transport infrastructure" *The Annals of Regional Science* 29 221–235.

Niskanen, E. (1987) "Congestion tolls and consumer welfare" *Transportation Research* 21B (2) 171–174.

Oates, W.E. (1983) "The regulation of externalities: efficient behaviour by sources and victims" *Public Finance* 38 362–375.

OECD (Organisation for Economic Co-operation and Development) (1993) *Environmental Data Compendium 1993*. OECD, Paris.

Opschoor, J.B. (1992) "Sustainable development, the economic process and economic analysis". In: J.B. Opschoor (ed.) (1992) *Environment, Economy and Sustainable Development*. Wolters-Noordhoff, Groningen, 25–52.

Opschoor, J.B. and R. Weterings (1994) (eds.) *Milieu* 9 (5) Special Issue on "Environmental Utilisation Space".

d'Ouville, E.L. and J.F. McDonald (1990) "Optimal road capacity with a suboptimal congestion toll" *Journal of Urban Economics* 28 34–49.

Pearce, D.W. and A. Markandya (1989) *Environmental Policy Benefits: Monetary Valuation*. OECD, Paris.

Pearce, D.W. and R.K. Turner (1990) *Economics of Natural Resources and the Environment*. Johns Hopkins University Press, Baltimore.

Pezzey, J. (1993) "Sustainability: an interdisciplinary guide" *Environmental Values* 1 321–62.

Pigou, A.C. (1920) *Wealth and Welfare*. Macmillan, London.

Poole, R.W. (jr.) (1992) "Introducing congestion pricing on a new toll road" *Transportation* 19 (4) 383–396.

Quinet, E. (1989) "The social cost of land transport" Draft, OECD, Paris.

Quinet, E. (1993) "Transport between monopoly and competition: supply side and markets". In: J. Polak and A. Heertje (eds.) (1993) *European Transport Economics*. Blackwell, Oxford.

Richardson, H.W. (1974) "A note on the distributional effects of road pricing" *Journal of Transport Economics and Policy* 8 82–85.

Richardson, H.W. (1975) "A note on the distributional effects of road pricing: a rejoinder" *Journal of Transport Economics and Policy* 9 188.

Rienstra, S., J. Vleugel and P. Nijkamp (1996) "Options for sustainable passenger transport; an assessment of policy choices" *Transportation Planning and Technology* forthcoming.

Rietveld, P. (1989) "Infrastructure and regional development: a survey of multiregional economic models" *Annals of Regional Science* 23 255−274.

RIVM (Rijksinstituut voor Volksgezondheid en Milieuhygiëne) (1993) *Nationale Milieuverkenning 3 1993−2015*. Samsom H.D. Tjeenk Willink, Alphen aan den Rijn.

Rothengatter, W. (1989) "Economic aspects". In: ECMT (1989) *Transport Policy and the Environment: ECMT Ministerial Session*. ECMT/OECD, Paris, 147−176.

Rouwendal, J. and P. Rietveld (1989) "Waiting time, monopolistic behaviour and optimality" Draft, Department of Spatial Economics, Free University, Amsterdam.

Samuelson, P.A. (1952) "Spatial price equilibrium and linear programming" *American Economic Review* 42 283−303.

Sandmo, A. (1975) "Optimal taxation in the presence of externalities" *Swedish Journal of Economics* 77 86−98.

Sandmo, A. (1976) "Optimal taxation: an introduction to the literature" *Journal of Public Economics* 6 37−54.

Scitovsky, T. (1954) "Two concepts of external economies" *Journal of Political Economy* 17 143−151.

Seale, K. (1993) "Attitudes of politicians in London to road pricing" Proceedings of Seminar F of the PTRC 21st Summer Annual Meeting, 117−128.

Segal, D. and T.L. Steinmeier (1980) "The incidence of congestion and congestion tolls" *Journal of Urban Economics* 7 42−62.

Shefer, D. (1994) "Congestion, air pollution, and road fatalities in urban areas" *Accident Analysis and Prevention* 26 (4) 501−509.

Shefer, D. and P. Rietveld (1994) "Congestion and safety on highways: towards an analytical model" TRACE discussion paper TI 94-92, Tinbergen Institute, Amsterdam−Rotterdam.

Sheldon, R., M. Scott and P. Jones (1993) "London congestion charging: exploratory social research among London residents" Proceedings of Seminar F of the PTRC 21st Summer Annual Meeting, 129−145.

Siebert, H. (1982) "Nature as a life support system: renewable resources and environmental disruption" *Journal of Economics* 42 (2) 133−142.

Small, K.A. (1983) "The incidence of congestion tolls on urban highways" *Journal of Urban Economics* 13 90−111.

Small, K.A. (1992a) *Urban Transportation Economics*. Fundamentals of Pure and Applied Economics 51, Harwood, Chur.

Small, K.A. (1992b) "Using the revenues from congestion pricing" *Transportation* 19 (4) 359−381.

Small, K.A. and J.A. Gomez-Ibañez (1996) "Road pricing for congestion management: the transition from theory to policy". In: K.J. Button and E.T. Verhoef (eds.) (1996) *Road Pricing, Traffic Congestion and the Environment: Issues of Efficiency and Social Feasibility*. Edward Elgar, Aldershot (forthcoming).

Starkie, D. (1986) "Efficient and politic congestion tolls" *Transportation Research* 20A (2) 169−173.

Sullivan, A.M. (1983) "Second-best policies for congestion externalities" *Journal of Urban Economics* 14 105−123.

Takayama, T. and G.G. Judge (1971) *Spatial and Temporal Price and Allocation Models*. Contributions to Economic Analysis 73, North-Holland, Amsterdam.

Takayama, T. and W.C. Labys (1986) "Spatial equilibrium analysis". In: P. Nijkamp (ed.) (1986) *Handbook of Regional and Urban Economics* (1) Elsevier Science Publishers, Amsterdam.

Tertoolen, G. (1994) *Free to Move...?! A Field Experiment on Attempts to Influence Private Car Use and the Psychological Resistance It Evokes* (in Dutch). Ph.D. Dissertation, University of Utrecht.

Tietenberg, T.H. (1994) *Environmental Economics and Policy*. HarperCollins College Publishers, New York.

Toman, M.A., J. Pezzey and J. Krautkraemer (1994) "Neoclassical economic growth theory and "sustainability"". In: D. Bromley (ed.) (1994) *Handbook of Environmental Economics*. Blackwell, Oxford, 39−65.

Turvey, R. (1963) "On divergences between social cost and private cost" *Economica* **30** 309−313.

Tweede Kamer der Staten-Generaal (1989−90) *Structuurschema Verkeer en Vervoer; Deel D: Regeringsbeslissing*. Vergaderjaar 1989−1990, 20.922 nrs. 15 en 16, Sdu, Den Haag.

Tweede Kamer der Staten-Generaal (1991−92) *Uitvoeringsnotitie Parkeerbeleid. Hoeksteen en Toetssteen van het Verkeers- en Vervoersbeleid*. Vergaderjaar 1991−1992, 22.383 nrs. 1 en 2, Sdu, Den Haag.

UNCED (United Nations Conference on Environment and Development) (1992) *Declaration on Environment and Development*. United Nations, New York.

UN (United Nations) (1994) *Framework Convention on Climate Change*. United Nations, Geneva.

Van den Bergh, J.C.J.M. (1996) *Ecological Economics and Sustainable Development: Theory, Methods and Applications*. Edward Elgar, Aldershot.

Van den Bergh, J.C.J.M. and P. Nijkamp (eds.) (1994) *Annals of Regional Science* **28** (1) Special issue on "Sustainability, Resources and Region".

Van den Bergh, J.C.J.M., P. Nijkamp and P. Rietveld (eds.) (1996) *Recent Advances in Spatial Equilibrium Modelling: Methodology and Applications*. Springer-Verlag, Heidelberg.

Van Wee, G.P. (1995) "Pricing instruments for transport policy". In: F.J. Dietz, H.R.J. Vollebergh and J.L. de Vries (1995) *Environment, Incentives and the Common Market*. Kluwer Academic Publishers, Dordrecht, 97−124.

Varian, H.R. (1992) *Microeconomic Analysis*, third edition. Norton, New York.

Verhoef, E.T. (1994a) "External effects and social costs of road transport" *Transportation Research* **28A** (4) 273−287.

Verhoef, E.T. (1994b) "Efficiency and equity in externalities: a partial equilibrium analysis" *Environment and Planning* **26A** 361−382.

Verhoef, E.T. (1995) "The demand curve under road pricing and the problem of political feasibility: a comment" *Transportation Research* **29A** (6) 459−464.

Verhoef, E.T. and J.C.J.M. van den Bergh (1996) "A spatial price equilibrium model for environmental policy analysis of mobile and immobile sources of pollution". In: J.C.J.M. van den Bergh, P. Nijkamp and P. Rietveld (eds.) (1996) *Recent Advances in Spatial Equilibrium Modelling: Methodology and Applications*. Springer-Verlag, Heidelberg, 201−220.

Verhoef, E.T., J.C.J.M. van den Bergh and K.J. Button (1996) "Transport, spatial economy and the global environment". *Environment and Planning A* forthcoming.

Verhoef, E.T., R.H.M. Emmerink, P. Nijkamp and P. Rietveld (1996) "Information provision, flat- and fine congestion tolling and the efficiency of road usage" *Regional Science and Urban Economics* forthcoming.

Verhoef, E.T., P. Nijkamp and P. Rietveld (1994) "Second-best congestion pricing: the case of an untolled alternative" TRACE discussion paper TI 94-129, Tinbergen Institute, Amsterdam—Rotterdam.

Verhoef, E.T., P. Nijkamp and P. Rietveld (1995a) "Second-best regulation of road transport externalities" *Journal of Transport Economics and Policy* 29 147–167.

Verhoef, E.T., P. Nijkamp and P. Rietveld (1995b) "The economics of regulatory parking policies" *Transportation Research* 29A (2) 141–156.

Verhoef, E.T., P. Nijkamp and P. Rietveld (1996a) "Second-best congestion pricing: the case of an untolled alternative" *Journal of Urban Economics* forthcoming.

Verhoef, E.T., P. Nijkamp and P. Rietveld (1996b) "The trade-off between efficiency, effectiveness and social feasibility of regulating road transport externalities" *Transportation Planning and Technology* forthcoming.

Verhoef, E.T., P. Nijkamp and P. Rietveld (1996c) "Regulatory parking policies at the firm level" *Environment and Planning C (Government and Policy)* forthcoming.

Vickrey, W.S. (1969) "Congestion theory and transport investment" *American Economic Review* 59 (Papers and Proceedings) 251–260.

Viner, J. (1931) "Cost curves and supply curves" *Zeitschrift für Nationalökonomie* 3 23–46.

Vleugel, J.A., H.A. van Gent and P. Nijkamp (1990) "Transport and environment: experiences with Dutch policies". In: J.-Ph. Barde and K.J. Button (eds.) (1990) *Transport Policy and the Environment*. Earthscan, London, 121–156.

Walters, A.A. (1961) "The theory and measurement of private and social cost of highway congestion" *Econometrica* 29 (4) 676–697.

Wardrop, J. (1952) "Some theoretical aspects of road traffic research" *Proceedings of the Institute of Civil Engineers* 1 (2) 325–378.

Watling, D. and T. van Vuren (1993) "The modelling of dynamic route guidance systems" *Transportation Research* 1C (2) 159–182.

WCED (World Commission on Environment and Development) (1987) *Our Common Future*. Oxford University Press, Oxford/New York.

Weitzman, M.L. (1974) "Prices *vs.* quantities" *Review of Economic Studies* 41 477–491.

Willson, R.W. and D.C. Shoup (1990) "Parking subsidies and travel choices: assessing the evidence" *Transportation* 17 141–157.

Wilson, J.D. (1983) "Optimal road capacity in the presence of unpriced congestion" *Journal of Urban Economics* 13 337–357.